How to Do Everything
Facebook® Applications

About the Author

Jesse Feiler is the author of a number of books about the Web and new technologies, as well as Mac OS X and FileMaker. His books have been translated into Japanese, Chinese, Polish, German, Spanish, French, and other languages. His most recent books are *How to Do Everything with Web 2.0 Mashups* and *Special Edition Using FileMaker 9*. As the director of North Country Consulting, he has designed and implemented a variety of FileMaker solutions for small businesses and non-profits in fields such as production, marketing, the arts, printing and publishing, food service, and construction. He has taught and consulted widely on non-profit governance. He lives in Plattsburgh, New York.

How to Do Everything
Facebook® Applications

Jesse Feiler

McGraw
Graw
Hill

New York   Chicago   San Francisco   Lisbon
London   Madrid   Mexico City   Milan   New Delhi
San Juan   Seoul   Singapore   Sydney   Toronto

The McGraw·Hill Companies

Cataloging-in-Publication Data is on file with the Library of Congress

McGraw-Hill books are available at special quantity discounts to use as premiums and sales promotions, or for use in corporate training programs. To contact a representative, please visit the Contact Us pages at www.mhprofessional.com.

How to Do Everything: Facebook® Applications

1234567890   FGR FGR   0198

ISBN   978-0-07-154967-7
MHID   0-07-154967-6

Sponsoring Editor Roger Stewart	**Technical Editors** Michele Davis Jon Phillips	**Production Supervisor** James Kussow
Editorial Supervisor Jody McKenzie	**Copy Editor** Lisa McCoy	**Composition** International Typesetting and Composition
Project Manager Harleen Chopra, International Typesetting and Composition	**Proofreader** Divya Kapoor, International Typesetting and Composition	**Illustration** International Typesetting and Composition
Acquisitions Coordinator Carly Stapleton	**Indexer** Claire Splan	**Art Director, Cover** Jeff Weeks
		Cover Designer Jeff Weeks

Contents at a Glance

PART I   **Facebook Applications: What They Are and How to Use Them**

1   Use Facebook as a Social Utility 3
2   Find Your Way Around Your Facebook Home Page and Profile 13
3   Find Your Way Around Facebook 45
4   Find Your Way Around a Facebook Application: Groups 65
5   Use Other Facebook Applications 91

Part II   **Use Facebook Technologies**

6   Use XML, XHTML, and CSS 115
7   Use PHP 129
8   Understand Overall Facebook Architecture 143
9   Use Facebook Markup Language (FBML) 155
10   Use the Facebook API 169
11   Use Facebook Query Language (FQL), Mock-AJAX, FBJS,
      and Facebook Mobile 183

Part III   **Build Facebook Applications**

12   Get Started as a Facebook Developer 195
13   Build a Basic Interface 215
14   Integrate MySQL Data 253
15   Add More Features 287
      Index 321

Contents

Acknowledgments xv
Introduction xvii

Part I   **Facebook Applications: What They Are and How to Use Them**

Chapter 1   **Use Facebook as a Social Utility** **3**
              Understand the Facebook World   5
                  Social Utility   5
                  Virality   5
                  Social Graph   6
                  Web 2.0   6
                  The Size of the Facebook World   6
              Use Facebook Basics   7
                  Profile and Preferences   7
                  Facebook Applications   10
                  Networks   10
                  The Wall   11

Chapter 2   **Find Your Way Around Your Facebook Home Page
              and Profile** **13**
              Use Basic Navigation   15
                  The Facebook Frame   15
                  The Left-Hand Column (Left Nav)   17
                  The Footer Links   17
                  The Canvas   18
              Manage Your Account   19
                  Account Settings   19
              Use Your Home Page   21
                  Home Page Contents   21
                  Controlling Your Home Page   22
                  Platform Elements for the News Feed   28

Use Your Profile 29
Profile Page Layout 29
Profile Information 33
Visibility for Pokes, Messages, and Friend Requests 37
Friends and Search 39
Interact with Facebook Pages 42

Chapter 3   **Find Your Way Around Facebook** **45**
Use the Mini-Feed 47
Platform Elements for the Mini-Feed 47
Use the Wall 47
Platform Elements for the Wall 49
Use the Inbox and Messages 49
Work with Pokes 49
Platform Elements for Pokes 49
Handle Requests and Notifications 50
Platform Elements for Requests and Notifications 50
Use Friend Finder and Invite Friends 51
Use Social Ads 52
Get Started 53
Create a Facebook Page 53
Choose the Audience 55
Create the Ad 57
Set the Budget 58
Review the Ad and Pay 60
Develop Polls 61
Handle Subscriptions 63

Chapter 4   **Find Your Way Around a Facebook Application: Groups** **65**
Create and Manage Groups 67
Create and Edit Groups 68
Group Info 69
Picture 72
Use Groups 73
View Discussion Board 74
Message All Members 74
Edit Group, Members, and Officers; Invitations 75
Create Related Events 75
Use Facebook Identifiers 82
Use the Groups Application 82
Groups API 82
Launch Groups 84
My Groups 85

Browse Groups 86
Popular 87
Look at the Facebook Elements in Groups Pages 87

Chapter 5   **Use Other Facebook Applications** **91**
Add and Edit Applications and Their Privacy Settings 92
Add an Application 93
Control Application Privacy Settings 95
Photos 99
Photo Albums 100
Photos 102
Tags 102
Events 104
Integrate Facebook Using Notes and Mobile 107
Import a Blog 108
Use a Mobile Phone 109

Part II   **Use Facebook Technologies**

Chapter 6   **Use XML, XHTML, and CSS** **115**
Use XML for Data Transfer 117
Understand the Basics of XML 118
Understand XML Syntax 119
Use XML Elements 120
Use XML Namespaces 121
Use XHTML on Your Facebook Pages 122
Using div Elements 122
The id Attribute and Facebook 124
Validate Your Facebook Web Page Syntax 124
Debug Facebook XHTML 124
Use CSS to Format Your Facebook Pages 125
Facebook and Style Sheets 126
Learn the Facebook Style Basics 126

Chapter 7   **Use PHP** **129**
Understand PHP Basic Syntax 132
Use PHP Delimiters 132
Use Comments 132
Use Terminators 133
Use PHP Variables and Arrays 133
Use PHP Strings 133
Building Concatenated Strings 134
Use PHP Conditional Statements 135

	Use Multiple PHP Files	137
	Use PHP Functions	137
	Handle Exceptions	139

Chapter 8	**Understand Overall Facebook Architecture**	**143**
	Work with the Architecture	144
	How the Canvas Works	145
	How the Profile Page Works	147
	Use the Facebook Object	147
	Use the Facebook REST Object	149
	Parameters Are Provided for You	151
	Output Is Parsed for You	151
	How the Facebook REST Object Works Internally	152

Chapter 9	**Use Facebook Markup Language (FBML)**	**155**
	Use the FBML Test Tool	158
	Use FBML Data Elements	159
	Use FBML Control Elements	160
	Use the FBML Share Element	161
	Sharing a URL	163
	Sharing Data	163
	Use FBML Forms	164
	Use FBML Dialogs	166

Chapter 10	**Use the Facebook API**	**169**
	Use the User API	171
	users_getInfo	171
	users_getLoggedInUser	172
	users_isAppAdded	173
	Use the Profile API	173
	set_FBML	173
	get_FBML	173
	fbml_refreshImgSrc	173
	fbml_refreshRefURL	173
	fbml_setRefHandle	174
	Use Events API	174
	events_get	174
	events_getMembers	175
	Use the Feed API	175
	feed_publishStoryToUser	175
	feed_publishActionOfUser	176
	feed_publishTemplatizedAction	176

Use the Friends API 177
 friends_areFriends 177
 friends_get 177
 friends_getAppUsers 177
Use the Groups API 177
 groups_get 177
 groups_getMembers 178
Use the Notifications API 178
 notifications_get 178
 notifications_send 178
 notifications_sendEmail 179
Use the Photos API 180
 photos_get 180
 photos_getAlbums 180
 photos_getTags 181
Use the Marketplace API 181
 marketplace_createListing 181
 marketplace_removeListing 182
 marketplace_getCategories 182
 marketplace_getSubCategories 182
 marketplace_getListings 182
 marketplace_search 182

Chapter 11 **Use Facebook Query Language (FQL), Mock-AJAX, FBJS, and Facebook Mobile** **183**
Use Facebook Query Language (FQL) 184
Use Dynamic FBML Action Attributes 186
Use Mock-AJAX 186
Use FBJS 187
Use Facebook Mobile 189
Watch for Further Developments 190

Part III **Build Facebook Applications**

Chapter 12 **Get Started as a Facebook Developer** **195**
Add the Facebook Developer Application 196
Create a New Application 199
 Set Up the New Application 200
 Create the Application on Your Server 200
 Connect the Application to Facebook 203
 Test 206

Update the About Page 209
Add the Application 209
Create a Test Account 212

Chapter 13 **Build a Basic Interface** **215**
Decide What You Want to Do 216
Design the Application 218
Add Value to Facebook 218
Become Facebook-ish 219
Draw the Facebook Line 220
Obey the Rules 221
Iterate 222
Start to Build the Sample Application 222
Decide What You Want to Do 222
Decide How You Want to Do It 223
Design the Application 223
Set Up the Application Parameters 227
Implement the Basic Page and Navigation 228
Choose the Basic Design 228
Implement the Basic Design 231
Implement the Pages 234
Home Page 237
My Events 241
Friends' Events 242
Browse Events 242
Implement Utilities 243
Event Retrieval 243
Event Display 245
Begin to Test 251

Chapter 14 **Integrate MySQL Data** **253**
Understand SQL Basics 255
Use MySQL 257
Explore the Example Database 258
Work with the Schema 258
Build the Database (if necessary) 262
Use MySQL Query Browser for Testing 265
Construct and Test the First Query
(Adding/Removing Favorites) 269
Connect to the Database 270
Send Parameters to the Script 271
Add to the Table 272
Remove Items from the Table 275
Putting It Together 275

Finish the PHP Work: Overview 277
    function get_from_database_and_render
       ($nColumns, $owner, $user) 277
    function render_cae ($nColumns, $owner,
       $user, $results) 277
    function render_cae_columns 278
Finish the PHP Work: Details 278
    function get_from_database_and_render
       ($nColumns, $owner, $user) 278
    function render_cae ($nColumns, $owner,
       $user, $results) 283
    function render_cae_columns 285

Chapter 15   **Add More Features** **287**
Use Public Canvas Pages and Control Adding Applications 288
    Greet the User by Name 290
Update the Profile Page 290
    Update the Profile Box 291
    Get the User's Text 292
Add News Feed and Mini-Feed Items 294
    Actor and Target 295
    Title 295
    Body 296
    Images 297
    Targets 297
    Implement a Template Story 298
Paginate Results 302
    Design the Pagination Architecture 304
    Use the Facebook Pagination Styles 305
    Change get_from_database_and_render Parameters 306
    Change the Page That Calls
       get_from_database_and_render 307
    Implement Pagination in
       get_from_database_and_render 308
    Implement Let Friends Know 313
Implement the Share Button 314
    Add More SELECT Options 315
Add a Discussion Board 317
Improve Security 318
Get Started with Facebook Applications 319

Index **321**

Acknowledgments

Roger Stewart and his colleagues at McGraw-Hill have made writing this book a great experience. Carly Stapleton has helped move the process along from contract through production with her usual steady hand. Once the production process went into high gear, Lisa McCoy provided copy edits and suggestions to make the book's text as clear as possible. Jody McKenzie's advice on layout and style issues helped us to make the book consistent. Production manager Harleen Chopra oversaw the smooth-running process of converting the edited text to laid-out pages. And, of course, Jeff Weeks provided a great cover design. As she has for many years, Carole McClendon at Waterside Productions managed the business end of the project; no one could ask for a better agent.

Friends and colleagues have made valuable suggestions and put up with test runs of descriptions of Facebook and Facebook Platform on various occasions that ostensibly were to be devoted to other tasks (such as having dinner).

Others made suggestions about the sample application constructed in Part III of the book. In particular, Yvette McClendon provided great technical comments and review of the sample application as did intrepid early users Ewa Jankowska, Ted Goodman, and Patrick Gallagher.

Introduction

Facebook has grown rapidly in the few years of its existence, and its users have changed from U.S.-based students at colleges and universities to a broad spectrum of people around the world. Its fastest-growing demographic is people age 25 and over. This book provides an introduction to Facebook Platform, showing you how you can develop applications for Facebook as it is and will be—not Facebook as it was two years ago.

Facebook supports a large number of development environments, but this book focuses on two: PHP: Hypertext Preprocessor (PHP) and MySQL. Facebook itself is the second most-trafficked PHP site in the world, and it is one of the largest MySQL installations, so it seems logical to begin with them. If you are programming in another language or using another database, the architecture and Facebook components described in this book will still be available to you, but the interfaces will reflect the language or database (if any) that you use.

In addition to supporting various development environments, Facebook supports several different deployment options. In two of them, you use HTML-based code to create your application's interface, which is then displayed by Facebook. You can do this using an iframe or using Facebook Markup Language (FBML). You can also create a desktop application that runs on a user's computer and interacts with Facebook. This book focuses on Facebook applications using FBML.

Part I of the book looks at Facebook from the user's point of view, showing you the basic tools and walking you through a number of Facebook's own applications. Along the way, you will see tables that point out some of the Facebook Platform components that help implement the tools and components. In Part II, the Facebook Platform components themselves are looked at, along with the technologies such as Extensible Markup Language (XML), PHP, MySQL, and Representational State Transfer (REST) that are used to make everything work. Finally, in Part III, you will see how to build two Facebook applications: a barebones application in Chapter 12 and a fairly complex application in Chapters 13, 14, and 15.

Downloadable code for many of the chapters is available through the book's Facebook Page, the author's Web site, or the publisher's Web site. (The URLs are provided inside the back cover.) The book's Facebook Page also includes discussions and updates as well as links to other resources.

Several points about the downloadable code should be noted:

- Particularly in Chapters 13, 14, and 15, the code from one chapter builds on the code from previous chapters. Be careful that you use the correct chapter's code. Sections of code are modified, added, or removed from chapter to chapter, as described in the book.

- In order to test your code, you will need your own Web server and Facebook developer keys (this is all described in Chapter 12). The downloadable code requires customizing with your Web server and key information, as well as your database name and password. The major customization will be in a downloadable file called config.php.

In focusing on Facebook itself, the code in this book is designed to showcase features of Facebook as clearly as possible. It can be restructured and refactored to make it more concise or more efficient, but that could come at the cost of making it somewhat less clear. Likewise, there are some issues of security that are pointed out but not implemented in all cases because they, too, would add slight complexity (or at least more characters in the code). Do not think that because the section on security in Chapter 15 comes at the end of the book that it is an afterthought. As always, security planning needs to come right at the start of a project. It is given relatively little space in this book because the security issues you deal with in developing Facebook applications are the same issues you deal with in developing Web sites, programming with your language of choice, and running the database (if any) of your choice.

In early 2008, Facebook joined with ABC News to sponsor two back-to-back two-hour debates just before the New Hampshire primary. The US Politics Facebook application Debate Groups section let people join in, browsing debate topics, adding some to My Debates, and viewing My Friends' Debates. This is exactly the structure of the example application built in Part III of this book, except that application deals with arts and entertainment events rather than political debates. The architecture is suitable for a wide range of topics. Furthermore, sections of the example application can be used independently in simpler applications.

Part One

Facebook Applications: What They Are and How to Use Them

Chapter 1

Use Facebook as a Social Utility

How to…

- Understand the Facebook world
- Get started
- Use Facebook basics
- Get the most out of Facebook applications

It started at Harvard University. You may have heard how undergraduate Mark Zuckerberg started Facebook at Harvard in February 2004 and how it rapidly spread to other universities, then to high schools, on to corporations, and then, in September 2006, to anyone who wanted to register. But that's the second part of the Harvard Story. The first part dates back to 1967, when Harvard professor Stanley Milgrim began his *small world* experiments. In these experiments, people were asked to send a packet of information to someone they did not know in a distant city; the person was described, but no address was given. The participants sent the packet on to someone whom they did know who might know the target person or who might know someone who knew the target. The process was then repeated. It turned out that the packets that finally were delivered had made it to their destinations with an average of about six hops. This was close to the "six degrees of separation" among people in the world suggested by Hungarian author Frigyes Karinthy in his 1929 story "Chain-Links."

Facebook starts with real people and their real relationships. It helps people communicate in a variety of ways; as they do so, they often add new friends, join groups, and share information, ranging from photos to invitations to events and even classified ads. There are certainly more than six degrees of separation between any two randomly chosen Facebook members, but it is not unlikely that a replication of the small world experiments, in which people made an effort to contact someone they did not know, would find six or even fewer hops on Facebook (and without using tools such as the search capability, which might bring it down to one or two hops).

This book starts by describing Facebook and its features. Then you will see how to build applications on Facebook platform. These applications all add value in some way to the real people on Facebook. That value may be amusement; it may be information, or services. The application developers may be altruistic; they may want to make money by selling the amusement, information, or services; or they may choose to profit by selling advertising along with the amusement, information, or services.

Understand the Facebook World

The concepts and terminology of the Facebook world are few and simple. This section briefly describes four of the most important. It is interesting to note that only one of them is truly a computer or technology term.

Social Utility

Facebook describes itself as a "social utility." As founder and CEO Mark Zuckerberg said to *Time* magazine: "What we're trying to do is just make it really efficient for people to communicate, get information, and share information. We always try to emphasize the utility component."

A number of somewhat similar sites are referred to as social networking sites (and, in fact, Facebook is sometimes referred to that way, although they prefer the term social utility). One of the most distinguishing features of Facebook is that it starts from real people and real relationships. According to the Terms of Use, you may not:

> register for more than one User account, register for a User account on behalf of an individual other than yourself, or register for a User account on behalf of any group or entity;

> impersonate any person or entity, or falsely state or otherwise misrepresent yourself, your age or your affiliation with any person or entity

NOTE *Violations of the Terms of Use occur, but for the most part, you can rely on people on Facebook being who they say they are. If you have any doubt about someone's identity and the issue is important, it may be worth not pursuing a conversation or other transaction (which is true of all services online and off). But if you have the time and inclination, you can perform your own variation on the small world experiment. Contact someone you do know who might know the Facebook member and ask them if they know the member or might know someone who knows the member. You may be able to construct a list of people who you trust or who are trusted by people you trust that reaches to the Facebook member.*

Virality

This term refers to the spread of information through social networks in the same way that viruses causing disease are spread. Because of the links among friends in Facebook, information can spread in this way. The adoption of new Facebook applications can be phenomenally fast in this environment, in part, because as one person adds an application, that news can be passed along to friends automatically and they may choose to add the application themselves. Much of the excitement about Facebook applications comes from their rapid spread and use by scores of thousands of people within a few hours.

Social Graph

This is the term preferred by Facebook to describe the network of their members. Graphs are visual representations of numbers, but also can be visual representations of relationships. One of the major problems with modeling or graphing a group of people or objects is being able to unambiguously identify them so that you do not have two relationships where actually only one exists. The two items from the Term of Use cited previously mean that each person on Facebook should be there only once; this removes the problem in constructing a social graph.

Web 2.0

This is the only technical term in this section. It refers to the Internet as a platform as well as the growth of collaborative and sharing services, such as social networking sites, wikis, mashups, and the like. It uses technologies such as JavaScript, PHP: Hypertext Preprocessor (PHP), eXtensible Markup Language (XML), and Representational State Transfer (REST) to generate and receive highly structured data over standard Internet protocols.

One of the most important aspects of Web 2.0 is that it uses the Hypertext Transfer Protocol (HTTP) protocol to deliver pieces of pages when necessary. This is the technology that allows part of a Web page to be refreshed without resending the entire Web page. This makes for a much more responsive user experience and uses much less bandwidth.

The Size of the Facebook World

Although the small world experiments demonstrated that a relatively small number of people can forge a link between any two people in the real world, that only works when the real world consists of a large number of people among whom those links can be found. The Facebook world is very big, which means that you can quickly find individuals, but through them, you can meet a very large number of people very quickly.

You can get the most recent Facebook statistics by clicking the About link in the links at the bottom of the page, then clicking the Press link at the right of the page you have gone to, and looking at statistics.

Although the numbers will have changed by the time you read this, here are some samples as of late 2007:

- Over 58 million active users

- More than half of them use Facebook every day

- Over 55,000 networks

- It is the most popular photo-sharing service, with over 14,000,000 photos uploaded each day

- The countries with the most users are the United States, Canada, UK, Australia, Turkey, Sweden, Norway, South Africa, France, and Hong Kong [sic]

Perhaps the most important number for the readers of this book is this: 80 percent. 80 percent of the 58,000,000 Facebook users use at least one application built on the Facebook platform.

Use Facebook Basics

If you do not have a Facebook account, you can easily create one by going to www.facebook.com and clicking the Sign Up link. It will open the window shown in Figure 1-1.

NOTE
Facebook is growing rapidly and evolving as it does so. It is quite likely that the pages you see when you run Facebook will be somewhat different from the ones captured in the fall of 2007 when this book was written. Any substantive differences will be described on the book's Facebook Page. It and other resources are listed inside the book's back cover.

There is no charge to use Facebook, and minimal information is required. Note that you must accept the Terms of Use, which means that if you provide incorrect information, your account can be canceled.

Profile and Preferences

Once you have signed up, you can log in using your email address and password. You will have a Profile page to which you can add information, as shown in Figure 1-2.

In the next chapter, you will see how to create and modify your profile. As you can see by comparing Figures1-1 and 1-2, you can change your email address as needed. All of the email addresses you provide will be verified by sending an email to them. When you click the link in that email, the new address is added.

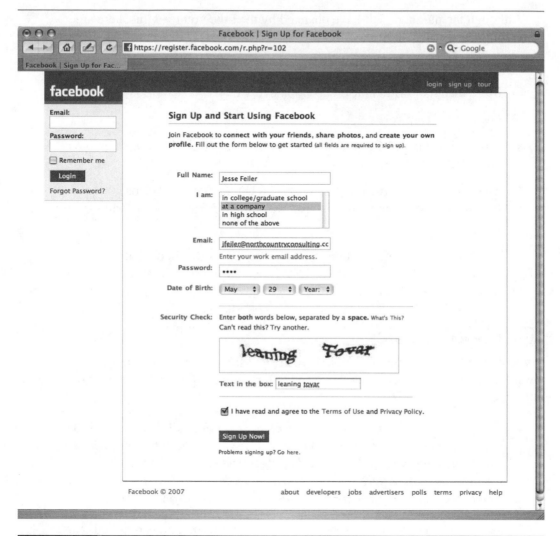

FIGURE 1-1 Facebook signup

You can delete addresses as needed; all current email addresses for an account can serve as logins (they share the same password).

For now, a high-level tour is in order. Some parts of the page will always be present and always be in the same places. These include the left-hand sidebar containing the Search box and the applications, the profile information itself (a photo, if you have uploaded one, and your name), your Friends list, and the

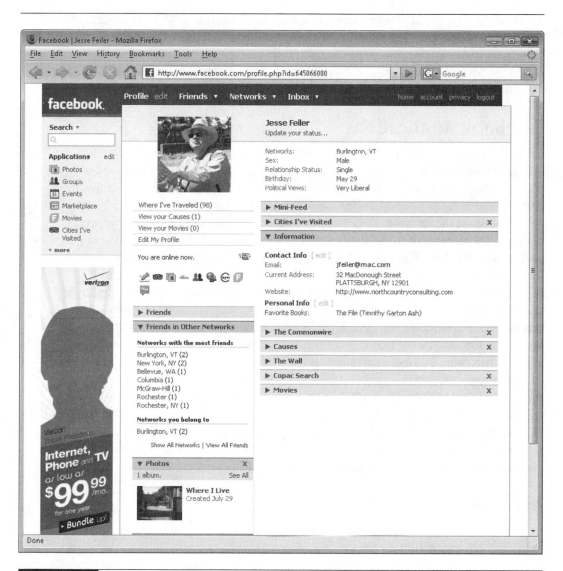

FIGURE 1-2   A Facebook Profile page

Mini-Feed (which is a list of recent news items about yourself). Although the Friends list and Mini-Feed will always be present and always be in the same places, you can minimize them using the blue triangles, as shown in Figure 1-2. The other items can be moved up or down and often from right to left. As you attempt to do so, you will be warned if you try to move them incorrectly.

With the exception of a few items (such as the Friends list, Mini-Feed, and the profile information itself), almost everything on the profile is customizable, not only in its location, but also in its content. You can control the information that is published about you as well as the information that you receive on the Mini-Feed and other items.

Facebook Applications

Each of the items on the profile has a headline, which is light blue with text that is a darker shade of blue. Many of them are *applications* that you can add to your profile. Applications are tools that help facilitate your interactions with friends on Facebook as well as your other Facebook adventures. They are similar to any other applications on the desktop or the Web in that they let you do the things you want to do with your computer and they are written in common programming languages, such as Java or PHP. They differ from applications such as word processors in that they are quite targeted and lightweight: they generally do one thing very quickly and simply. Some applications are provided by Facebook; others are provided by third parties (this book will show you how you can create such applications). You can move the applications around on your Profile page; you can also use the Close box (click the small ×) at the right of each title bar to remove the application from your Profile page or—more extreme—from your account.

Each application has its own settings that you can control. As you will see, the Profile Edit button takes you to the Edit My Applications page, shown in Figure 1-3, where you can control the settings.

Facebook lets you search among the thousands of third-party applications, as you can see in Figure 1-4. A click of the mouse provides more information; you can then choose to add the application to your profile.

Networks

You are encouraged to join a network on Facebook; in fact, you can join up to five networks, but you will have to choose one as a primary network. It is the network to which you feel most attached. Originally, it was the school you attended; now, networks include corporations and geographic areas. You can change networks from time to time. Certain information and messages are distributed to all members of a network.

Even if you are not a member of a network, you can browse its Network page. That page shows you events for the network, advertisements and the marketplace for that network, what is currently popular, and a variety of other information, including discussions and the network Wall. Members of a network see more information about the network than visitors do.

FIGURE 1-3   Edit your applications.

The Wall

The Wall is an area of your profile on which anyone (including you) can write. It is visible to anyone who looks at your profile, and is a good way of sharing brief news and comments among your friends. Network pages also have Walls onto which members of the network can write. A variety of third-party applications expand and extend the Wall functionality; you can add them if you want.

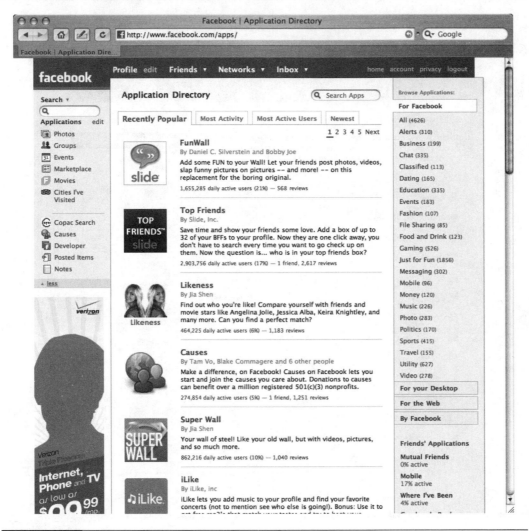

FIGURE 1-4   Find new applications.

Chapter 2

Find Your Way Around Your Facebook Home Page and Profile

How to...

- ■ Use basic navigation

- ■ Manage your account

- ■ Use your Home page

- ■ Use your Profile page

- ■ Interact with Facebook Pages

Facebook is easy to use. Its many features are intuitive, and its interface is clean and consistent. The basic overview from the previous chapter is enough to get most people started with Facebook. However, if you are going to start building applications on Facebook Platform, you need to know much more about Facebook and its interface. For example, it is safe to say that many, if not most, users of Facebook do not know what the dashboard is—at least not by name. In this chapter, you will begin to find the functionality and interface of Facebook described using the terms that you as a developer will need to know.

For each feature, you will also see the ways in which users can control it (often with preferences); you will also find a list of major Facebook Platform elements that are relevant to it. Those elements consist primarily of application programming interface (API) calls, Facebook Query Language (FQL), and Facebook Markup Language (FBML). Platform elements that are common to many areas or that are only tangentially related to specific areas are not included. You may find examples of the uses of these elements in the index; of course, the ultimate source is the Developer documentation—particularly the wiki—on the Facebook site.

Thus, this chapter and the ones that follow in this part of the book, provide you an overview of Facebook Platform as the user sees it. In Part II of this book, the details of Facebook Platform are described from a developer's point of view. What is important to know at this point is the difference among the three sets of elements:

- ■ API calls are generally function calls made through Facebook's REST interface.

- ■ FQL consists of SELECT statements modeled after SQL. They are sent through an API call.

- ■ FBML is a markup language that provides elements that can be specified by developers of Facebook applications.

When a Facebook application's page is requested by a user, Facebook requests the FBML code from the server where the developer's application runs, and its FBML code is uploaded to Facebook, where it is parsed, processed, and returned to the user as HTML. It is also important to note that all Facebook users are identified by a *user id* (`uid`) rather than a name. This is a standard technique of well-designed software: By using an essentially meaningless identifier for the user, everything about the user can be changed (names do change, as do addresses and even gender).

This chapter focuses on the Facebook basics. Facebook allows for a great deal of customization; it also allows you to control in great detail who can see specific types of information about you. The various privacy settings for the basic parts of Facebook are described in this chapter. As you move into other areas of Facebook in the following chapters, the complexity of the privacy settings drastically decreases. Most of the privacy settings described here are incorporated into the features that follow, and no further discussion of them is needed.

Use Basic Navigation

There are four major components to all Facebook pages: the frame at the top, the left-hand column (sometimes called Left Nav), the page footer links, and the Canvas.

The Facebook Frame

The Facebook *frame* is shown in Figure 2-1. It is at the top of the page. It contains the major Facebook navigation links.

At the left are the four main areas of Facebook: your profile, the list of your friends, the list of networks you are in, and your inbox. Click on each one to go to that area. Next to the Profile link, you will find an Edit button to edit your profile. Small arrows next to the Friends, Networks, and Inbox links let you go directly to sections of those areas (such as friends who are online or notifications from your inbox).

At the right, you find links to your Home page, your account settings, and your privacy settings, as well as a link to log out of Facebook (particularly useful if you are using a computer other than your own).

Links in Facebook are not underlined as they are in some other environments. On the body of pages where the background is generally white or a light color, links are distinguished by being shown in blue. On the frame, where the background color is dark blue, links are white or a light color.

FIGURE 2-1   Facebook frame

Much Facebook navigation begins with clicking on one of the frame links. In this book, whenever you find a suggestion to go to your profile or to adjust your privacy settings, you start by clicking on the relevant frame link.

The Left-Hand Column (Left Nav)

There is a left-hand menu on most Facebook pages; it is sometimes called *Left Nav*. It contains the Search field and a list of your applications. It may also contain advertisements.

The Footer Links

Across the bottom of Facebook pages are basic links to information about Facebook, information for developers, and more. These links are informational. Thus, the privacy link in the footer links to the privacy policy page for Facebook, and the privacy link in the frame at the top of the page links to your privacy settings.

Did you know?

How Navigation Is Described in This Book

It is possible to describe Facebook navigation in great detail. For example, to set News Feed privacy preferences, move your mouse to the top of the page where you find the blue bar and then click on Privacy in order to go to the Privacy Overview page. From there, click Edit Settings next to the description of News Feed and Mini-Feed privacy settings.

It is also possible to describe Facebook navigation more simply: set News Feed privacy settings. Where the primary link is one of the frame links and where any subsequent navigation is clearly indicated, the book does not waste your time with the intermediate steps. Rest assured, however, that the actual settings and functional details are described and shown at length.

The Canvas

The *Canvas* is the rectangle below the frame, located to the right of the left-hand column and above the page footer links. It is where most of the information you care about is displayed by an application.

For applications, the *dashboard* is the section at the top of the canvas that shows the application's name as well as buttons that let you create things (such as Create An Event in the Events application dashboard, shown in Figure 2-2), perform a navigation action (such as Browse Events, Popular Events, and Export Events), or get help (always at the right of the dashboard). Applications may instead have a *header* in this location which simply contains the application name. One reason for doing this is to use an FBML element such as `fb:if-user-has-added-app` to find out whether to display the dashboard with its actions, create button, and help buttons or the header which does not contain these items. You can make the decision based on complex logic so that an added application's particular user settings determine which dashboard elements are included.

FIGURE 2-2   The dashboard

Manage Your Account

The Account button at the right of the frame lets you manage your account. There are four tabs:

- Settings
- Networks
- Notifications
- Mobile

Account Settings

Much of this information is collected during the sign-up process, but you can change it if you need to later on. It also can interact with your profile and the News Feed and Mini-Feed.

Settings Tab

This is the basic information. It consists of:

- Your real name
- Contact email address. This is the place where you change your email address for your account and for your profile. If you are editing your profile's email entry, you will be taken to this page
- Password
- Credit card information. You can choose to store it for use when making purchases through Facebook

There is also a button to deactivate your account.

Networks Tab

You can join up to five networks on Facebook, including one regional network. If you join a workplace or school network, you need to register from an email address of that organization.

NOTE   *Regional networks are sometimes difficult to manage. You can only change regional networks twice in 60 days, and you can only belong to one at a time. There are places where no appropriate regional network applies, so you need to work with Facebook groups and visit networks that you do not join to find out what is happening in regions you are interested in.*

Notifications Tab

Facebook can notify you by email of a variety of events that involve you. These are set from the Notifications tab, and you can turn any of these on or off:

- Sends me a message
- Adds me as a friend
- Writes on my Wall
- Pokes me
- Tags me in a photo
- Tags me in a note
- Tags one of my photos
- Invites me to join a group
- Invites me to an event
- Requests to join a group of which I am an admin
- Requests to join an event of which I am an admin
- Comments on my notes
- Comments on my photos
- Comments on my posted items
- Comments on a photo of me
- Comments after me in a photo
- Comments after me in a note
- Comments after me in a posted item
- Tags me in a video
- Comments on my videos
- Comments on a video of me
- Replies to my discussion board post
- Posts on the Wall of an event I admin
- Invites me to be an administrator
- Makes me an event admin
- Makes me a group admin

Mobile Tab

Finally, the Mobile tab lets you control how your mobile phone works with Facebook.

Use Your Home Page

The first page you see is the Home page. Unlike your profile, your Home page cannot be rearranged. However, you can control the amount and type of information that is presented to a certain extent. A typical Home page is shown in Figure 2-3.

Home Page Contents

The larger of the two columns is given over to your News Feed. Basically, it consists of stories about your friends' activities on Facebook. The stories are generated

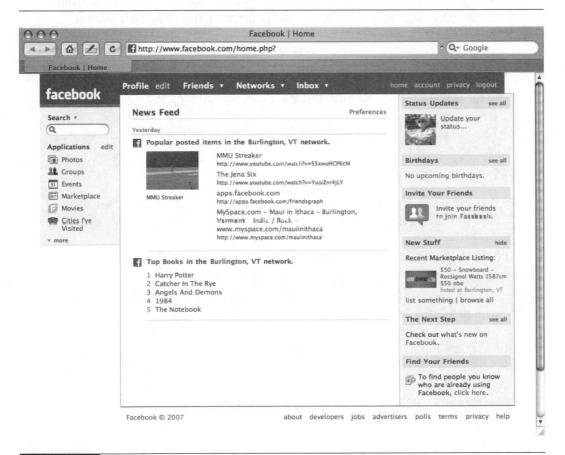

FIGURE 2-3   Facebook Home page

automatically; you see them based on the interaction of your preferences and your friends' preferences. Not everyone wants all of their activities shown in their friends' News Feeds, and not everyone wants to see everything about their friends. The next section details this interplay of preferences.

In addition to the News Feed, the right-hand column contains a number of elements that vary from time to time. At the top, you may receive notifications and requests of various sorts: friend requests, invitations, messages, pokes, and event alerts (including your friends' birthdays). You can set your status and see your friends' status (where you are, how you are feeling, or anything else that you can express in a few words and want to share with your friends). In addition to your Home page, you also see notifications on the Notifications tab of your inbox. After you have clicked on a notification from your Home page, it will disappear from there, but you can still see it on the Notifications tab of your inbox.

Controlling Your Home Page

There are three things you can control with regards to Home pages:

■ You can control the information about you that appears in others' News Feeds on their Home pages.

■ You can control your status updates.

■ You can control your News Feeds (subject to settings others have set about their information).

Controlling Your Information in Others' News Feeds

The News Feed uses a variety of settings to determine what is displayed. The first set of preferences is not under your control: They are the preferences of your friends who determine what activities of theirs can show up in News Feeds. They (and you) set these preferences from the Privacy page. (You can also get here from the Privacy link at the right of the frame at the top of Facebook pages, and then clicking News Feed and Mini-Feed.) It has a variety of settings; the ones that matter here are the News Feed and Mini-Feed settings, shown in Figure 2-4.

This controls what can be published about you. That is the first step in determining what people see in their News Feeds.

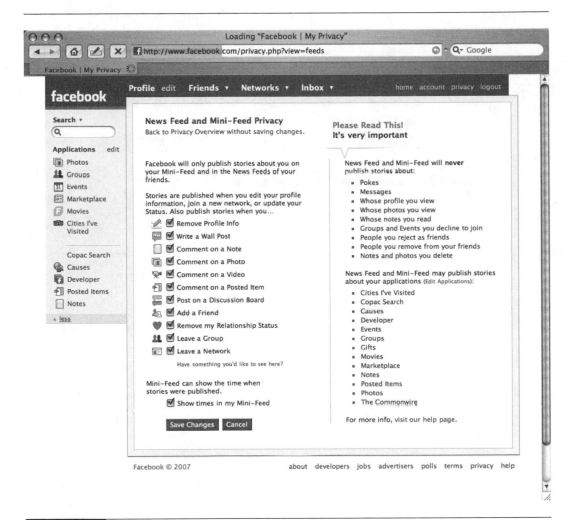

FIGURE 2-4   Privacy settings related to the News Feed and Mini-Feed

Applications sometimes post stories about your interactions with them. If they do, you can control them. Open the Edit My Applications page by clicking Edit at the top of the Applications list in the Left Nav. Click Edit Settings for the application you want to control. A pop-up window will open, as shown in Figure 2-5.

Set application privacy.

The pop-up menu at the top of the small window has the following settings:

- All my networks and all my friends

- Some of my networks and all my friends (in which case, checkboxes for your networks are shown)

- Only my friends

Thus, you can control what each application can publish about you.

You can set privacy settings for each application. You also can set privacy settings in great detail for applications other than those for which you have customized settings (such as new applications as soon as you add them). See Chapter 4 for more details.

Controlling Your Status Updates

There is a similar privacy setting for status updates. In the Profile section of the Privacy page (not in your profile itself), you can control the publication of your status updates. It has a pop-up menu with the same choices as that for application privacy, as shown in Figure 2-6.

There is one big difference among these settings. Stories are published for your News Feed and Mini-Feed when you interact with Facebook and your friends, so you need a way to specify in a good bit of detail what can be published, because the process is automatic. The publication of your status updates occurs when you explicitly change your status yourself, so you are already in control. If you never change your status, it will never be published, regardless of the settings.

Controlling Your News Feed

Once stories are published in accordance with the privacy settings of the users, you use News Feed preferences, shown in Figure 2-7, to control what you want to see. You can get to them from the Preferences button at the upper-right corner of the News Feed.

You adjust whether you want to see stories more or less often based on the following categories:

- Events
- Groups
- Photos
- Notes
- Relationships
- Friends
- Wall posts
- Profiles
- Status
- Posts

You can also see more or less information about specific friends.

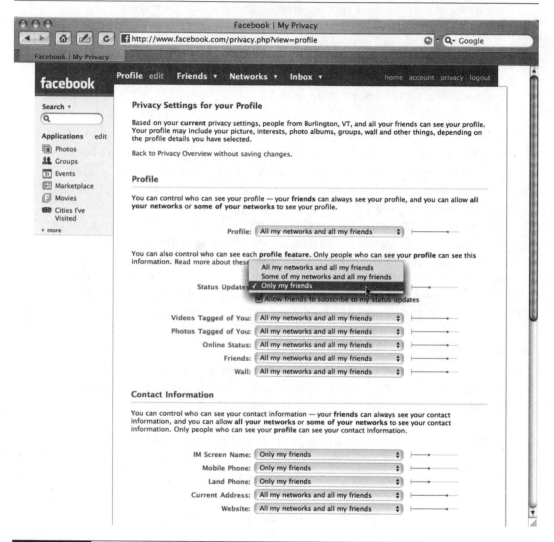

Set privacy settings for your status updates.

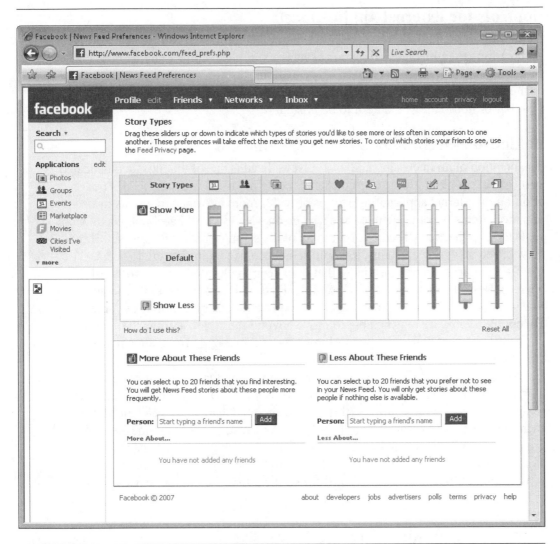

FIGURE 2-7   News Feed preferences

Controls for External Applications

Beginning in the Fall of 2007, Facebook implemented the capability of external applications to publish items to your news feed. You can control this at both ends of the transaction: when the external application asks you whether you consent to the publication of the item, and at the Facebook end, where you can decide whether or not to allow the item to be posted.

Behind-the-Scenes News Feed Development

The creation of an interesting and useful News Feed is one of the most sophisticated parts of Facebook Platform; it is constantly being modified and enhanced. The addition of external applications' stories provides more information, but as more and more items become eligible for each person's News Feed, Facebook needs more tools to keep the News Feed relevant to all of the settings that users have set. If the News Feed just grew and grew, it would soon become less interesting to users.

Two features are now available that help keep the limited number of stories in a user's News Feed as relevant as possible. First, you can click small icons next to each story's title that indicate whether you like that story or not. Over time, Facebook's software may be able to move beyond the slider settings that you control in the preferences shown in Figure 2-7, to analyzing for each candidate story whether you are likely to like it or not.

Another feature affects developers who are writing the code that creates the stories. Instead of totally free-form stories, developers are now encouraged to use templates to create those stories (this is described in Chapter 15). Developers can then register these templates with Facebook. As a result, when it comes time to create a user's News Feed, Facebook can be smart enough to aggregate similar stories (instead of "Dick went up the hill," and "Jane went up the hill," this information helps Facebook generate one of the most fascinating possible stories: "Dick and Jane went up the hill").

Platform Elements for the News Feed

Developers can control the News Feed using the Platform elements shown in Table 2-1. You can also control notifications and requests that appear in the right side of your Home page; they are described in detail in Chapter 3.

Platform Element	Category	Notes
feed.publishActionOfUser	API	Publishes a Mini-Feed story to the user and (possibly) News Feed stories to the user's friends.
feed.publishStoryToUser	API	Publishes a News Feed story to the user.
feed.publishTemplatizedAction	API	Possibly publishes and aggregates structured actions to the News Feeds of the user's friends, as well as a Mini-Feed story to the user.

TABLE 2-1   Home Page Platform Elements

Use Your Profile

In Facebook, your profile is the information about yourself that you provide. Your Profile page is based on that information (but not all the information is used), as well as on other features, many of which you can control.

NOTE   *The profile and the Profile page are two separate but highly related concepts. When there is a possibility of confusion, this book will refer to the profile information or the Profile page.*

Profile Page Layout

Figure 2-1 showed a typical Profile page. Certain elements will always be there in addition to the standard page elements.

The top of your Profile page has your photo (if you have uploaded one) and your basic profile information. In the upper-right area, an Update Your Status link lets you do just that. Below your photo, your online status is shown. As you can see in Figure 2-8, applications may insert information below your photo, such as "Where I've Traveled." These are *Profile Action Links* that provide information and that you can click to go to the application.

FIGURE 2-8   Expand or collapse a box.

The Friends box appears below your Profile Action Links. You can expand or collapse it, but you cannot move it. Likewise, your Mini-Feed appears directly below your basic information; you can expand or collapse it, but it too, cannot be moved. When you hover the mouse over a box's title bar, you can see what you can do by way of moving or expanding it, as you can see in Figure 2-8.

FIGURE 2-9   Move boxes up or down.

As you can see in Figure 2-9, some boxes, such as the Friends In Other Networks box, can be dragged up or down in the column (note the two vertically oriented arrows to the left of the title bar in Figure 2-9).

As Figure 2-10 shows, some boxes can be moved up and down as well as from column to column. Note the four-way arrow in the margin of Figure 2-10.

Some boxes that you have added to your profile can be closed and removed by clicking the × at the right of the title bar. If a box does not have an ×, it cannot be closed or removed from your Profile page.

FIGURE 2-10   Move boxes from side to side.

You can use the privacy settings at the right of the Facebook frame at the top of the page to control the visibility of your profile:

- All my networks and all my friends
- Some of my networks and all my friends (in which case, checkboxes for your networks are shown)
- Only my friends

Profile Information

You create your basic profile information when you sign up for Facebook. You can update it at any time using the Edit button next to the Profile link at the top of the page. Your information is divided into eight tabs, as shown in Figure 2-11. (The eighth tab, Layout, provides help on rearranging your profile; it contains no data.)

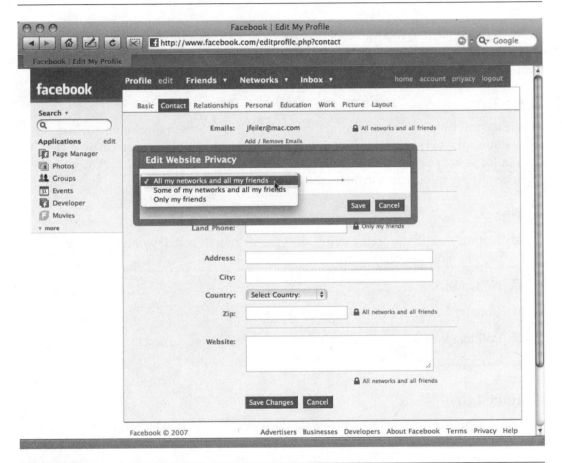

FIGURE 2-11   Enter and update your profile information.

As you can see from Figure 2-11, some of the information can be limited to the choices described previously by clicking on a padlock next to the data:

- All my networks and all my friends

- Some of my networks and all my friends (in which case, checkboxes for your networks are shown)

- Only my friends

In the sections that follow, items that allow these privacy choices to be set are indicated with (*). You can set them by clicking the padlock next to the item on your profile, or you can set them from the Privacy Settings page.

Basic Tab

This is the information that appears at the top of your Profile next to your photo. You cannot control its visibility, but you do not need to provide all of the information (except for your age, which Facebook requires for its internal use and which you can suppress). Basic information includes the following:

- Sex

- Birthday (with the option to not show; show month and day only; or show month, day, and year)

- Hometown

- Country

- Political views

- Religious views

Contact Tab

The information in the Contact, Personal, Education, and Work tabs is shown on your Profile page in the Information box.

The contact information consists of the following:

- Email (*) Note that this is set in the account settings; if you click on the Add/Remove Emails in the Contact tab, you will go to the account settings

- Screen names for AOL Instant Messenger (AIM), Google Talk, Skype, Windows Live, Gadu-Gadu, and ICQ (*)

- Mobile phone (*)
- Land phone (*)
- Address, city, state, country, and ZIP (*)
- Website (*)

Relationships Tab

Here is where you can provide information about relationships you have or are looking for:

- Interested in men/women
- Relationship status
- Alternate/maiden name (used only in searching; not displayed in your profile)
- Looking for friendship/a relationship/dating/networking

Personal Tab

This information consists of free-format text that you can enter about the following items:

- Activities
- Interests
- Favorite music
- Favorite TV shows
- Favorite movies
- Favorite books
- Favorite quotes
- About me

If entered, this information is visible in the Information box to anyone who can see your profile.

Education Tab

Like the personal information on the previous tab, this information is visible in the Information box to anyone who can see your profile:

- College/university and class/year
- Attended for (college or graduate school)
- Concentration
- High school and class/year

TIP   *Adding education information can help out-of-touch friends find you, and vice versa.*

Work Tab

This also appears in the Information box to anyone who can see your profile:

- Employer
- Position
- Description
- City, state, country
- Time period (whether you work there now and when you started)

There is a button to add another job on this tab. For other jobs, you can specify a date range during which you worked.

TIP   *Adding jobs can help you find former colleagues, and vice versa.*

Picture Tab

This tab lets you upload a picture of yourself. A small thumbnail is displayed; you can drag the image around in the small frame to adjust it. You can also remove the picture if you want.

Platform Elements for Profile Pages

Developers can interact with a Profile page in various ways. Table 2-2 shows the Platform elements that control whether or not data is displayed on a user's Profile page.

Table 2-3 shows Platform elements that let you add information to a user's Profile page. An application's box on the Profile page is specified by FBML that is sent to Facebook by an application when the application wants to change the data; it is used by Facebook whenever it is needed.

Platform Elements for Profile Data

Table 2-4 shows the most common elements used to access data from within a user's profile.

Visibility for Pokes, Messages, and Friend Requests

When you send a poke, message, or friend request, some parts of your profile are visible to those people, even if the entire profile would normally not be seen.

Platform Element	Category	Notes
fb:if-is-own-profile	FBML	Displays content if the owner is the user.
fb:narrow	FBML	Displays content if the box is in the narrow column of the Profile page.
fb:wide	FBML	Displays content if the box is in the wide column of the Profile page.
fb:visible-to-added-app-users	FBML	Contents of the element are visible only if the user has added the application.
fb:visible-to-app-users	FBML	Contents of the element are visible only if the user has allowed the application full permission.
fb:visible-to-friends	FBML	Contents of the element are visible only if the user is a friend of the profile owner.
fb:visible-to-owner	FBML	Contents of the element are visible only if the profile owner is the user.
fb:visible-to-user	FBML	Contents of the element are visible only if the viewer is a specified user.

TABLE 2-2   Profile Platform Elements That Control Visibility

Platform Element	Category	Notes
`fb:profile-action`	FBML	Specifies a link on a Profile page under the user's photo.
`fb:subtitle`	FBML	Subtitle for a Profile page box.
`fb:user-table`	FBML	A table of user names and thumbnails on a Profile page.
`profile.getFBML`	API	Returns the FBML for a user's profile.
`profile.setFBML`	API	Sets the FBML for a user's profile.
`fb:ref`	FBML	Retrieves FBML from a URL or a handle. Use it to insert constant code for your application in many users' Profile pages.
`fbml.setRefHandle`	API	Sets a handle and FBML to be used by `fb:ref`.
`fbml.refreshRefUrl` and `fbml.refreshImgSrc`	API	For ref handles that come from URLs, refreshes FBML or image from the external server.

TABLE 2-3 Profile Platform Elements for Applications

As you can see in Figure 2-12, from the Privacy Overview page, you can adjust the Poke, Message, and Friend Request settings.

Also on this page, in the lower-right area, you can see who can view these parts of your profile because you have contacted them recently with a friend request.

Platform Element	Category	Notes
`fb:name`	FBML	Renders the name of the given user. Options allow first name, last name, and other choices.
`fb:pronoun`	FBML	Renders a pronoun for the user, with options for reflexive, possessive, objective, and other forms.
`fb:profile-pic`	FBML	Returns an HTML img tag, with the user's profile picture and an optional link.

TABLE 2-4 Profile Platform Elements for Profile Data

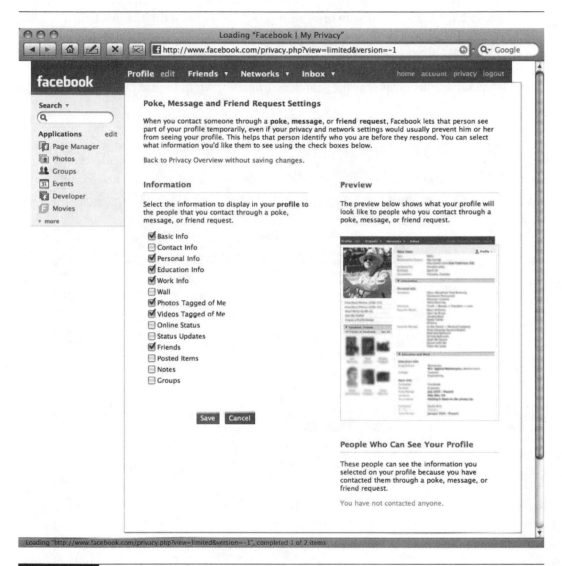

FIGURE 2-12   Poke, Message, and Friend Request privacy settings

Friends and Search

Friends are a key element of Facebook. Your profile shows the total number of friends that you have; six are shown just below your photo. Clicking See All opens the Friends page.

You also have a display of networks with your friends in them; it is just below your Friends box. There are many ways to find new friends. You may encounter people as friends of your friends or as members of groups or networks; you also may search for them using various criteria. The last part of the privacy overview to be discussed in this chapter is the search settings, shown in Figure 2-13. This is

FIGURE 2-13   Privacy-related search settings

where you control who can see you in a search and what they can do when they find you.

It is now possible for people to search Facebook without being logged in. They can also find you from search engines. The privacy settings shown in Figure 2-13 allow you to control the visibility of your information in the public search, as well as what actions can be taken. The public search listing preview is shown in Figure 2-14.

FIGURE 2-14   Public search listing preview

Platform Element	Category	Notes
fb:friend-selector	FBML	Input field where you can start to type a friend's name. It will automatically complete as you type. Compare to fb:multi-friend-input.
fb:if-is-friends-with-viewer	FBML	Displays content if the user is friends with the user specified.
fb:multi-friend-input	FBML	As you start to type a name, you see a drop-down list of matching names, from which you can select one. Compare to fb:friend-selector.
fb:multi-friend-selector	FBML	A graphical selector of friends for requests or invitations. Three to 10 rows shown; maximum selected is 5 to 20.
fb:name	FBML	Renders the name of the given user subject to options such as first or last name.
fb:visible-to-friends	FBML	Content of the element is visible only if the user is a friend of the profile owner.
friends.areFriends	API	Returns whether pairs of users are friends.
friends.get	API	Returns user IDs of user's friends.
friends.getAppUsers	API	When called by an application, returns the user's friends who are signed up for the application.

TABLE 2-5   Profile Platform Elements

Platform Elements for Friends

Developers can interact with friends using the components shown in Table 2-5.

Interact with Facebook Pages

Each Facebook user has a Profile page. It is built from data the user has entered, as well as information provided by applications that the user has added (all subject to privacy constraints, of course).

Facebook has added the ability for users to create Facebook Pages (note the capital P), which are similar to Profile pages, but that represent entities: businesses, politicians, nonprofit organizations, and even writers.

Figure 2-15 shows a Facebook Page.

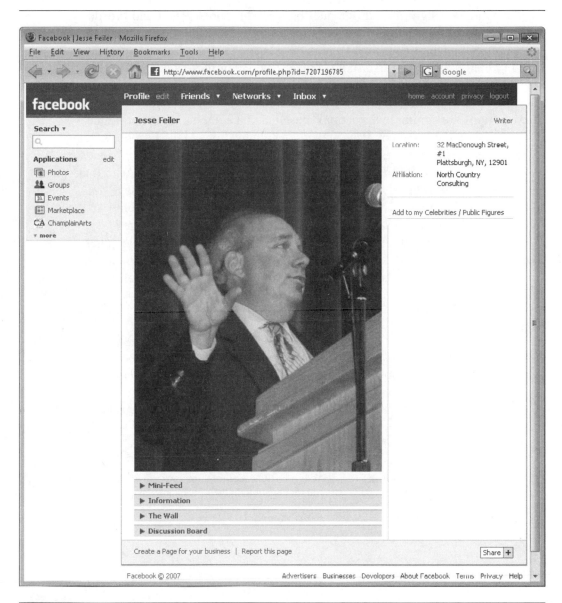

FIGURE 2-15   A Facebook Page

There are two significant differences between Facebook Pages and Profile pages. Most obviously, a Profile page is for a single user, whose identity is shown on that page. A Facebook Page is for a business, organization, or other entity (which might be a person); it is created by one or more *admins*. These are Facebook users whose identity, therefore, is verified. Actions taken by "the Facebook Page" are actually taken by the admins on behalf of the Facebook Page. These actions are similar to the actions a user can take, including updating the information on the Facebook Page and adding applications to the Facebook Page.

The other difference has to do with the social graph. Users can have friends on Facebook: You send a friend request and may receive a confirmation. After that, the two of you are friends. Facebook Pages do not have friends: they have *fans*. If you want to become a fan of a Facebook Page, you just click on add link to the right of the picture, as shown in Figure 2-15. No confirmation is required.

Most of Facebook works the same for Facebook Pages as for Profile pages. The News Feed, Mini-Feed, and an application's Profile box all function as you would expect. There are Platform elements that are specific to Facebook Pages. They are listed in Table 2-6.

Platform Element	Category	Notes
pages.getInfo	API	Returns visible pages for a user.
pages.isAppAdded	API	Given a Facebook Page ID, returns whether or not it has added the application.
pages.isAdmin	API	Whether or not the current user is an admin for a Facebook Page you specify.
pages.isFan	API	Whether or not a user is a fan of the Facebook Page you specify.
fb:page-admin-edit-header	FBML	Adds an edit header for admins to use when editing your application on their Facebook Page.

TABLE 2-6   Platform Elements for Facebook Pages

Chapter 3

Find Your Way Around Facebook

How to…

- ■ Use the Mini-Feed
- ■ Use the Wall
- ■ Use the inbox and messages
- ■ Work with pokes
- ■ Handle requests and notifications
- ■ Use Friend Finder and invite friends
- ■ Use Social Ads
- ■ Develop polls
- ■ Handle subscriptions

The previous chapter showed you how to find your way around your Home page and profile. In doing so, you were introduced to a number of the fundamentals of Facebook, including news feeds, status updates, and certain aspects of notifications. You also found out how your own profile information is handled and what you can do to protect your privacy. The concepts of friends and networks showed you how you can interact with other people on Facebook.

Building on those basics, this chapter explores most of the rest of Facebook, with the exception of applications, which are discussed in the next chapter. As in the previous chapter, for each aspect of Facebook, you will find a description of it from the user's point of view; in most cases, these descriptions are followed by a table showing some of the Facebook Platform elements that you, as an application developer, can use to interact with the Facebook features. The Platform elements are discussed in more detail in Part II.

NOTE   *Most of the privacy settings for Facebook apply to your profile and were described in the previous chapter. From now on, when you read about information that you can see on a Facebook page, you should remember that it is always subject to privacy settings; that phrase is not repeated unless there is a substantive change you need to know about.*

Use the Mini-Feed

The Mini-Feed is located just under your status updates and basic information on your Profile page. You can collapse or expand it, but you cannot move it. It contains the latest news about you.

The News Feed on your Home page consists of your friends' doings. Your doings appear in the Mini-Feed on your profile. Anyone who can view your profile will be able to see your stories in your Mini-Feed. In addition to your general privacy settings, you can remove an individual Mini-Feed story by clicking the × at the right of it. This will hide the story from your Mini-Feed and from anyone who views your Profile page.

In November 2007, Facebook introduced Social Ads, Facebook Pages, and Facebook Beacon. Facebook Beacon allows external Web sites to post stories to your Mini-Feed (and thence to your friends' News Feeds) if you permit it. These stories may reflect your purchases or other actions on the external Web site. In addition to setting privacy settings for external Web sites in your privacy settings, you also have an opportunity on the external Web site to approve or disapprove an individual story. You also can remove such a story the next time you log into Facebook.

If you want to see all of your Mini-Feed stories, you can click See All to open the window shown in Figure 3-1. Here you will be able to select from your Mini-Feed stories using the buttons at the right (useful if you've been really active!).

Platform Elements for the Mini-Feed

These are the same elements shown in Table 2-1 in the context of the News Feed.

Use the Wall

The Wall is an area of your Profile page on which you and your friends can write messages. You can also add attachments to those messages that use various applications that you or the owner of the Wall's profile has added. You can delete any of the postings on your Wall by clicking Delete at the bottom of the post.

Facebook Platform also supports Walls on application pages. They are sometimes referred to as Wall-like objects to distinguish them from the Wall on your Profile page. In all cases, Walls allow anyone with the proper access to write on them.

FIGURE 3-1   See all your Mini-Feed stories.

Platform Element	Category	Notes
fb:attachment-preview	FBML	A link in a Wall or message attachment that can be clicked on to fetch new content.
fb:comments	FBML	A Wall-like object you can place onto a page and post comments to.
fb:wall	FBML	Renders a Wall-like page section. See also fb:wallpost.
fb:wallpost	FBML	Renders a Wall-style post.
fb:wallpost-action	FBML	Displays a link at the bottom of a Wall post.

TABLE 3-1   Platform Elements for the Wall

Platform Elements for the Wall

Table 3-1 shows the Platform elements for the Wall.

Use the Inbox and Messages

Your inbox and its messages are available from the Facebook frame. The inbox functions much as email does, but there are some important differences. Although you can include links in your messages, you cannot add attachments to them. Also, you can send a message to any individual on Facebook (whether that person is a friend or not), but if you are sending a message to a group of individuals, you can only send it to a maximum of 20 recipients, who must be your friends.

Work with Pokes

A poke is a content-less message sent to another Facebook user. It can mean "hello," "what's new," or whatever either of you chooses to interpret it as. You can send pokes from a number of places, including lists of photos and other media contributed by Facebook users. If Facebook Mobile is activated, pokes go to mobile phones.

Platform Elements for Pokes

Table 3-2 shows the basic Platform element to receive pokes. More elements that can be used for pokes are described in the following section.

Platform Element	Category	Notes
notifications.get	API	Returns notifications for the current user, separated into messages, pokes, shares, friend requests, and group or event invitations.

TABLE 3-2 Platform Elements for pokes

Handle Requests and Notifications

Requests include friend requests, invitations to groups and events, and friend detail events (such as how you know someone). They are sent to you by others (or by others to you). In general, one person sends a request to another, and the other person receives a notification. Notifications show up on at the upper-right of your Home page; they also show up on the Notification tab of your inbox. Using the Notifications tab of your account settings, you can control what, if any, actions cause notifications to also be sent to your email address.

Platform Elements for Requests and Notifications

Table 3-3 shows the Platform elements for requests and notifications.

Platform Element	Category	Notes
notifications.send	API	Send a notification to one or more users.
fb:notif-email	FBML	Content to be sent via email; specified in notifications.send.
fb:notif-page	FBML	Content to be sent via a Facebook notification; specified in notifications.send.
fb:notif-subject	FBML	Subject for email notification; specified in notifications.send.
fb:request-form	FBML	A form to send requests or invitations to friends. Usually contains an fb:multi-friend-selector or similar element.
fb:req-choice	FBML	Button to be shown on the bottom of a request on the requests page. (Ignore is added by default.)
fb:request-form-submit	FBML	Submit button for an fb:request-form.
notifications.get	API	Returns outstanding notifications.

TABLE 3-3 Platform Elements for Requests and Notifications

Use Friend Finder and Invite Friends

You can find your friends on Facebook using the Find Friends tab on Friends, as shown in Figure 3-2. Facebook can read email address books from Hotmail, MSN, Yahoo!, Gmail, and AOL, and search for the addresses in its directory. There are also instructions on this page for how you can export addresses from other address books.

You can also use the Invite Friends command next to Friends in the frame to compose email messages to one or more of your friends, inviting them to join Facebook, as shown in Figure 3-3.

FIGURE 3-2   Use Friend Finder to locate friends on Facebook.

FIGURE 3-3 Invite friends to join Facebook.

Use Social Ads

Social Ads appear in *ad space* (the left-hand column, or Left Nav, below Search and the menu of applications) or in the News Feed. They were introduced in November 2007, replacing the basic version of flyers on Facebook and incorporating new features that allow integration with the activities of users and their friends (all, of course, subject to the users' privacy preferences). You can use Social Ads to promote anything (subject to Facebook's Terms of Service). Social Ads take advantage of stories in users' News Feeds. As a result, it is important for you to understand the process, not just to be able to promote your Facebook application, but to understand how to post stories to the News Feed from your application so that they can be integrated with advertising, if you desire.

Get Started

To create a Social Ad, you click on the Advertisers or Businesses links at the bottom of any Facebook page. That begins the process shown in Figure 3-4.

You can choose to advertise an external Web site or a Facebook Page or application. If you want to advertise a Facebook Page and do not yet have one, the third option will launch you into the process of creating a Facebook Page.

Create a Facebook Page

The first step in creating a Facebook Page is identifying who or what will be the subject of the page, as shown in Figure 3-5.

You then proceed through a series of pages that are similar to the pages on which you enter profile data for your personal account. In this case, depending on the type of business you are setting up, you have varying types of data to enter. For example, as you can see in Figure 3-6, for a local business, you can enter the hours of operation.

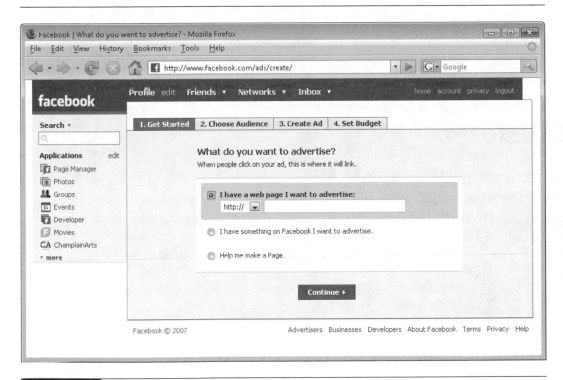

FIGURE 3-4   Start to create a Social Ad.

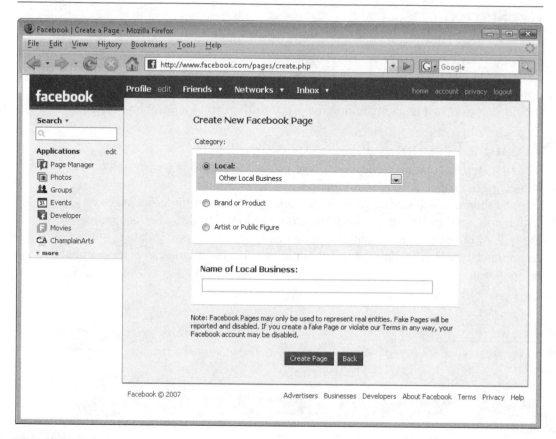

FIGURE 3-5 Identify the Facebook Page's subject.

NOTE

This process can be launched from several places in Facebook. You can create the Facebook Page, as described here, in the context of creating a Social Ad. Alternatively, you can create a Facebook Page from the Businesses link at the bottom of any page and then, having created the Facebook Page, you can create a Social Ad based on it. You can also create the Facebook Page and come back to it later to create one or more Social Ads based on the page.

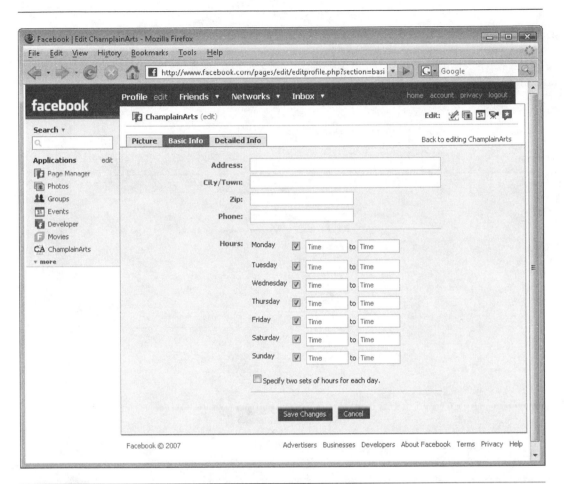

FIGURE 3-6   Enter data for the business.

Choose the Audience

Now that you have identified what you want to advertise (an external Web site or a Facebook Page or application), you start describing your audience and how you want the ad to be placed. The next page in the Social Ads creation sequence is shown in Figure 3-7; it lets you identify the people who should see your ad.

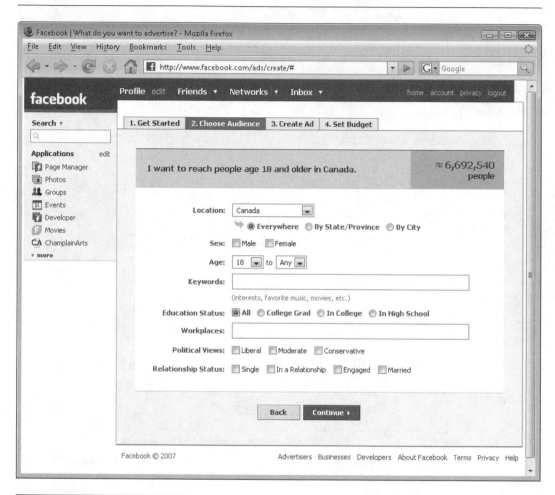

FIGURE 3-7   Specify your audience.

NOTE   *As you change the settings, the number of people you have identified is shown in the upper-right area of the page. This is not the number of people who will actually see your ad; rather, it is the number of people you have identified. If you are a sophisticated advertiser or demographer, you may have such information at your fingertips. But for most people, the size of the group you are identifying can be a big help. Changing a few settings may drastically enlarge or decrease the group you are targeting.*

Did you know?

More on Your Ad's Performance

Advertisers often talk about "reach and frequency," meaning the scope of an advertisement's reach to a given target group and the frequency with which it is seen by a given individual within that target group. There is generally a trade-off: to have individuals see your advertisement several times (frequency), you may want to send it to a smaller group of people (reach) so that the chances of any individual seeing the advertisement more than once are greater. Part of the theory behind Social Ads is that their impact may be increased because of their integration with friends and their actions. If that is the case, the frequency may be able to be decreased in an advertising campaign. There are many books, articles, and Web sites on the theories of marketing and advertising. In addition, Facebook Insight, the statistics that you can see about your advertisement's performance, can be an enormous help in the necessary and ongoing evaluation of your advertisement.

Create the Ad

As you can see in Figure 3-8, the next step is to create the Social Ad. Towards the bottom of the page is the option to add social actions to your ad.

If you want more information, you will see the example shown in Figure 3-9. This is the key integration point between applications and Social Ads. It can sometimes lead to surprising results for users whose actions are used in this way if they have not set their privacy settings appropriately. On the other hand, if someone has thought briefly about privacy settings and set them appropriately, this integration can be powerful not just for the advertiser but also for the user who initiated the social action. From the advertiser's point of view, it may launch a business transaction. But, from the users' points of view, this type of integration, along with News Feed stories, may launch purely social interaction, such as an email inquiring, "How did you like the concert," or "Interested in dinner afterwards?" Remember: Facebook is all about the social graph, in all of its guises and permutations.

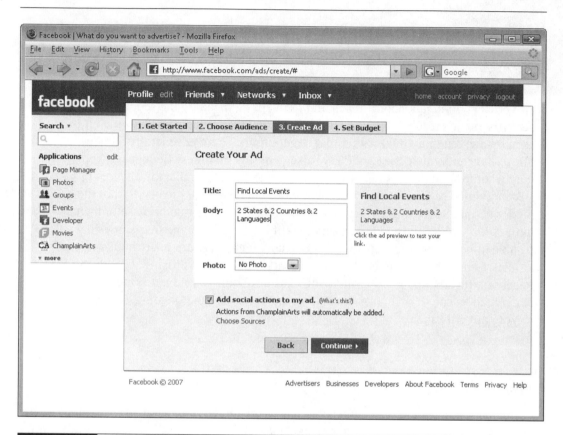

FIGURE 3-8   Create the ad.

Set the Budget

The last step is to set the budget for the ad. You have two choices here. You can pay by the click or by the view. If you pay by the click (Cost-Per-Click or CPC), you pay up to a specified amount for each click your ad receives. (Remember that all ads have some kind of link or another in them.) You can set a maximum daily amount for this, as shown in Figure 3-10. You can also specify when the ad runs.

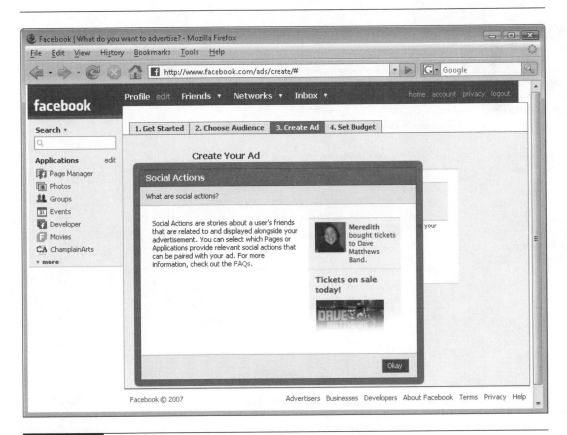

FIGURE 3-9   Use Social Actions with your ad if you want.

If you pay by the view, you pay every time the ad is presented to users, regardless of whether they click. Cost-Per-View (CPM) is based on a thousand views, not a single click. You also can specify whether the ad runs in ad space or in the News Feed (see Figure 3-11).

NOTE   *Traditional advertising terminology talks of* cost-per-thousand *(impressions), abbreviated as CPM. That is how Cost-Per-View for a thousand views can wind up being abbreviated as CPM.*

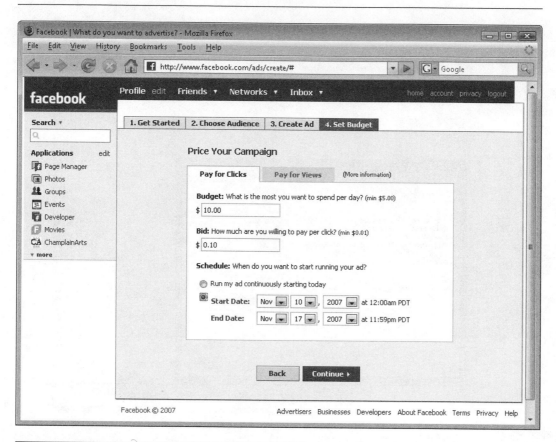

Set a budget for a CPC ad.

Facebook determines what advertisements to display based on the available advertisements and the costs that the advertisers are willing to pay.

Review the Ad and Pay

The last page, shown in Figure 3-12, lets you review your advertisement settings and enter your credit card information.

FIGURE 3-11   Set a budget for a pay-by-view ad.

Develop Polls

You can develop polls to be placed in users' News Feeds. Like social ads, you
must pay for these. You will find polls in the Businesses link at the bottom
of Facebook pages. You will find a brief description and then be offered an
opportunity to create a poll with up to five answers. You can then choose how
it will be run, as shown in Figure 3-13.

FIGURE 3-12   Review and pay.

There is a $1 charge to set up the poll; you then pay a certain amount for each response, up to a limit that you specify. These are unscientific polls, but they can provide interesting results for promoting products and services. In addition, depending on where the polls are shown and what the substance is, they may provide information that is actionable. (Internet polls for electoral candidates are particularly vulnerable to manipulation.)

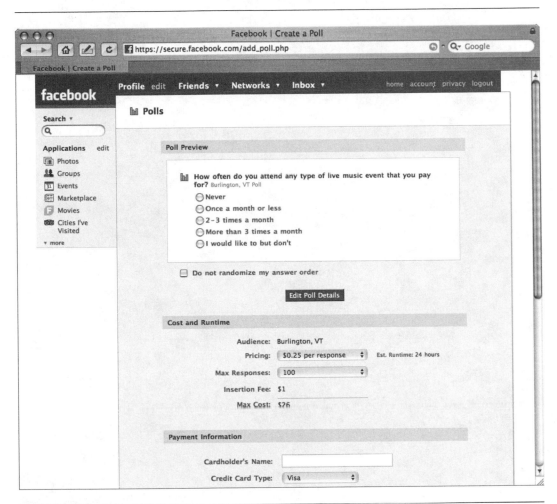

FIGURE 3-13   Create a poll.

Handle Subscriptions

You can create Really Simply Syndication (RSS) or Atom feeds from a variety of places on Facebook. These include your notifications, your friends' status updates, and your friends' posted items. You can then use the subscription URL that is generated in your browser to keep up to date with the Facebook information to which you are subscribed.

Chapter 4

Find Your Way Around a Facebook Application: Groups

How to...

- Create and manage groups
- Use groups
- Use Facebook identifiers
- Use the Groups application

One of the reasons for Facebook's popularity is the fact that its complexity and power are derived from the combination and recombination of a small number of common objects and concepts. Each component is consistent with every other component in functionality as well as in look and feel. Nowhere is this more evident than in Facebook applications. The features and functionality described in the previous chapters are implemented directly in code written by Facebook. Everything else is written as a Facebook application, whether it is written by Facebook or by a third-party developer such as yourself.

Even such core components of Facebook, such as groups, events, photos, and the marketplace, are implemented as applications built on Facebook Platform. This chapter walks you through the basics of Groups, one of the most commonly used and reasonably complex applications. Although the code is proprietary to Facebook, you will see how you could use Facebook Platform to implement the functionality of the Groups application. You will notice that some of the functionality of groups (the Facebook feature) is not exposed in Facebook Platform. For example, you cannot add a group with Facebook Platform. Many of the core Facebook functions are not exposed—particularly if their uncontrolled use has the potential to corrupt the Facebook database. Thus, as you start to plan your Facebook applications, check to make certain that the calls you need to make are available. Do not fret much about this: So much is available and you can add so much functionality of your own, that this is not much of an issue. In fact, it is often the case that if you want to use calls that are not available (such as creating new groups), you may be trying to duplicate functionality that already exists in Facebook and which requires no modification.

NOTE   *Facebook includes the concept of groups, and it includes elements to manipulate groups. It also includes the Groups application, which lets you use those internal elements to manipulate groups. Groups (capitalized) refers to the application; groups (lowercase) refers to the Facebook concept. This practice is used throughout the book: Events is the application that controls Facebook events, for example.*

Thus, this chapter serves as a fairly detailed description of many of the elements of Facebook Platform that you can use to implement an application. Continuing the technique of the previous chapters, you will walk through the interface and then see the routines that could be used to implement it from an operational point of view. In the next part of the book, the structure is reversed: You will find the details of the code taking center stage.

That part of the book also deals with the markup elements that you use to display data on a page. It also explores the Facebook API that you can access through the REST interface, either directly from any language that supports REST calls or through the Facebook objects that handle all of this for you if you are using PHP. If you use the Facebook objects, the results of API calls are usually returned in PHP arrays. However, the actual results of the API calls are XML documents, which are parsed by those objects. In this chapter, the actual XML that is returned is shown. In that way, you can use it as a model for any language that you use to write your applications. You will find out what calls return what items (the members of a group, for instance). The complete syntax and structure of the returned XML is described in Chapter 6.

But first, a close look at what groups are is in order.

Create and Manage Groups

If you have not joined a Facebook group yet, join one now. There is no substitute for observing someone using a product like software, and you have the perfect test subject: yourself.

You can browse the list of groups to find one that interests you. Figure 4-1 shows the FileMaker Developers group displayed in the Groups application, and it illustrates a variety of features of groups.

First of all, there is basic information about the group, such as the name and description. Groups also have a type and subtype; in Figure 4-1, they are separated by a hyphen.

Photos, videos, and posts can be added to a group. Many groups also have discussion boards. They also may have officers and administrators. You will see how to set up a group and set these options in this section. Figure 4-1 shows the group in action—that is, with photos and members-added information, all subject to the constraints you set up when you create a group.

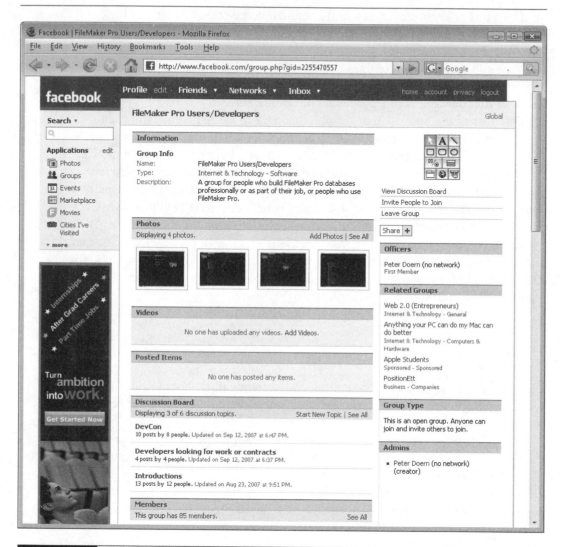

FIGURE 4-1   FileMaker Developers group

Create and Edit Groups

You create a group from Groups by clicking Create A New Group in the upper-right area of a page, such as the one shown in Figure 4-2, which is the page that opens when you first open Groups.

FIGURE 4-2   Create a group in the Groups application.

Group Info

When you create or edit a group, you start with the Group Info tab, as shown in Figure 4-3.

Each group has a name, and it must either be associated with a specific network or flagged as global. Neither of these settings can be changed. Non-global groups will be limited to members from the specified network, so make certain

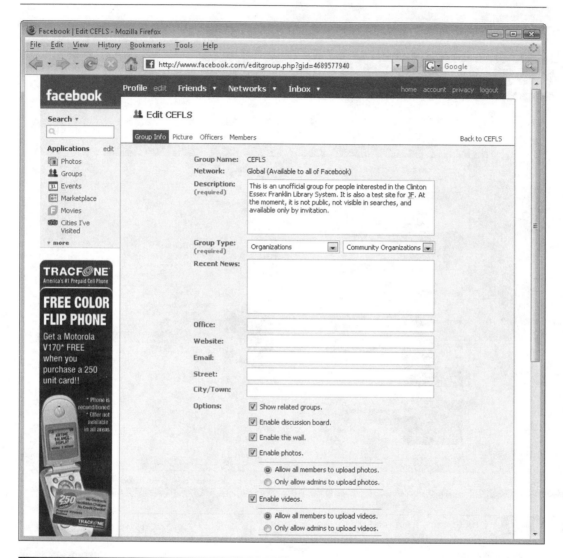

FIGURE 4-3 Begin providing information about your group at the top of the Group Info tab.

that you really want to do this. (It is a useful tool if the network is an organization and you want the group to be invisible from the outside.)

Other settings are shown in Figure 4-3 and are self-explanatory in most cases. The basic options control what Facebook features are enabled: the Wall, photos, videos, posts, and a discussion board. Related groups can be shown: they are calculated from the membership by Facebook.

Figure 4-4 shows the bottom of the Group Info tab. Here you see the basic privacy settings for the group itself. Publicize lets you control whether the group is visible on the network page (if you have chosen a network) and visible in searches. Access has three settings: open, closed, and secret. Open is just that: Anyone can join, and anyone can see the group's information. Secret means that only members can see the group's information, and they must be invited to join. Closed means that only members can see the discussion board, photos, videos, and posted items, but anyone can see the rest of the information. Furthermore, requests for membership must be approved by an administrator.

TIP   *Setting up a group as secret is often a good idea if you are testing a group idea. You can change the access later.*

FIGURE 4-4   Set privacy settings at the bottom of the Group Info tab.

Picture

The next tab lets you associate a picture with the group. It must be under 4 megabytes (MB).

Officers and Administrators

In Figure 4-5, you see the Officers tab. On the underlying page is a list of group members. If you click the Make Officer link at the right of each line, the dialog shown here opens for the person selected. You can enter a title for this person. You can later remove this person as an officer if you want.

Facebook also recognizes administrators for the group, such as the creator. If you are an administrator, you can go to the list of members and make other members administrators. Administrators actually can control the group; officers have a title but no powers (unless they are also administrators).

Members

The final tab lets you view the members of the group. It also shows you a list of your friends, with checkboxes next to each one. You can select those friends

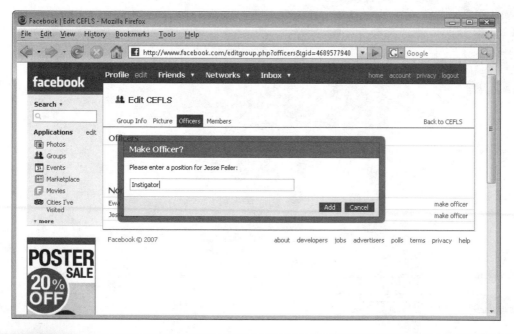

FIGURE 4-5   Create officers

you want to invite to the group with a single click of the mouse. You also can invite people who are not Facebook members to join; they will receive an email invitation from you, but will have to join Facebook before joining the group.

Use Groups

You can use a group if you are a member, or if it is an open group to which you have access. Figure 4-6 shows a group's page as it appears to an administrator. Compare it with Figure 4-1, which shows a group as it appears to a member.

At the right are a number of links that let you work with the group.

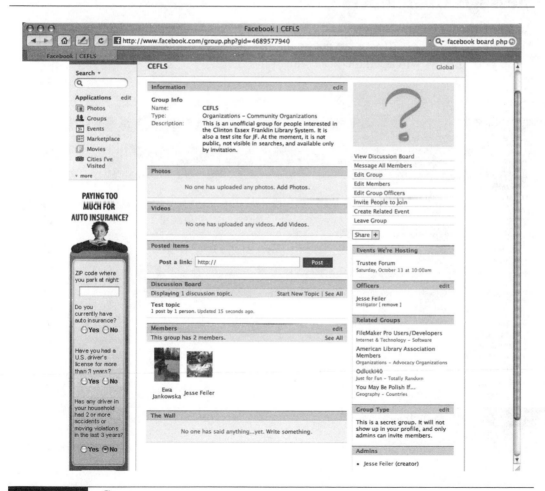

FIGURE 4-6   Group page

View Discussion Board

If a discussion board was enabled in the Group Info tab, then you can view it, as shown in Figure 4-7. You can see a list of topics, or you can click one and see all of the posts.

> **NOTE** *Even if the discussion board is enabled for the group, View Discussion Board will not show up until the first post has been created. If the discussion board is blank, it will contain a link saying "Start the first topic." If you do so, it will create the topic and View Discussion Board will then appear.*

Message All Members

As an admin, you can send a message to all members of a group by clicking Message All Members. If you are not an admin, you can send messages using the Share button. This will open the page shown in Figure 4-8.

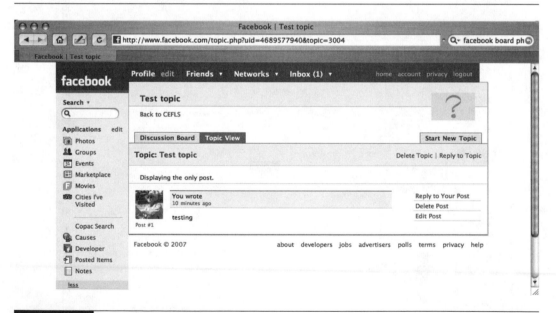

FIGURE 4-7   Discussion board

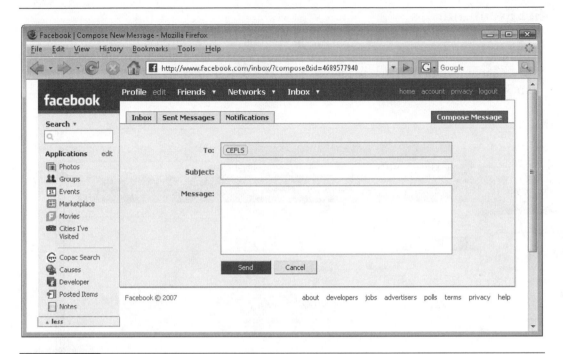

FIGURE 4-8   Send a message to all group members.

> **NOTE**   *There is a limit of 1,000 recipients to a message, so if your group contains more than 1,000 members, Message All Members cannot be used. You can post a notice on your group's Wall, but your members may not see it.*

Edit Group, Members, and Officers; Invitations

These topics were discussed in the previous section, "Create and Edit Groups."

Create Related Events

This is one of the most useful features of groups: You can create events for them. Events are standard Facebook events, with a date and time, place, title, and a list of invitees. If your group is conceptual (for example, devotees of William Dean Howells), events may not matter to you. However, if your group represents an organization, events may be a critical feature. (Only admins can create events for groups.)

Set Event Info

Start by clicking Create Related Event and opening the page shown in Figure 4-9.

There are subtle differences between the pages to create and edit events. When you create an event, the tabs are labeled Step 1: Event Info, Step 2: Picture, and Step 3: Guest List.

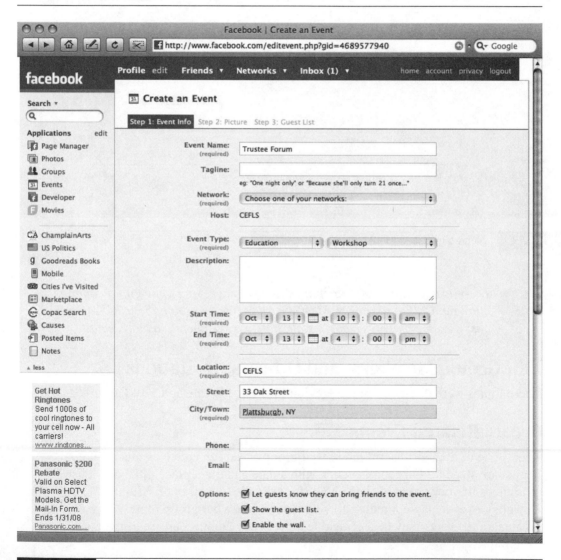

FIGURE 4-9   Begin providing information about your event at the top of the Event Info tab.

As you can see from Figure 4-9, the basic information is what you would expect for an event. Figure 4-10 shows the bottom of this page, with the same types of settings available as on the Group page itself.

Access here requires a little more thought than for the group itself, although the settings are the same. If you make the group and its events public or secret, you do not have to worry. Your only concern is if there is some combination of settings. There are cases in which you want events to be more visible than the group itself (a fund-raiser, perhaps); there also are cases in which you want events to be less visible than the group itself (a meeting of a subcommittee, perhaps).

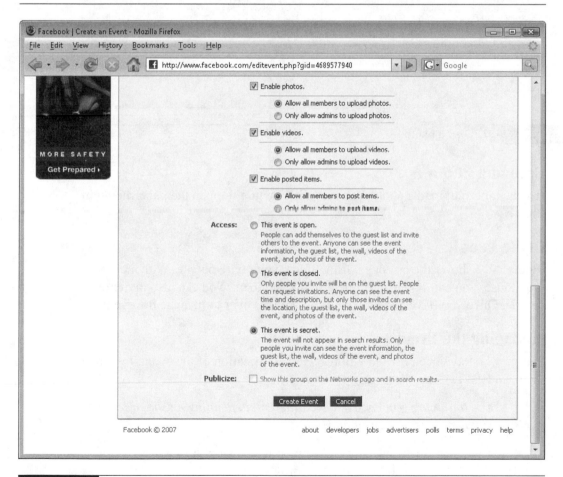

FIGURE 4-10   Set privacy settings at the bottom of the Event Info tab.

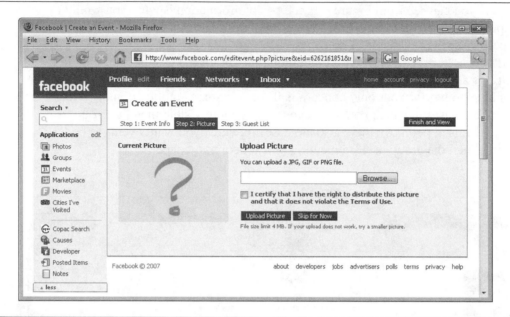

FIGURE 4-11   Upload a photo

Upload a Photo

If you want to upload a photo, you can click Picture to open the page shown in Figure 4-11.

Invite People

Figure 4-12 shows the last page, from which you invite people. With a click of the mouse, you can invite all of the group's members. You can also invite other people. Once you have done this, Facebook takes over to manage the event.

Managing the Event

People who have been invited will receive a notification of the event, to which they can RSVP.

NOTE   *The following sequence may be different, depending on the order in which you respond to an event and edit it.*

When you see the event, you can look at it and view it in a brief display. Figure 4-13 shows the brief listing, from which you can RSVP or view the entire event.

If you want to see the full event, you can look at it by clicking on the event title, as shown in Figure 4-14.

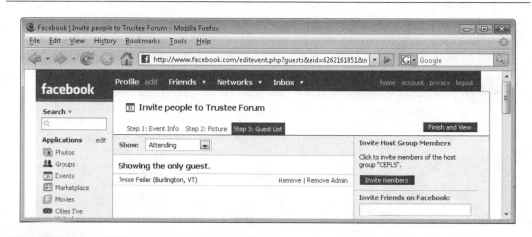

Invite people to an event

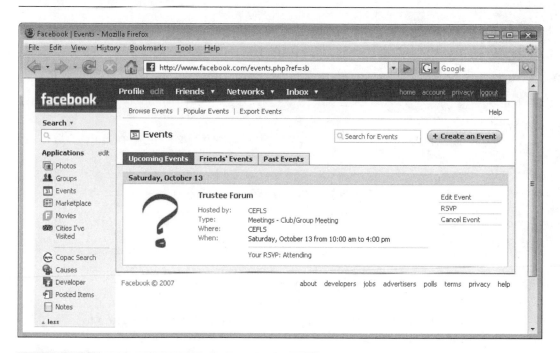

You can RSVP to the event

FIGURE 4-14 View all of the information for the event.

You will notice that at the right of Figure 4-14, you now have the option to cancel the event. Clicking that link will open the dialog shown in Figure 4-15.

Finally, notice that beneath the cancel link you can share or export the event. Sharing the event allows you to send it as a message or to post it to your profile, as shown in Figure 4-16.

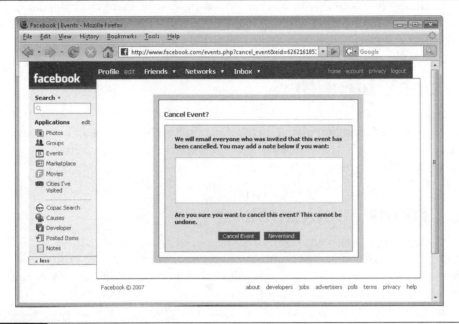

FIGURE 4-15   You can cancel an event

FIGURE 4-16   Share an event as a message or a post.

If you choose to export it, you will download an ICS file that your calendar program can most likely read (certainly Windows Calendar and iCal on Mac OS X can read it).

Use Facebook Identifiers

Each element of the Facebook Platform has a unique identifier. They are used to identify objects that are manipulated by the API and Facebook Markup Language (FBML) elements. Table 4-1 shows the basic identifiers that are referred to in the balance of this book.

Use the Groups Application

As noted previously, groups are just that: groups of people with something in common. You can join up to 200 groups on Facebook. You can create groups, join them, and leave them. Groups can have administrators and officers—you can become either. And, just as with everything else on Facebook, privacy has been built in from the ground up. All calls respect privacy settings; you need do nothing else. In this section, you will look in some detail at the Groups application and how it implements the functionality of Facebook groups.

Groups API

The concept of groups is part of the Facebook Platform API, and is accessible to any application using the API—including the built-in Groups application. Table 4-2 shows the Groups API calls that implement groups in Facebook Platform.

Like all API calls, these return XML or JSON arrays, although as you will see in Part II, if you use the PHP Facebook object, that XML will be transformed into

Identifier	Meaning
uid	User ID
nid	Primary network ID
eid	Event ID
gid	Group ID
pid	Photo ID
aid	Photo album ID

TABLE 4-1 Facebook Identifiers

Platform Element	Category	Notes
groups.get	API	Get all groups for a user, a list of gids, or a uid/gid list combination.
groups.getMembers	API	Returns a group's membership list.

TABLE 4-2   Groups API Calls

a PHP array before you have to deal with it. (If you do not use a client library that implements some version of a Facebook object, you will need to parse the XML that is returned.) It is worth looking at the structure of the results for these two calls so that you can see that almost all of the information that is needed to display group information is provided.

Here is the result of a call to groups.

```
<?xml version="1.0" encoding="UTF-8"?>
<groups_get_response xmlns="http://api.facebook.com/1.0/"
  xmlns:xsi="http://www.w3.org/2001/XMLSchema-instance"
  xsi:schemaLocation="http://api.facebook.com/1.0/
  http://api.facebook.com/1.0/facebook.xsd" list="true">
    <group>
      <gid>12345</gid>
      <nameE. F. Benson Fans</name>
      <nid>0</nid> //network
      <description>
        Fans of Benson's Lucia (and other) novels.
      </description>
      <group_type></group_type>
      <group_subtype> </group_subtype>
      <recent_news/>
      <pic>http://www.yoursite.com/images/benson.jpg</pic>
      <pic_big>
        http://www.yoursite.com/images/benson.big.jpg
      </pic>
      <pic_small>
        http://www.yoursite.com/images/benson.small.jpg
      </pic>
      <creator>98765432</creator>
      <update_time>1156543965</update_time>
      <office/>
      <website/>
```

```
  <venue>
    <street/>
    <city/>
    <state> </state>
    <country></country>
  </venue>
</group>

<group>
  //...another group
</group>
</groups_get_response>
```

And here is the result of a call to Groups.getMembers:

```
<?xml version="1.0" encoding="UTF-8"?>
<groups_getMembers_response xmlns="http://api.facebook.com/1.0/"
  xmlns:xsi="http://www.w3.org/2001/XMLSchema-instance"
  xsi:schemaLocation="http://api.facebook.com/1.0/
  http://api.facebook.com/1.0/facebook.xsd" list="true">
    <members list="true">
      <uid>1234</uid>
      <uid>2345</uid>
      <uid>3456</uid>
      <uid>4567</uid>
    </members>
    <admins list="true">
      <uid>1234</uid>
      <uid>8765</uid>
    </admins>
    <officers list="true">
      <uid>1234</uid>
    </officers>
    <not_replied list="true"/>
</groups_getMembers_response>
```

Launch Groups

You can launch the Groups application—just like any other application—by
clicking it in the Left Nav list of applications. Applications can also be

launched from URLs or links; the interconnectedness and virality of Facebook is demonstrated, for example, when a News Feed story contains a link to an application that generated information in the News Feed. When you launch Groups, the page shown previously in Figure 4-2 opens. (Of course, the specific groups shown will vary, depending on what, if any, groups you have joined and what groups, if any, your friends, if any, have joined.)

Inside the Facebook frame, you will see the *dashboard* at the top of the page. A dashboard contains the basic controls for the page:

- **Actions** appear at the upper-left area of the dashboard. In Figure 4-2, the actions are My Groups, Browse Groups, and Popular Groups.

- **Create** elements appear at the right. No more than one can exist in the dashboard, which means that you can only create one type of new entity (a new group, a new photo album, and so forth). The create element does not have to exist, but if it does, it looks like Create a New Group in Figure 4-2.

- **Help** elements are located at the right of the dashboard.

- The application name and icon (if one has been uploaded) are automatically inserted into a dashboard by Facebook.

These elements are created with FBML elements into which you can place strings to be displayed in the `title` attribute (which will be the name of the create button, action, or help link; you also specify an `href` attribute, which is the page to link to to implement the functionality of the create button, action, or help link. You cannot specify a font, style, or location—all of these are determined by the Facebook interface, which enforces consistency

My Groups

If you click My Groups, you will open the page shown in Figure 4-17.

This is a typical Facebook page, containing a variety of graphical elements generally created using FBML. (The display elements are described in Chapter 9 and in the examples throughout Part III.) As you can see from Figure 4-17, you can see groups to which you belong and their characteristics. You can also search groups and create a new group.

FIGURE 4-17 Open the My Groups page.

Browse Groups

Figure 4-18 shows the Browse Groups page. There is more data than will fit on one page, so pagination controls let you go from page to page. You will see how to implement this in Chapter 15.

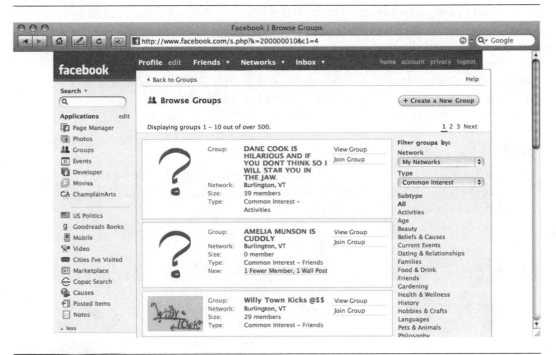

FIGURE 4-18   The Browse Groups page

Popular

The last page is actually a Network page. If you go to a Network page, you will see what is popular in its posted items, groups, events, and notes.

Look at the Facebook Elements in Groups Pages

Now that you have seen the basics of how you can use the Groups application, take a few moments to go back through the process and see how it is accomplished. Although the actual code inside Groups may be different, you can create the effects that you have seen on the pages in this chapter using standard FBML.

FBML Header Elements

First, look at the headers of the pages. There are three major types shown in this chapter. In Figure 4-2, you see a dashboard with the application name and icon, actions, help items, and a create button. There is also a search button that has been added to the basic dashboard elements. Compare Figure 4-2 with Figure 4-17, which contains a media header. The media header contains the user's picture, a title, and—when it is viewed by the user—an action. A third type of header exists: it contains only the application name and icon; it is like a dashboard with no actions, help items, or create button (it is called simply fb:header).

Table 4-3 summarizes the FBML elements involved in headers.

FBML Tabs

Although the page shown in Figure 4-19 is not constructed specifically for the Groups application, it does use a new interface element: tabs, as shown in Table 4-4. (Posted Items, Groups, Events, and Notes).

Platform Element	Category	Notes
fb:dashboard	FBML	A dashboard element. It can contain any of fb:create-button (no more than one),fb_action, and fb_help. Contains no attributes.
fb:action	FBML	The href attribute provides the link to the page that implements the action.
fb:create-button	FBML	The href attribute provides the link to the page that implements the create button.
fb:help	FBML	The href attribute provides the link to the page that implements the help item.
fb:header	FBML	This element looks exactly like a dashboard with no create button, action or help links.
fb:mediaheader	FBML	Shows the user's picture. Normally contains both fb:header-title and fb:owner-action elements.
fb:header-title	FBML	Must be contained within an fb:mediaheader element.
fb:owner-action	FBML	Contains an href that is visible when the viewer of the page is its owner.

TABLE 4-3 Page Header Elements

FIGURE 4-19   See what's popular on Facebook.

Platform Element	Category	Notes
fb:tabs	FBML	This is the container of the tab_item elements, of which there must be at least one.
fb:tab_item	FBML	Each tab_item has a URL and a title string (there are four fb: tab_items in Figure 4-19: Posted Items, Groups, Events, and Notes). They must be in an fb:tabs element.

TABLE 4-4   Tab Elements

FBML Page Body

Much of the layout and styling of the Canvas happens automatically because your FBML (including the HTML that you write within it) uses the standard Facebook styles. Thus all of these elements have the standard Facebook blue color and font for links. The Facebook interface is remarkably clean, which makes it pleasant to look at and easy to use. As a developer of a Facebook application, you can make it even easier to use by not trying to change the styles as well as by laying out your pages in a way that is similar to those of the built-in applications such as Groups.

In the center of the page shown in Figure 4-17 is a list of My Groups; the same type of formatting can be used for any list of items. Beneath the header or dashboard at the top of the page, there are some frequently used controls (such as Show: All Groups) and status information (such as You Are In 3 Groups). Within the list, the links set off at the right such as Edit Group or Leave Group are clear links not only because of their Facebook style but also because their wording is imperative.

Perhaps less obvious is the collection of links under Find A Group at the bottom right of the page. Each of these is a standard element with an `href` attribute going to the appropriate section of Facebook.

The bottom of the Canvas (above the bottom links that are not shown in Figure 4-17) contains additional links and actions such as Create Group, the links for Find Groups, and the Search Groups form.

Chapter 5

Use Other Facebook Applications

How to...

- Add and edit applications and their privacy settings
- Use Photos
- Use Events
- Integrate Facebook using Notes and Mobile

In the previous chapters, you saw the basics of Facebook: learned how to work with your Profile and Home pages; found out about the Wall, News Feed, requests, and notifications; learned about polls, Social Ads, and subscriptions; and got deeply into the concept of groups, as well as the Groups application. This chapter concludes the first part of the book by summarizing many of the other built-in Facebook applications.

You will find some of the major applications here: Photos, Events, and so forth. As in the previous chapters, you will find an overview of the application from a user's point of view, and you will see some of the Facebook Platform elements that can be used in creating the user interface. (Remember that because the code is proprietary, this is only a suggestion of how Facebook Platform could be used.) Facebook Platform elements that have already been described in the previous chapter are not pointed out here again.

Add and Edit Applications and Their Privacy Settings

The Groups application discussed in the previous chapter, along with the applications discussed in this chapter, are already added to your Facebook profile when you create your account. You can add others (and remove these) as you see fit. You click the Edit link or the Applications link in the Left Nav to edit your applications and search for new ones.

NOTE *You will not see Facebook Platform elements in this part of the chapter. That is because the process of adding applications and controlling their general settings is an internal Facebook process. You can find out if an application has been added, and you can put code in your application's Post-Add URL which lets you know when someone has added it, but the settings in this section simply work for you and the user. If a setting does not permit something to happen or be shown, you cannot make it happen or show it. You do not have to do any testing or checking of settings.*

Add an Application

When you search for applications, you will see the application's About page, which provides basic information, such as that shown in Figure 5-1 for the Video application.

FIGURE 5-1   The Video application's About page

This page has a button that you can use to add the application. When you begin to add an application, you see a page like the one in Figure 5-2 which provides more information about the application and, most importantly, lets you control what it can do. (These settings can be changed later in the Edit Settings link in the list of applications that is opened when you click Edit in the applications list.)

Once you have chosen your settings, your new application is added to the list of applications shown in the Left Nav (provided you have chosen that option in the settings shown in Figure 5-2). The initial page of a just-added Video application is shown in Figure 5-3.

At any time, you can edit your applications to change their settings or remove them by clicking Edit at the top of the application list to open the page shown in Figure 5-4. As you can see, you can reorder them as you want. You can also choose which applications show up in the Left Nav applications list so that it is a manageable size and logically ordered for you.

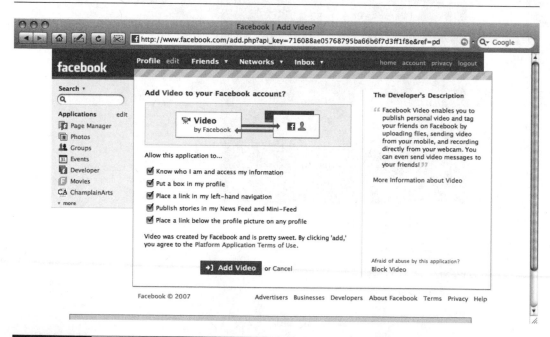

FIGURE 5-2   Choose your initial application settings.

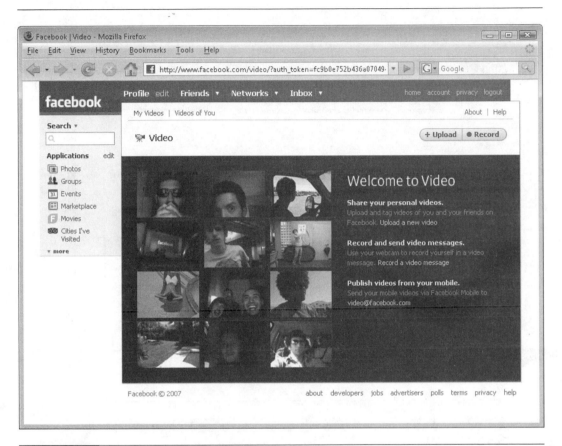

FIGURE 5-3   The added Video application

If you choose to edit an application's settings, the dialog shown in Figure 5-5 appears.

As an example, if you choose not to allow the Movies application to add a link below your profile picture, the View Your Movies link shown in Figure 5-6 would not appear.

Control Application Privacy Settings

From the Privacy link at the top of Facebook pages, you can go to the Privacy Overview page. There you will find a link to edit application settings, which opens the page shown in Figure 5-7.

As you can see, you can remove applications from here (as well as from the Edit Applications page shown in Figure 5-4). You can also control privacy settings

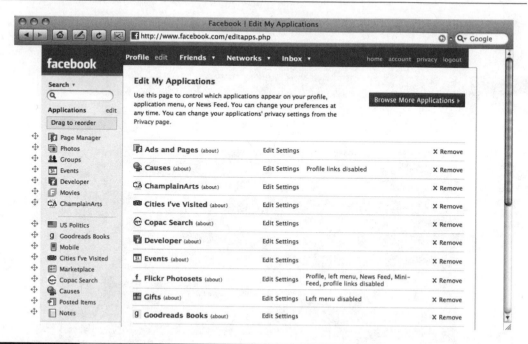

FIGURE 5-4   Edit applications.

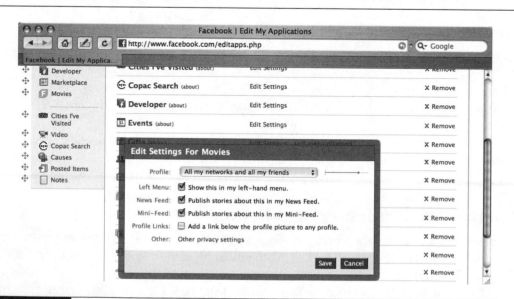

FIGURE 5-5   Edit application settings.

FIGURE 5-6   Control links below your picture.

FIGURE 5-7   Control application privacy settings.

for some applications that have additional controls beyond the standard Facebook settings. For example, the Notes application has additional settings that you can control, as shown in Figure 5-8.

You can use the Authorized Applications tab to remove the access you previously authorized for unadded (but used) applications. You cannot modify the settings, because that is only allowed for added applications. In the case of authorized but unadded applications, all you can do is remove that access and then, if you want, restore new access settings the next time you use the application.

Finally, the Other Applications tab, shown in Figure 5-9, is an important control. It adjusts settings for all applications for which you have not otherwise specified settings, including those you may use in the future. In general, it is a good idea to configure these settings to the most restrictive ones you want to use and then to loosen them on an application-by-application basis. That way, you maintain your privacy in the areas where it matters to you.

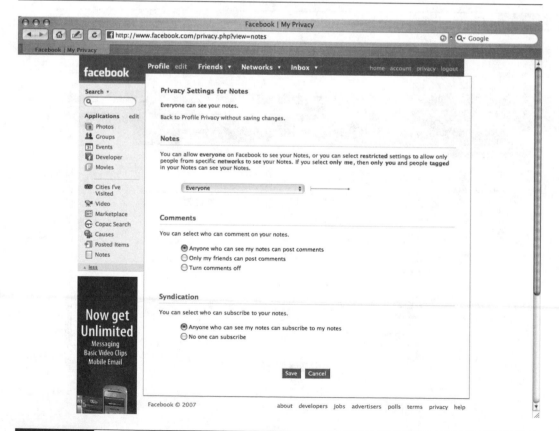

FIGURE 5-8   Control Notes privacy settings.

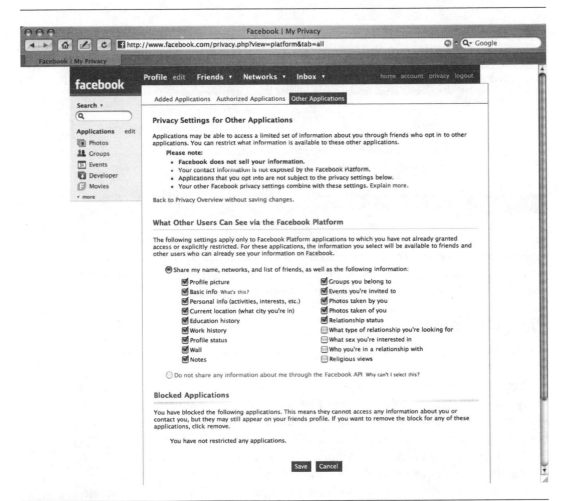

FIGURE 5-9 Configure application privacy settings for Other Applications.

> **NOTE** *There is an option to not share any information through applications built on Facebook Platform. If you have already granted access to applications of this type, you cannot revoke it with this blanket setting until you remove added applications and revoke privileges you have granted to unadded applications.*

Photos

Facebook is one of the biggest photo-sharing sites (sometimes it is ranked the biggest). The Photos application is one of its most popular applications, and, just as with groups, there is support for photos built into Facebook itself so that other applications can be built to do work with photos. There are three primary aspects of the photos

FIGURE 5-10   The Photos application page

implementation: photos, the albums into which you can arrange them, and tags for the photos to identify and categorize them. Albums are identified by album identifiers (usually referred to as `aid`), and photos are identified by photo identifiers (`pid`).

Photo Albums

When you click Launch The Photos Application, you see the page shown in Figure 5-10.

You can see recent albums of your friends as well as newly tagged photos. In many ways, this page is like the News Feed on your Home page: It is automatically generated from your friends' actions. You can use the tab at the top to go to your photos, and that is where you can create albums, as shown in Figure 5-11.

You can create and edit the album information, as shown in Figure 5-12.

As always, you can set visibility options as to who can see the album. Those options are respected by Facebook Platform. Table 5-1 shows the album manipulation elements.

Platform Element	Category	Notes
`photos.createAlbum`	API	Creates an album for the current user (you cannot create an album for someone else).
`photos.getAlbums`	API	You can specify a user ID and/or one or more `aids` and retrieve data about the selected photo albums.

TABLE 5-1   Manipulate Albums with Facebook Platform

FIGURE 5-11 Manage your albums.

FIGURE 5-12 Edit album information.

Photos

Photos (actually any graphic, including PDFs) can be uploaded to albums: You need the album first before you upload the photos. As you can see in Figure 5-13, the Photos interface lets you browse your computer for the file(s) to be uploaded. Table 5-2 shows the photo elements.

Tags

You can tag parts of photos, as shown in Figure 5-14. The tag consists of text, as well as the x,y coordinates of the spot in the photo where you have clicked.

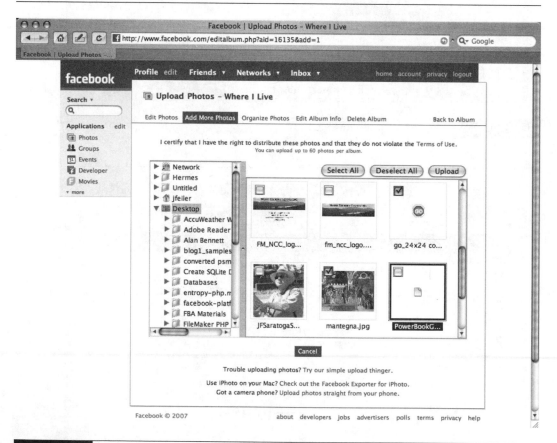

FIGURE 5-13 Upload photos to an album.

Platform Element	Category	Notes
photos.get	API	Retrieve photos based on a subject name, pid, aid, or other filters.
photos.upload	API	Upload photos to an album.
fb:if-can-see-photo	FBML	This brackets conditional code. You can use it to control whether or not a photo and accompanying text is displayed. If the photo cannot be shown, you may not want to display the text; alternatively, you may want to display special text, such as "Photo Unavailable."
fb:photo	FBML	This renders the photo for a page.

TABLE 5-2 Photo Elements

FIGURE 5-14 Tag people in photos.

Platform Element	Category	Notes
photos.addTag	API	Given a pid, you can add a uid or text (not both) to that photo. You need to pass in the mouseclick x and y coordinates to indicate the place on the image to which the tag applies.
photos.getTags	API	Given one or more photos, this call returns all of the tags, including the text and x,y coordinates.

TABLE 5-3   Tag Elements

Most of the time, you tag your friends in your photos, and that is how they and your other friends can see who they are and where they are.

Table 5-3 shows Facebook Platform photo tag manipulations

Events

Like groups and photos, events are a built-in part of Facebook. You can use the Events application to manipulate them, and you can use Facebook Platform to manage them programmatically. When you open Events, you see upcoming events, your friends' events, and past events, as shown in Figure 5-15. You can also create new events from here.

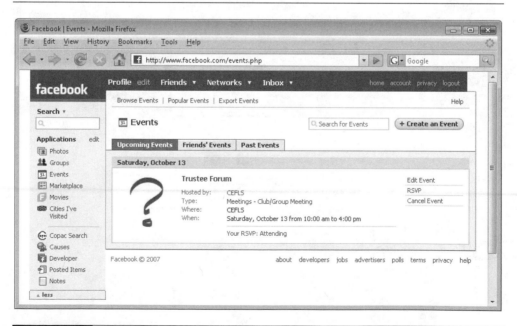

FIGURE 5-15   Use the Events application.

FIGURE 5-16   Browse to find events.

You can also browse events, as shown in Figure 5-16.

If you look at an event, as shown in Figure 5-17 you will see that not only can you share it, as you can share so many Facebook objects, but you can also export it. If you click Export, you open the dialog shown in Figure 5-18.

Table 5-4 shows the Facebook Platform elements for events.

NOTE   *Although events are a major component of Facebook, this section is brief. In large part, that is because of Facebook's architecture: The same objects are used and reused throughout. Thus, you have already seen in Chapter 4 how to create events in the context of groups. You have also seen how events interact with your Home page, profile, and notifications. This means that the truly event-specific code is short and sweet.*

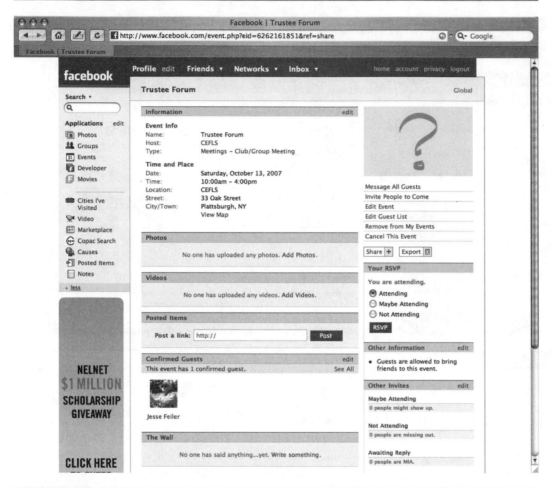

FIGURE 5-17 View an event.

Platform Element	Category	Notes
events.get	API	Retrieve events by RSVP status, uid, and start/stop time.
events.getMembers	API	Retrieve members (invitees), with their RSVP status for a specific event.

TABLE 5-4 Event Elements

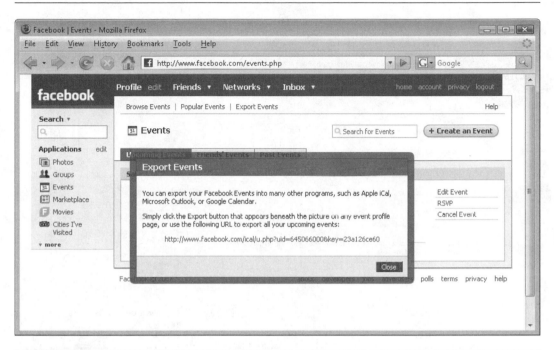

Export events to other applications and formats.

Integrate Facebook Using Notes and Mobile

As you have seen, each new Facebook application builds on Facebook Platform and existing features, so that by this point, there is nothing new to discuss in applications such as Marketplace, Gifts, or Posted Items. The interface is the same as it is for the other applications, and the Facebook Platform features, such as the News Feed, notifications, and so forth, function exactly the same way.

But the Notes application, although it has nothing new in the way of Facebook Platform elements in its implementation and nothing new in its user interface, provides a good place to look at Facebook's integration with the outside world. You have seen how you can share objects and export data in some cases (such as calendar data for events), but Notes can automatically import data from a blog, and it is a good example of how a mobile phone can be used to send data to Facebook. Both the blog import and the mobile settings are shown at the right of the Notes page, which you can see in Figure 5-19.

FIGURE 5-19   Use Notes to view notes, import them from a blog, or write new notes.

Import a Blog

You can choose to import data from a news feed generated by a blog. This is controlled at the right of the Notes page, shown in Figure 5-19. If you choose to import data, you will be asked for the URL of the blog and confirm it in the dialog shown in Figure 5-20.

Most blogging software today has the option to create RSS or Atom news feeds to which people can subscribe. Of course, subscriptions are not limited to people: Mashups can read news feeds and process the information automatically to reformat or even analyze it. In general, the most complicated part of an automated system is the first step: data entry. Once information has been entered, modern technologies can manipulate it so that the subsequent steps are all automated.

NOTE   *For more information on mashups, see the author's book* How to Do Everything with Web 2.0 Mashups.

There is a certain overlap between Facebook functionality and blogs: Both can contain periodic updates, and both can contain pictures. A comment structure is built

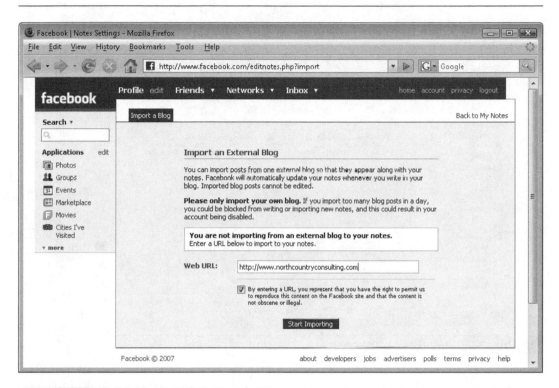

FIGURE 5-20   Enter the blog URL.

into Facebook at many points, and comments are available in blogs. It makes a great deal of sense not to duplicate your efforts—decide what information will go where, and then set things up so that the data flows where it should go. If you set Facebook to read your blog's news feed (which is simple to create—just select a checkbox in your publishing profile on the blog), your blog entries will show up as notes, and Facebook's news and notification features will then perform as they always do.

Also, at the right of Figure 5-19, you can see that you can subscribe to notes—your own or your friends'. This is the reverse data flow: Enter a note in Facebook, and have it become part of a news feed that can be viewed in a news reader or processed by other software. Either way, Facebook fits neatly into a data flow that you construct so that your notes or blog entries are entered once and then sent on the route that you have determined for them.

Use a Mobile Phone

In the Account link at the top of Facebook pages, one of the tabs lets you configure a mobile phone, as shown in Figure 5-21.

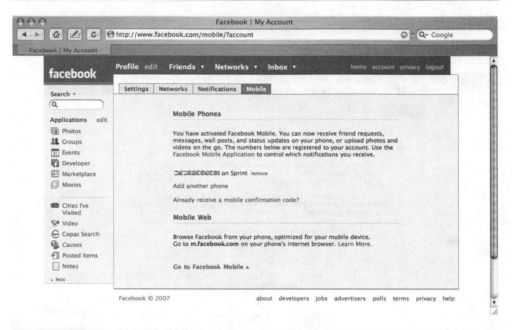

FIGURE 5-21   Configure your account's mobile settings.

There are two sets of mobile settings. The first uses your phone's text-messaging system; the second lets you use a version of the Facebook interface that is designed for the challenges of a mobile phone's Web browser.

Configure Messages

On the page shown in Figure 5-21, you can enter the phone numbers you want to use for text messages. Note that text messages from Facebook are a push technology (they are sent to the mobile phone, which simply delivers them); the mobile Web interface is a pull technology (you browse the Web on your phone and request information, even though some of it—like your News Feed—is pushed to you).

At the bottom of the page is a link to the Mobile application; click Go To Facebook Mobile to open the page shown in Figure 5-22.

You can use text messages to upload photos and videos to Facebook (as shown at the right of Figure 5-22). You can also subscribe to your friends' uploads by editing your mobile settings (at the left). Just as with blogs and news feeds, you can place Facebook in the center of a data flow. If you edit your mobile settings, the page shown in Figure 5-23 opens.

You can configure what you want to have sent and even the times of day and a maximum number of messages.

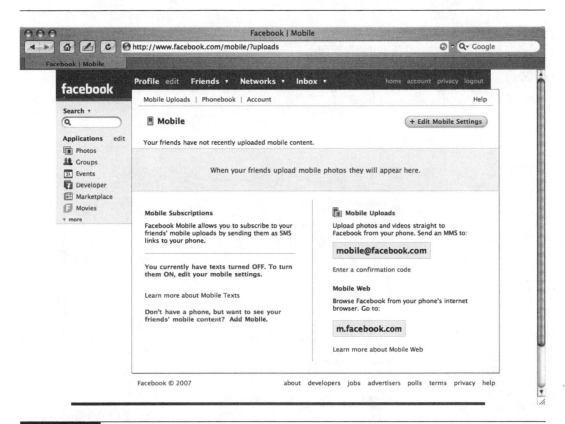

Facebook | Mobile

FIGURE 5-22   Use Facebook Mobile.

Configure the Mobile Web

Configuring the mobile Web is a matter of using your phone's Web browser to go to http://m.facebook.com, which is the basic mobile Web page. Depending on your phone, you may also be able to view the regular Facebook page. It will not fit on the screen, but you may want to see it on your phone.

NOTE *The Facebook mobile Web page may not display on a computer's browser because it is designed to be shown on a mobile device.*

There may be yet another choice open to you. If you use an iPhone, you can go to the regular Facebook URL. Facebook will recognize that you are using an iPhone, and you will be redirected to http://iphone.facebook.com, which provides an interface specifically designed for the iPhone.

There is only one mobile-specific element of Facebook Platform. It lets you create an element that is only shown on a mobile Web page, as shown in Table 5-5.

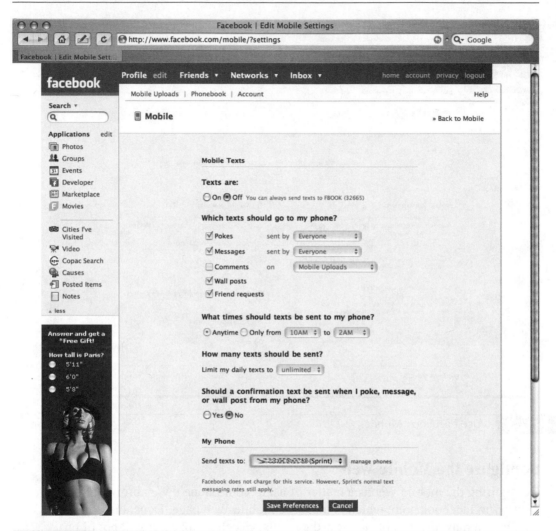

FIGURE 5-23   Edit mobile settings.

Platform Element	Category	Notes
fb:mobile	FBML	An element, the contents of which are only displayed in a mobile Web page. May contain other FBML elements.

TABLE 5-5   Mobile Web Settings

Part II

Use Facebook Technologies

Chapter 6

Use XML, XHTML, and CSS

How to...

- Use XML for data transfer
- Use XHTML on your Facebook pages
- Use CSS to format your Facebook pages

This part of the book helps you understand the technologies involved in building a Facebook application. This chapter introduces you to XML, XHTML, and CSS—or serves as a reminder; the next one focuses on PHP. All of these technologies are open-source technologies that are used in many modern applications. Another key open-source technology, MySQL, is used internally at Facebook as well as by many Facebook applications. It is described in the next part of the book, specifically in Chapter 14.

After the first two chapters of this part, you will find specific Facebook technologies: the general architecture (Chapter 8), Facebook Markup Language, or FBML (Chapter 9), the Facebook API for use with REST (Chapter 10), and Facebook Query Language, or FQL (Chapter 11).

Each of the three technologies described in this chapter has special considerations when used to develop Facebook applications. Thus, even if you know your way around them, it can be useful for you to see how they are specifically used in Facebook applications.

All three of these technologies in one way or another address a fundamental issue that arose as the Web grew. The initial technology for developing pages, Hypertext Markup Language (HTML), combines content and formatting controls. This was fine for the original hand-crafted Web pages, but as it became necessary to generate pages programmatically, and as it also became increasingly common to need the content for one page presented in a slightly different format on another page, the limitations of this combination became troublesome. Thus, you will find all three of this chapter's technologies addressing various aspects of the need to separate content from presentation.

NOTE *If you use the Developer application in Facebook (and you should, not just for getting API keys), browsing the discussion board will show you a number of cases in which the specifics of these technologies in the Facebook world have sometimes caused confusion. That is a good resource if you are already having trouble, but this chapter is a good starting point to avoid trouble.*

Use XML for Data Transfer

XML addresses one of the content/presentation concerns that became apparent early on: the need to separate presentation information from syntactical information. It was easy to specify a bold font face or a larger font size to indicate a heading or the start of a section, but it was impossible in HTML (and remains so to this day) to separate the bold font face that indicates the beginning of a document section from the bold font face that may indicate emphasis on a specific word to clarify the meaning of a sentence.

XML by itself has no presentational information; it is often combined with style sheets in order to be displayed or printed, but on its own, it consists only of content and structural information.

NOTE *An example of the use of XML is in RSS or Atom feeds. They deliver their information as XML documents, and the display of the content is determined by style sheets in browsers or news feed readers. Thus, while the goal of browser and Web page designers is for HTML pages to look as similar as possible in different browsers on various platforms, when it comes to news feeds, the formatting can be quite different. The provider of the HTML page specifies the layout and hopes that the browsers render it accurately and consistently. But the author of a news feed (which frequently is software that pulls the data from a blog or other changing resource), determines nothing whatsoever about the formatting.*

As you will see, the structural information in an XML document is hierarchical, starting from a single document root and then branching out into various sub-elements and their sub-elements. Because of this very clear and very simple structure, XML documents can easily be read by scripts and programs (such as PHP, the topic of the next chapter).

XML documents were originally designed to stand next to HTML pages, with style sheets for the XML documents adding presentation information to the XML content and structure in order to assemble an HTML page automatically. That is still the case in many areas. In other areas, however, XML is used to deliver content and structural information for information that is less than a full Web page (a news feed, for example, or internal Facebook information). For that reason, this section focuses on the parts of XML that are most relevant to Facebook—the relatively small pieces of information that are presented, for example, in a response to a query for a specific Facebook user's friends.

Find More Information about XML

The primary source for information about XML is www.w3c.org—the World Wide Web Consortium. At the XML section, you will find the language specification, as well as links to other resources.

If you use the `friends.get` API call to get a user's friends, the response comes back in an XML document (which, although it is a complete document, might appear to you to be a fragment, because it only contains the data for the response). Listing 6-1 shows a sample of the XML returned from a `friends.get` call. It will be referred to in the sections that follow.

Listing 6-1

```xml
<?xml version="1.0" encoding="UTF-8"?>
<friends_get_response
  xmlns="http://api.facebook.com/1.0/"
  xmlns:xsi="http://www.w3.org/2001/XMLSchema-instance"
  xsi:schemaLocation="http://api.facebook.com/1.0/
    http://api.facebook.com/1.0/facebook.xsd" list="true">

  <uid>12345</uid>
  <uid>54321</uid>

</friends_get_response>
```

Understand the Basics of XML

XML documents contain both content and semantic information—that is, the meaning of the data. There are, therefore, two structures: a logical structure and a physical structure.

The XML Physical Structure

The physical structure of an XML document is the simpler structure. It consists of *entities*, which begin with the *root* or document entity. All other entities of the document are contained within the root. Some of those entities may have entities within them. Each entity in an XML document is contained within another entity, with the exception of the root.

The XML Logical Structure

The logical structure of an XML document consists of *elements, tags, comments, declarations, character references,* and *processing instructions.* What you would normally consider the content of an XML document (such as words) is contained within the elements.

The First Line

In addition to the two structures, all XML documents begin with a line that specifies the version of XML used in the document and the encoding used. This is a common first line. (In Facebook, remember that XML is used to deliver information from the API to you, the developer. Therefore, you are not constructing XML documents, so the first line does not matter to you.) When you parse the XML as described in the next chapter, the parser will just skip over it.

```
<?xml version="1.0" encoding="UTF-8"?>
```

Understand XML Syntax

XML is a markup language like HTML, XHTML, and their precursors, such as Standard Generalized Markup Language (SGML), which was the best known of the markup languages that were developed in the 1960s and '70s. All of these languages separate content from formatting, generally by the use of < and > symbols.

In markup languages through HTML, capitalization does not matter in the markup information (it is respected, of course, in the content). For XML, as for most other modern markup languages, such as XHTML, capitalization does matter. Thus,

```
<name>
```

and

```
<Name>
```

are two different tags in XML.

Also, in part because XML and its contemporaries need to be parsed by software, the rules for the order of tags are different: They must match up. In HTML, you can specify bold and italics for some text, as follows (spacing is used for clarity):

```
<b>
  <i>
This is some bold, italicized text.
  </b>
</i>
```

As you can see, when you spread out the tags, they are not aligned. Most HTML browsers will correctly handle this situation, but it is not valid for XML or XHTML. The order of the tags must be:

```
<b>
  <i>
This is some bold, italicized text.
  </i>
</b>
```

Use XML Elements

XML elements, the primary components of the logical structure of an XML document, are composed of three pieces:

- An opening tag
- The content of the element
- A closing tag

If there is no content for the element, the opening tag can close the element, as in

```
<name / >
```

This would be a name element that opens and closes with a single tag and contains no content.

There is a logical difference between an empty element and a non-existent element. In one case, there is non-existent content, but in the other, there is neither content nor an element.

Referring back Listing 6-1, in the center of the document are two `uid` elements:

```
<uid>1234</uid>
<uid>54321</uid>
```

Each has an opening tag and a closing tag; in addition, each has content. They are located within the `friends_get_response` element.

Opening tags of elements may also have *attributes*. Attributes have keywords and values. Both are required. In HTML, you can specify `checked` for the state of a checkbox, as in:

```
<input type="checkbox" checked />
```

But in XML or XHTML (which use the same syntax for attributes), you would need to rewrite that code as:

```
<input type="checkbox" checked="checked" />
```

The value must always be enclosed in quotation marks, even if it appears not to be a string, as is the case with:

```
maxlength="50"
```

Although you can see that 50 is a number, it is treated as a string in the markup. (And it is read as a string by the parser.)

Use XML Namespaces

Although a structure for elements is specified in XML, the actual elements depend on the content of the document. You can create `uid` elements, `owner` elements, or anything that you want.

In order to avoid confusion, you use *namespaces*. Namespaces are unique identifiers, which, combined with an element name, produce a unique namespace-qualified name. Thus, in the example used here, all of the element names used are part of the Facebook namespace for version 1.0:

```
xmlns="http://api.facebook.com/1.0/"
```

NOTE   *Although the namespace is expressed as a URL, it does not have to exist and is merely used to indicate the namespace. In this case, this means that an element such as* uid *has a unique meaning within the Facebook world. If the namespace were identified with another namespace environment,* uid *might have another (or no) meaning.*

Two additional attributes in the element are used for validation. This line indicates that the XML document can be validated:

```
xmlns:xsi="http://www.w3.org/2001/XMLSchema-instance"
```

The following line indicates the location of the specific schema to use in validation:

```
xsi:schemaLocation="http://api.facebook.com/1.0/
  http://api.facebook.com/1.0/facebook.xsd" list="true">
```

Taken together, these three attributes mean:

- The namespace for the document is Facebook

- The document can be validated using the W3C validation rules

- The specific schema is the Facebook schema, located at api.facebook.com/1.0/facebook.xsd

Use XHTML on Your Facebook Pages

XHTML has most of the same new syntax rules as XML, such as the difference between upper- and lowercase letters, the quoting of attribute values in opening tags, and the need to balance opening and closing tags. In general, it is a good idea to use the stricter rules of XHTML in all the Web pages that you construct.

With Facebook applications, you are creating pieces of Web pages that will be placed inside the Facebook frame. The exception to this is when you create a stand-alone page—often in your own Web site—to which links from your Facebook application point.

> **NOTE**   *There are three flavors of XHTML:* strict, transitional, *and* frameset. *Unless your page is using framesets, most people today use the transitional version, which includes some deprecated features that make it easier to move existing HTML pages into the world of XHTML.*

Using div Elements

One of the hallmarks of Web 2.0 and Asynchronous JavaScript and XML (AJAX)—among other design paradigms—is the use of div elements on Web pages. These elements are divisions or sections of the page. Whatever their original purpose was, today they are used very often to identify a section of the Web page that can be located and updated by a script. For example, when creating a mashup using one of the mapping APIs, you lay out the page with a div where you want the map to go. When you have gathered the information from the user to go out and create the map, you let the mapping API know the id of the div into which to place it, and that is where it ends up. By having addressable sections of Web pages, AJAX technologies can update them without refreshing the entire page. They are very important in the design of Web pages like this—and in Facebook application pages.

Find More Information about XHTML

The primary source for information about XHTML is www.w3c.org—the World Wide Web Consortium. At the XHTML section, you will find the language specification as well as links to other resources.

In addition to their addressability, `div` elements can receive styles, which may then be applied to all of the elements within them. As is the case with all tags and elements, a `div` cannot contain parts of an element—only complete elements can be contained within a `div` (or within any other container).

The `align` attribute is not fully supported for `div` elements. It is only supported in transitional and frameset XHTML, not strict XHTML. It is a good idea to steer clear of it.

You can add a variety of attributes to `div` elements:

- `id`
- `class`
- `title`
- `style`
- `dir`
- `lang`
- `xml:lang`

- `onmouseover`
- `onmousemove`
- `onmouseout`
- `onkeypress`
- `onkeydown`
- `onkeyup`
- `onclick`
- `ondblclick`
- `onmousedown`
- `onmouseup`

The event attributes (those starting with "on") can reference JavaScript—either in inline code or a script that is created elsewhere on the page. Because the page and its scripts can be created dynamically using PHP (as shown in Chapter 7), you can construct scripts and interactions that are specific to the data that you have retrieved from Facebook. Taken together, the addressability of a `div` element and the ability to add a script make it an important tool. (Of course, if an element within a `div` also responds to mouse clicks or key events, that inner element gets first crack at an event that happens to it; the handlers for the `div` come into play only if an internal element does not handle the event.)

Although you can apply styles directly to a `div` element, the more common method is to create styles for `div` elements with specific classes or that have a particular `id` as described later in this chapter. Not only is this more common, but it is more maintainable.

The id Attribute and Facebook

As you will see, attaching a style to a certain class of div can be a way of providing consistency. To make a div addressable, or to apply a style to a specific div, you can use the id attribute for that div. However, in the world of Facebook, you should be aware that internally, Facebook will add your application id to the id you create for a div. What that means is that the id you create is guaranteed to be unique within the Facebook page of which it is a part, and your style cannot accidentally (or deliberately!) override the Facebook styles on the page.

Validate Your Facebook Web Page Syntax

Because the syntax for XHTML (like the syntax for XML) is strict, these pages can be validated. Facebook application pages are parts of the final Web page, and they tend to be relatively short, so visual inspection or a little trial and error can often manage syntax checking. (And if you use a tool such as Dreamweaver that flags mismatched quotation marks and tags, that makes it even easier.)

If you want to validate an XHTML page, you can do so at http://validator .w3c.org, as shown in Figure 6-1. You can direct the page to the document or paste the document into it for validation. On the page, the More Options area lets you choose to validate an HTML or XHTML fragment just by pasting it into the page. Because your Facebook code is likely to be just a fragment, this is the option you would most often use.

Debug Facebook XHTML

If you use the techniques described in Chapter 7 to dynamically create your Facebook page with PHP, you may very well not have a page or even a page fragment to validate. Facebook has an additional tool for you.

If there is an unrecoverable error in processing your page as it is inserted into the Facebook frame, an error will be displayed. This type of error often has to do with mismatched quotation marks or tags.

More subtle errors may be manifest only because the page does not look right or does not behave correctly. If you are the developer of the application and you are running under your own Facebook id, you can use your browser's View Source command to look at the source of the page. Your raw source will appear at the top of the page inside a comment—this is the code that your application sent to Facebook and that it parsed into the standard page source code that anyone can see.

What follows is the source code for the page that is displayed in your browser. That is, it is the page that is a combination of what you have provided to Facebook and what it has created dynamically. This allows you to see the final styles that are used to display the page. If you have a program that formats HTML automatically, that will make this code easier to read. Even if you have to manually line up the starting and

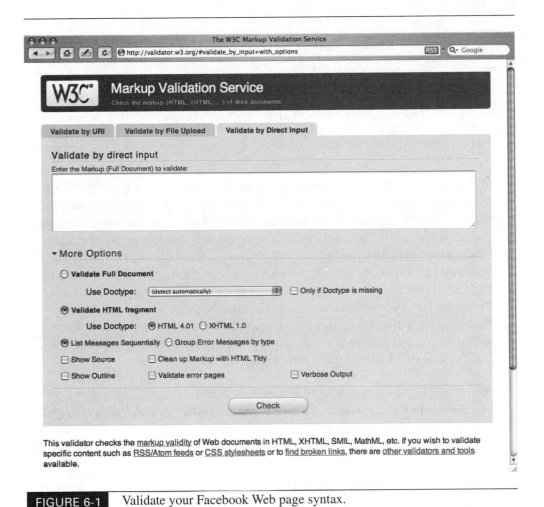

FIGURE 6-1   Validate your Facebook Web page syntax.

ending tags, that is a relatively mindless pursuit that (hopefully) you do not have to do often. Being able to compare the code you send to Facebook with the munged code it returns can help you solve problems and learn more about how Facebook works.

Use CSS to Format Your Facebook Pages

As noted at the beginning of this chapter, separating the munged-together, old-fashioned HTML pages with their content, structure, and formatting into their component parts has been an integral part of recent Web developments, including Web 2.0 and AJAX. The formatting (or presentation or styling) part of the issue is handled with style sheets—cascading style sheets (CSS) in particular.

Styles can be specified in external style sheets or in a `style` element of a Web page; they can also be specified for individual elements. By using styles attached to specific types of page elements, you can enforce consistency across a series of pages—even those built by a variety of developers, which is precisely the case with Facebook application pages.

For example, Figure 6-2 shows the Home page of the application that will be built in Part III of this book.

This page has a Facebook look and feel, partly because it lives within the Facebook frame, but also because it adopts the Facebook look and feel in terms of colors, graphics, and functionality. Some of this look and feel is not optional—you have no way to avoid adopting it. Other parts of it are up to you.

NOTE   *Perhaps the biggest issue in designing a Facebook application that is integrated in some way with an external Web site or application is deciding where to draw the line between two separate interfaces: Facebook and the external application or Web site. There is much more on this in Chapter 13.*

Facebook and Style Sheets

Facebook uses a multitude of styles in its style sheets; if you view the source of your application pages as described previously, you will see the style sheets at the top of the head element of the generated page.

The styles that you use on your pages must be placed in `style` elements in your page. You cannot use external style sheets (except the external Facebook style sheets, which are included by default).

Learn the Facebook Style Basics

As long as you use basic HTML syntax for the elements on your page, and as long as you use classes for your `div` elements that correspond to the classes of the comparable Facebook elements, your page will adopt the Facebook look and feel, almost without further ado.

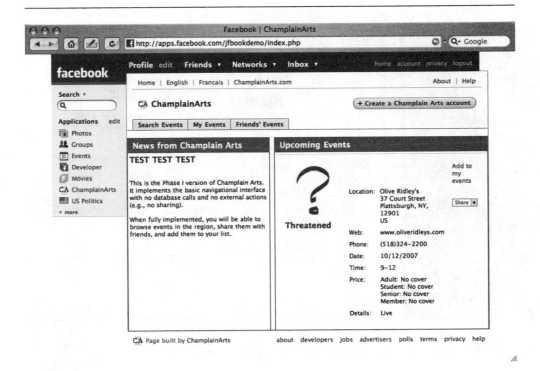

FIGURE 6-2   The ChamplainArts Home page

If you do need to construct your own styles, make them as close to Facebook styles as possible. One way of doing this is by using the colors that Facebook uses. Some of them are shown in Table 6-1.

If you are using Apple's Safari browser, you have an important tool to help you explore the styles and elements of the Facebook interface. Control-clicking on a Web page opens a contextual menu, as shown in Figure 6-3.

If you choose Inspect Element, the floating window appears that shows you where the element you have clicked on appears in the document's hierarchy. It also

Hex Color	Usage
#0e1f5b	Frame
#3b5998	Header, links
#7f93bc	Line between "Facebook" and "Search" (at the top of Left Nav)
#f7f7f7	Background of Left Nav, inactive tabs, and canvas backgrounds, such as on photos (and your applications, for consistency)

TABLE 6-1   Colors for Various Facebook Elements

FIGURE 6-3   Safari can show you the details of the page's elements.

shows you all the attributes that apply to that element, including its styles, metrics, and properties—even scripts. The specific element (or document node) on which you have clicked is identified, and its attributes (often a class and id) are displayed in the Node tab. This is a particularly useful way of discovering what and where the div elements are without reading code. While the mouse button is held down, the bounds of the selected element are shown in red on the Web page.

NOTE   *The Web Developer extension for Firefox provides similar functionality.*

Table 6-2 shows another important set of Facebook style settings: the widths of the various elements of standard Facebook pages.

Facebook Object	Width
canvas	646 pixels
narrow profile column	190 pixels; left margin of 10 pixels, no right margin
wide profile column	388 pixels; left margin of 8 pixels, no right margin

TABLE 6-2   Widths of Facebook Objects

Chapter 7

Use PHP

How to...

- Understand PHP basic syntax
- Use multiple PHP files
- Use PHP functions
- Handle exceptions

The previous chapter described how you can use XML, XHTML, and CSS both to format Web pages and to manage data. PHP is frequently used to help generate the pages for Facebook applications. You can use it to construct Facebook Markup Language (FBML) and HTML that is sent to Facebook for parsing and processing before it is returned to the user as standard HTML. In fact, the FBML specification identifies those elements of HTML that will be parsed by Facebook. It is fair to say that you send only FBML to Facebook and that the FBML that you send may contain allowable HTML within it. This chapter introduces you to the basics of PHP that you will use most in working with Facebook. (PHP classes are described in the following chapter.)

You can write a Facebook application that uses only bare-bones PHP. Here, for example, is the basic page for the minimal Facebook application in Chapter 12:

```php
<?php
  // the facebook client library
  include_once '../php4client/facebook.php';

  // keys and other setup
  include_once 'config.php';

  $facebook = new Facebook($api_key, $secret);
  $facebook->require_frame();
  $user = $facebook->require_login();
?>

<div style="padding: 10px;">
  <p>Hello.</p>
</div>
```

There is some boilerplate PHP code at the beginning of the file that you will probably use unchanged in many of your Facebook applications. The only other code consists of the last three underlined lines of code.

As you can see, this is just a `div` element with a text string. It works, and it helps prove the point that implementing the basics of a Facebook application is simple.

Did you know?

Find More Information about PHP

PHP is free software (in the sense defined by the Free Software Foundation, www.fsf.org) supported by The PHP Group (www.php.net). The current implementation, downloadable from www.php.net, is the de facto specification of the language (there is no separate formal specification, as there is for some other languages and for many Internet standards at www.w3c.org). The Web site contains documentation, discussions, and further information about PHP. It also contains download and installation links. This is the primary source for more information about PHP.

If you need to install PHP, installation instructions are provided on their Web site. If you have specific problems, look at the Frequently Asked Questions (FAQ), as well as the messages posted by people encountering and solving problems. If you do not find an answer there, feel free to post your own question.

But most of the time, you are not displaying constant text. What you need to display is specific data that is relevant to the user. This data needs to be retrieved either from Facebook or from an external data source. Then, you need to write some code that will generate the FBML and HTML that incorporate the changeable data rather than a static text string. That is where PHP comes in.

NOTE   *PHP is certainly not required for Facebook. What you need to do is generate the variable HTML that reflects the data you need; any language (scripted or compiled) that can access the data and then generate HTML can be used. PHP is probably the most common language, but you need not be constrained by it. The only constraint you have is that the language you use must be able to generate the code, and that means that it must run on the server that you will be using to serve your pages for Facebook. In addition, the language must also be able to interact with Facebook through its REST interface. Look at resources in the developer documentation, and you will find a variety of interfaces in a variety of languages.*

Also note that the current version of PHP is version 5; version 4 is not supported by PHP after 2007, but it is supported with PHP 4 libraries in Facebook for a while. If you have a choice, you should use PHP 5. (Your decision may be made by which version is running on your Web server.)

Understand PHP Basic Syntax

This chapter focuses on those parts of PHP that are most useful in developing Facebook applications. This section touches on the main points you should know (or which refresh your memory).

Use PHP Delimiters

PHP code normally is placed in files with the *.php* suffix. When a request for such a file is received by a Web server, it normally passes the file over to PHP, which processes the file and typically returns an HTML page, which can then be sent by the Web server to the user or on to Facebook and thence to the user. Within the PHP file, PHP code is delimited by

```
<?PHP
```

and

```
?>
```

Text outside these delimiters is assumed to be HTML code, which is passed through as-is. There are other ways of delimiting the PHP code in a file, but this is the most common and reliable. It also has the advantage that applications such as Dreamweaver recognize it and can color-code the PHP syntax as you write it. (In the case of Facebook, the HTML code outside PHP delimiters also includes the FBML elements.)

 The other commonly used delimiters are <? and ?> or <% and %>. The first pair has been deprecated. Stick with the standard <?PHP and ?> delimiters

A single PHP file may have several sections of PHP code in it, each one delimited.

Use Comments

PHP supports comments on a single line, starting with //, wherever it is in the line of text, and continuing to the end of the line. The common /* and */ delimiters are used for multiline comments. As in all programming languages, it makes sense to document your code thoroughly.

Use Terminators

All PHP statements are terminated by a semi-colon (;).

Use PHP Variables and Arrays

PHP variables start with a dollar sign; after that, they contain letters, numbers, and underscores, although the first character after the dollar sign cannot be a number. They cannot contain spaces or other special characters. Case matters in PHP. It is good practice to settle on a convention for naming variables that is consistent.

Arrays in PHP can be accessed with numeric subscripts or associative subscripts. Numeric arrays start at zero, as in the following examples:

```
$myArray [0] = "value 1";
$myArray [1] = "value 2";
```

Associative arrays can take strings for their subscripts, as shown here:

```
$myArray ["giraffe"] = "neck";
$myArray ["anteater"] = "nose";
```

Variables need not be declared; they are typed depending on their use.

Use PHP Strings

Strings in PHP are enclosed within single or double quotes. They must match. Thus, the first two lines of code are legitimate, but the third is not:

```
$myString = 'test';
$myString = "test";
$myString = 'test";
```

Within a single-quoted string, double quotes are treated like any other character, and variable names are treated as text. Within a double-quoted string, variable names are expanded.

The following three lines of code demonstrate this:

```
$myVariable = "dog";
$myDoubleString = "The animal is a $myVariable."
  // The animal is a dog
$mySingleString = 'The animal is a $myVariable.'
  // The animal is a $myVariable.
```

Building Concatenated Strings

Using variables and quoted strings, you often use PHP to develop concatenated strings; frequently, these are FBML or HTML. In order to build a concatenated string, you can use the concatenation operator, which is a period.

If you are building a complex string, you can do so in several steps, which can improve readability. The first line uses the replacement operator to set a variable; the following lines concatenate each line onto the previous value. Here is an example:

```
$myString = '<table>';
$myString .= '</table>';
```

The result is:

```
<table></table>
```

This is a useful way of building a long string, but it can be tedious and hard to read. For a long section of code, the *heredoc* construct lets you set a string that respects line feeds and spacing. Basically, you type your text (often HTML) just as you normally would, and the whole thing is placed in a variable.

The first line begins with an identifier preceded by <<<; the last line (after the text) begins with that same identifier *at the beginning of the line*, followed by a semicolon. PHP variables (such as $caeName in this listing) are automatically expanded inside heredoc code.

Here is an example:

```
$myString = <<<fbmlhd
<table>
  <tr>
    <td width="100">
      <img  src="http://www.mysite.com/default.jpg" />
      <H1>$caeName</H1>
    </td>
fbmlhd;
```

You can use either style—or both. For a long section of text, heredoc can be much easier. You can then end that section and use concatenation for small amounts of text (the next section provides an example of this).

CAUTION *The syntax for heredoc is very strict. The initial <<< cannot begin in the first character position on a line, and the closing identifier must begin in the first character position on its line. Furthermore, the lines of a heredoc construct must be terminated with a newline character (sometimes referred to as a line feed or LF character). If you are using a Macintosh computer, you must save your PHP document as a UNIX document or as a document with line breaks. In Dreamweaver, you set this in Preferences in the Dreamweaver menu in the section called Code Format. The specific setting is Line Break Type, and the choice you want is LF (Unix). In BBEdit, you use the Options button in the Save or Save As dialog, and then choose UNIX for Line Breaks.*

Use PHP Conditional Statements

As is the case with most languages, you have a variety of control, loop, and conditional statements you can use. The most common for many Facebook pages is the `if` statement, and it is frequently used in conjunction with heredoc. If you have a long section of HTML code that has a condition in the middle of it, you can use heredoc for the first part, then perform the test, and then continue with another heredoc.

Here, for example, is some code that is used in Chapter 13. It is used to make a multipurpose function display data either in one or two columns in a single row of a table, with an image at the beginning of the line. It is generating HTML code, and if it will be displayed in one column, the width is set to 446, but in two columns, the width is 223 for each column. If the data is displayed in a single column, it is displayed in a table element, but if it is shown in two columns, there is a table element for each column. Thus, the common code begins with an opening tag for a table, and it ends with a closing tag for a table. If it is the two-column display, in the middle of the code the first table is closed and a second one is opened for the second column. In schematic form, here is the one-column display:

```
<table>
  <tr>
    <td>
      //image
    </td>
    <td width="446">
      <table>
        //single-column data
      </table>
    </td>
  </tr>
</table>
```

Here is the two-column display. Except for the column width, the data is going to be generated in exactly the same way as for the one-column display, but the underlined code will be inserted in the middle of it to close the first table and column and to open the second one:

```
<table>
  <tr>
    <td>
      //image
    </td>
    <td width="223">
      <table>
        //first part of two-column data
      </table>
    </td>
    <td width="223">
      <table>
        //second part of two-column data
      </table>
    </td>
  </tr>
</table>
```

Here is how the code begins (it is all within `<?PHP and ?>` delimiters):

```
$myString = <<<fbmlhd
<table>
  <tr>
    <td width="100">
      <img src="http://static.ak.facebook.com//pics/s_default.jpg"
        alt="event_image" class=""/>
      <H1>$caeName</H1>
    </td>
fbmlhd;

if ($nColumns == 1) {
  $myString .= '<td width="446">';
} else {
  $myString .= '<td width="223">';
}

$myString .= <<<fbmlhd
        <table class="infotable" valign="top">
```

... more code follows

It is not uncommon to have a long run of HTML split up with several `if` statements. In fact, this one is split a second time in the middle. If the data is to be displayed in two columns, at a certain point, the first column is terminated and the second begins.

```
if ($nColumns == 2) {
  $myString .= '</table>';
  $myString .= '</td>';
  $myString .= '<td width="223">';
  $myString .= '<table>';
}
```

Everything is being concatenated into $myString, which will eventually be returned from the function.

Use Multiple PHP Files

For the purpose of reusability as well as clarity, you can separate your PHP code into several files. You can use the `include` statement, but more often, you use the `include_once` statement; this means that if a single file is referenced several times, it is only included once:

```
include_once '../php4client/facebook.php';
```

Variables that have been set in an included file can be referenced in the main file.

Use PHP Functions

Whether in a single file or multiple files, you can build large PHP scripts and applications. For the purpose of building Facebook pages, you frequently are putting together fragments of PHP. You can provide a certain level of organization using multiple files. You can also provide more robust structuring by using functions and objects.

As in most languages, you can create functions in PHP; they behave just as they do in other languages, with a definition that you can then call as needed. Functions often return values, as in this simple example:

```
function get_and_render_cae (
  $nColumns,
  $uid = 12345,
  $caeid = null)
```

```
{
  //body of function here...set $functionResult
  return $functionResult;
}
```

As you can see, you can assign default values for arguments in a function. However, you must supply default values for the rightmost arguments if you use this feature. It can improve readability, but make certain that there are no non-default-valued arguments to the right of your default-valued arguments.

In general, making functions as specific as possible is a good idea. It is usually better to have a single function that performs a multistep process by calling several subsidiary functions than to put them all into the high-level function.

In addition, although you can use global variables inside your functions, if you confine yourself to using variables that are passed in as parameters, you will make your code even more robust.

The reasons for making functions specific and for using only parameters are many; some of the most important are readability, testing, and reuse.

Readability   A self-contained function can be read and understood on its own because it does not rely on global variables. You should not have to search through other code, or even other files, to find out what the meaning of the global variables is. And, it should go without saying that you should clearly comment each of the parameters passed into the function, not only describing what they are, but making clear any assumptions that you make about them. (For example, is raw data passed in or do you assume that certain error checks have been performed so that you do not need to repeat them within the function itself.)

Some people take readability one step further, suggesting that no function should be longer than a single page. This is an arbitrary limit, but it makes sense in many cases. Whether you are reading the function in a window or on a page, being able to see the entire function at one time can be very, very useful.

Also, make certain that you indent brackets and other delimiters so that the structure of the function is clear—indentation makes loops and conditional sequences very clear (and are much easier to see on a single page image). Of course, there are some functions that will never fit on a page, such as functions that are designed to create a large amount of output to an HTML page. In such cases, consider using a technique such as heredoc and placing each heredoc component in its own function. If you are interspersing heredoc with conditional statements, as described earlier, your debugging of the conditional sequence is very different from your debugging of the actual HTML code that is emitted.

Testing   The more readable code is, the easier it is to test (and the less testing is involved, because you can visually spot misaligned loops and conditions).

Furthermore, if a function does one clearly defined thing, there is likely to be a single path through its code (conditional statements may be in another, controlling function). When there is a single path—or only one or two branches—your testing can be short and sweet. When you have a multitude of paths and conditions, you need to test every combination, and those combinations increase rapidly with each additional test or condition.

Reuse   After all the work you put into coding your functions, you should get the most out of them. By making them self-contained (using parameters rather than globals) and making their purpose specific, you can maximize their reusability. One point to watch out for is the factoring of your application. Functions that interact with the user should normally be separate from functions that do not. This means that error conditions should be caught, but internal functions should return a result code to their calling function, and it, in turn, should interact with the user if necessary. In the world of Facebook applications, you frequently are integrating a database with your Facebook application; interaction with the database should normally be in its own functions. This allows you to do any back-stage manipulation of data before it is passed into the operational functions.

NOTE   *The issue of globals has one exception for many people. In Facebook and many other environments, you need one or more keys to access the external interface. These keys are needed throughout the application that you create, and they are well defined: You cannot do anything with a Facebook application without your keys. If you define the keys and other global environmental values as PHP defines or variables in a separate file (such as config.php), they are available to any file that includes that config.php file. Because they are needed so frequently in your code, you can argue that using these defines or variables instead of passing the keys in as parameters to every function actually increases readability. There is no mystery as to what they are (provided that they are named properly), and having a few extra and identical parameters in every function call can obscure the parameters that are specific to that function.*

Handle Exceptions

Like many modern languages, PHP uses *try/catch* structures to handle exceptions and errors. This allows the developer to write code that can handle exceptions on its own and keep going. Because your PHP code is primarily used to generate the FBML that will be returned to Facebook in response to a user request, it is important that you send something back to Facebook that will at least provide the user with some information as to what has happened. (If you provide invalid FBML to Facebook, it may generate an error for the user that is too esoteric for the user's taste.)

The principle of try/catch structures is that code that may fail is enclosed in a `try` block. If it does not fail, it executes as it normally would. If it does fail, control immediately transfers to a matching `catch` block. Here is the basic structure:

```
try {
  //code that may fail
} catch (Exception $theException) {
  //code to handle the exception
}
```

When an exception occurs, an `Exception` object is created. The catch block retrieves that `Exception` object and gives it a name such as `$theException` (more commonly, just `$e`). Once you have the Exception object in hand, you can use it in the `catch` block. The most common use of this object is to get the message associated with the exception. You could do that in the example shown here by using this line of code:

```
$theError = $theException->getMessage();
```

This is useful for telling the user what has happened, but because your PHP is so far removed from the user (who, after all, merely wants to view a Facebook page), you may not want to provide that message. If the exception has been raised (or *thrown*) by code that you have written, you have more options available to you.

When an error is encountered in code that you are writing, you start the try/catch processing by throwing an exception using code such as this:

```
throw new Exception ('Error message that you write', $errorCode);
```

You should supply an integer for `$errorCode`, and then, having thrown such an exception, you could retrieve that code from the `Exception` object using this line of code.

```
$theErrorCode = $theException->getCode();
```

You can then use your `catch` block to test the code that is returned and take appropriate action. That action may be some kind of default behavior, or it may be a message that the user can understand.

NOTE   *The default value for the message is* null, *and the default code is* 0.

Whatever you do, make certain that your PHP code completes and returns something logical to Facebook and thence to the user.

TIP   *Make certain that you record exceptions in some way so that you can tell if your application is in trouble.*

NOTE   *Most of the code described in this book omits try/catch blocks in order to focus on the Facebook code. Before moving your application into production, you should make certain that any code that could fail with negative consequences is protected by a try/catch block.*

In this chapter and the previous one, you have found some information about the important open technologies that are used in Facebook (MySQL will be discussed in Chapter 14). You have now seen a few snippets of Facebook code. It is time to move on into Facebook and explore the general architecture and specific technologies that Facebook has developed.

Chapter 8

Understand Overall Facebook Architecture

How to...

- Work with the architecture
- Use the Facebook object
- Use the Facebook REST object

You can describe the Facebook architecture in various ways—as an example of Web 2.0 functionality, as a modern implementation of what was called component software 15 years ago, or by talking about its implementation on the Facebook site using mostly open-source software. This chapter provides an overview of the Facebook architecture from the Facebook application developer's point of view (in other words, it does not worry about how the server load is distributed across Facebook's site). After the overview, you will find some specifics on how to use the two primary Facebook objects: the Facebook object itself and the Facebook REST object. Download and installation instructions for the files discussed in this chapter are provided in Chapter 12.

 In this chapter and the ones that follow, HTML refers generically to both HTML and XHTML. Most of the "HTML" produced by Facebook is now XHTML.

Work with the Architecture

In many ways, it is much easier to work with a large monolithic architecture than with the elegant, component-based Facebook application. With a large monolithic architecture, you can basically do what you want. You control everything, and if you choose to implement something idiosyncratically, there is no one to criticize you. All that matters is how the application performs: You only have to worry about pleasing your users.

With the Facebook architecture, you are responsible not only to your users, but also to Facebook and your Facebook Platform colleagues. Fortunately, this responsibility is managed by the architecture of Facebook Platform, so it will happen automatically for you. But there are boundaries you are unable to cross; these protect the rest of Facebook.

Your primary technical resource is the documentation on the Facebook site (that documentation is reached through the Developers link at the bottom of Facebook pages, as well as through the Developer application, where discussions and news are available). This chapter and the three that follow provide an overview of that architecture.

From a Facebook Platform developer's point of view, you need to worry about two main parts of the architecture: the Canvas and the Profile page.

How the Canvas Works

When you create an application on the Facebook Platform, you are actually writing components that will be presented as part of Facebook pages. The Canvas is the area that you use most directly. This is the rectangle below the frame, located to the right of the Left Nav and above the footer links. It is all yours—sort of.

The "pages" you create for your application generally consist of FBML, which is described in Chapter 9. You can hard-code the FBML, but more often it is generated by PHP or another language that you write, and it may include variable data from a database or other external source, as well as the results of calls to the Facebook API. No matter how you generate it, you send the FBML to Facebook. Remember that FBML can include many HTML elements without any changes. Thus, you can hard-code a page that consists of allowable HTML elements and send it to Facebook. From the Facebook side, it is FBML. If you hard-code HTML in this way, you can test your page outside the Facebook environment by opening it in any browser.

A browser cannot display FBML—it can only display HTML and run any JavaScript or other scripts that are part of the page. Thus, the page that is sent back to the user must have only browser-manageable features. The way this works is that when a user requests a page from your application, it goes through a Facebook URL, such as http://apps.facebook.com/yourapp/yourpage. The section of the URL ending with yourapp is your *Canvas Page URL*. Facebook then goes to the directory you have listed in your application's settings (your *Callback URL*) and requests the appropriate page such as http://www.yoursite.com/yourFBsupport/yourpage. (The callback url is the section of the URL up to and including yourFBsupport.) The page is returned to Facebook (not to your browser). When Facebook receives your page, it parses your page and converts the FBML to JavaScript and HTML. It adds the frame, Left Nav, footer, and any advertisements, and downloads a traditional page to your browser.

Facebook's parsing of your page includes more than just translating FBML into JavaScript and HTML. It also includes providing some additional features to keep the Facebook environment intact. It removes valid HTML syntax that is not valid on Canvas pages (external style sheets, for example). If you use the `id` attribute (in, for example, a `div` element), this parsing will modify the attribute's value by prefixing it with a string including your application's id. Thus:

```
<div id="ranking">
```

becomes

```
<div id="app1234567_ranking">
```

Similarly, rules in `style` elements are prefixed so that the styles you create in your application can affect only your application, not the rest of Facebook.

> **NOTE**
>
> *Facebook prevents your styles from affecting its page elements. However, if you use Facebook styles (which you should do, either directly or through FBML elements), none of this comes into play. It only affects styles that you define.*

When your page is requested by Facebook, all of the normal server-side processing that happens for any page request occurs. Thus, your server-side scripts or programs are run, and they generate the HTML and FBML that is passed through to Facebook. The server-side scripts or programs can also use REST to communicate with Facebook itself to gather data to be output in the page.

Thus, although the process has more steps than a simple request from a Web server, each of those steps is basically the same as in a non-Facebook Platform page:

- User requests your Facebook application page through a Facebook URL (or by clicking on a link on a Facebook page to your application through its Facebook URL).

- Facebook requests the appropriate page from your server, just as any HTTP request would be sent. Specifically, the request is made through a form sent with a POST request.

- Your server prepares the page. If necessary, it runs scripts or programs, and it may request data from Facebook via REST and from databases or other resources using other protocols. The page is prepared just as any HTML page is prepared, but it may include FBML.

- The page is returned to Facebook as any page is returned, using HTTP.

- Facebook parses the returned page, converts FBML to HTML and JavaScript, strips out Facebook-invalid HTML, and adds identifiers. It also adds the Facebook frame and other features.

- The finished composite page is returned to the user.

NOTE *All of the communication links here are standard Web protocols: requests and responses through HTTP and, possibly, REST. The server-side processing that occurs on your server when a page is requested by Facebook can be handled as any server-side processing is handled. That means you can implement it in PHP (perhaps the most common way), in Python, in C#, or, if you are quite imaginative, you probably could implement it in BASIC, FORTRAN, or COBOL. Facebook is language- and script-agnostic.*

How the Profile Page Works

The Profile page has a different flow. Your application may call the `setFBML` method in the API with a string of the markup for the Profile box of the application (the markup can consist of HTML and FBML). This markup can be produced at any time; it may be updated in response to user actions in your application (setting a Favorite, adding data, and so forth). The Profile box's markup is pushed to Facebook when it is appropriate for your application to do so, and there it sits. When the user's Profile page is requested, the markup that has been pushed there previously is displayed. It may be minutes old, or it may be months old. Your application is not called at this point.

NOTE *If you use the mock-Asynchronous JavaScript and XML (AJAX) calls described in Chapter 11, you can force a call back to your application. In general, Profile pages work best if you push the data when it is right for your application to do so. Forcing many mock-AJAX calls when the Profile page loads can theoretically cause performance problems.*

Use the Facebook Object

In Chapters 10 and 11, you will see details of the Facebook API calls. These are made by your server-side script or program as needed to prepare the page. If you are using PHP, you can download the client files that help you access the API calls easily. (Step-by-step instructions are provided in Chapter 12.) These files contain two important classes: a Facebook class and a REST class to implement the Facebook calls. There are separate versions for PHP 4 and PHP 5; the PHP class and object structure is very different in the two versions. It is preferable to use PHP 5, but your choice may be limited by your Web server, which may only support PHP 4.

Did you know?

PHP Object Basics

Object-oriented programming (OOP) makes code easier to read, write, and reuse. It consists of *objects,* which can contain both data and functionality. Objects are self-contained, and you can use them without knowing much, if anything, about how they perform the functionality. Objects are defined as *classes,* and those classes can contain *methods* (PHP functions) and *members* (PHP variables). The methods implement the functionality, and the members store the data.

At run time, a script or program *instantiates* a class; this causes an *instance* of the class to be created (*instantiated*). In the definition of the class, a special function called a *constructor* may have been defined. If so, it is automatically called each time an object is instantiated; it is used to set default values, which may be passed in as parameters in the new statement. (In PHP 5, a class's constructor is named __construct(), with two underscores at the beginning of the name.) Accessing a method or member of a class is done by using the -> operator. Thus, if you have instantiated the Facebook class and assigned it to a $facebook variable (a common practice), you can invoke one of its methods by writing:

```
$facebook->friends_get();
```

Within a method of a class, you can call another method of that class by using the reserved word, this, as in:

```
$this->friends_get();
```

Objects sometimes correspond to real-life concepts—in an inventory program, for example, objects may represent items in the inventory. Other objects encapsulate utility functions and are instantiated only once for a program. The Facebook and Facebook REST objects are of this type.

At the beginning of each of your Facebook Platform pages, you normally instantiate an instance of the Facebook class. You will need to include the appropriate file (PHP 4 or PHP 5). The instantiation call uses your two keys. Having instantiated the Facebook object, you then call its require_frame method (which makes certain that you are inside a frame and, if not, makes the necessary calls). In many cases, you then call `require_login` to make certain the user is logged in; that method returns the user id, which is typically stored in a variable (such as $user). You may also force the user to add the application:

```
// the facebook client library
include_once '../client/facebook.php';
// or
include_once '../php4client/facebook.php';

// note parameters passed into the constructor
$facebook = new Facebook($api_key, $secret);
$facebook->require_frame();
// if you want to require the user to be logged in to Facebook
// call this
$user = $facebook->require_login();
// if you want to require the application to be added call this
$facebook->require_add();
```

Facebook gives you this high-level interface so that you do not have to worry about making API calls. In the case of these calls, it is probably a bad idea to reinvent the code that requires a frame, login, or adding the application. Your customized code should be relevant to your application, not to standard Facebook functionality.

> **NOTE** *The includes and calls with the Facebook object are included at the beginning of any script that will be using the Facebook API or REST calls. If you have subsidiary files for configuration, library or utility routines, and so forth, these includes and calls are not included in those files, but only in the master file.*

You can browse the code of the Facebook class if you want, but these are the key calls that most applications make.

Use the Facebook REST Object

As part of the instantiation of the Facebook object, its constructor creates a subsidiary object, the Facebook REST object and stores it in the Facebook object's `$api_client` variable. It also performs a few other calls that are important to you. The constructor stores the two keys in variables that are part of the Facebook object. The REST object is what actually makes the API calls back to Facebook and, in the Facebook object constructor, several calls are made immediately through the REST object.

REST Basics

An acronym for Representational State Transfer, REST is an architecture that
uses the HTTP protocol to retrieve XML from a URL. The URL may be a
static Web page, but, more often, it is an address that causes a Web server to
execute a script or program to generate the XML data.

The URL to which the HTTP request is sent usually has parameters
attached to it. As is always the case, those parameters are name-value pairs,
separated from one another by & and introduced by ? at the beginning of the
set of parameters. Standard URL encoding applies. This means escaping any
character that might be interpreted as having meaning in the URL (such as a
space, a ? or an &) with an escape code such as %20 (for a space), %3F (?), or
%26(&).

Thus, a URL that implements a REST request might be:

```
http://www.yoursite.com?
  firstparam=firstvalue&secondparam=secondvalue
```

By using the Facebook object and the Facebook REST object, you will find
your life made much easier: They will construct the API calls for you and parse the
output from them before returning it to you.

A variety of parameters may have been passed into your page when it was
called from Facebook (they are parameters in the POST HTTP request). They are
unloaded and stored in variables, in cookies, or passed through to the Facebook
REST object. They include the user, whether or not the application has been
added, and the user's friends. This last is a key point to remember: The Facebook
REST object has a list of friends, ready to be accessed when you need it.

Data such as the session key, the expiration time, and so forth are needed for
subsequent API calls, but because all of this is handled for you by the two objects,
you can generally ignore many of the parameters you would normally need to
worry about if you were constructing an API call yourself.

The Facebook REST object is accessible through the Facebook object itself.
For example, if you have instantiated the Facebook object and assigned it to the

variable $facebook, as in the code previously shown in this chapter, here is how you would call friends_areFriends in PHP:

```
$facebook->api_client->friends_areFriends
  ($friends1id, $friend2sid);
```

Parameters Are Provided for You

The api_client->friends_areFriends function wraps the API call friends.areFriends. Table 8-1 shows the parameters that are used in the full API call.

Because the Facebook REST object has stored so much data itself, it can construct the entire call if you pass in just the last two parameters: the same-length lists of user ids that will be matched with one another.

Output Is Parsed for You

The result will be returned in XML, with each pair of user ids presented in an XML element followed by an <are_friends> element, with either 1 (they are friends) or 0 (they are not friends):

```
<?xml version="1.0" encoding="UTF-8"?>
<friends_areFriends_response xmlns="http://api.facebook.com/1.0/"
  xmlns="http://api.facebook.com/1.0/"
```

Type	Name	Required
string	api_key	X
string	session_key	X
float	call_id	X
string	sig	X
string	v	X
string	format	
string	callback	
array	uids1	X
array	uids2	X

TABLE 8-1   Parameters for friends.areFriends

```
xmlns:xsi="http://www.w3.org/2001/XMLSchema-instance"
xsi:schemaLocation="http://api.facebook.com/1.0/
  http://api.facebook.com/1.0/facebook.xsd"
  list="true">

<friend_info>
  <uid1>12345</uid1>
  <uid2>54321</uid2>
  <are_friends>1</are_friends>
</friend_info>
<friend_info>
  <uid1>09876</uid1>
  <uid2>67890</uid2>
  <are_friends>0</are_friends>
</friend_info>
</friends_areFriends_response>
```

Although the result from the API call is XML, the Facebook REST object can parse it so that the data that is actually returned from the call you make consists of an array, each element of which consists of a three-element array containing:

- uid1 - the nth id from uids1

- uid2 - the nth id from uids2

- are_friends - 1 / 0

Just as most of the complexity of the calling parameters is hidden from you, the task of parsing the returned XML is taken care of for you.

How the Facebook REST Object Works Internally

All of the API calls function in the same general way. Each call is wrapped in a method of the Facebook REST object, such as this one:

```
public function friends_areFriends($uids1, $uids2 ) {
  return $this->call_method(
    'facebook.friends.areFriends',
    array('uids1'=>$uids1, 'uids2'=>$uids2 )
  );
}
```

As you can see, all that happens here is that another method, `call_method`, is called. Here is the code in PHP 5:

```php
public function call_method($method, $params) {
  $xml = $this->post_request($method, $params);
  $sxml = simplexml_load_string($xml);
  $result = self::convert_simplexml_to_array($sxml);
  // debugging code removed
  if (is_array($result) && isset($result['error_code'])) {
    throw new FacebookRestClientException($result['error_msg'],
     $result['error_code']);
  }
  return $result;
}
```

Here is the code in PHP 4. As you will see in Chapter 12, you will need to download the IsterXmlSimpleXMLImpl code if you are using PHP 4.

```php
function call_method($method, $params) {
  $this->error_code = 0;
  $xml = $this->post_request($method, $params);

  $impl = new IsterXmlSimpleXMLImpl();
  $sxml = $impl->load_string($xml);
  $result = array();
  $children = $sxml->children();
  $result = $this->convert_simplexml_to_array($children[0]);
  // debugging code removed

  if (is_array($result) && isset($result['error_code'])) {
    $this->error_code = $result['error_code'];
    return null;
  }
  return $result;
}
```

The filling in of the parameters is done in `post_request`, which also sends the actual REST call and retrieves the result. The XML returned from `post_request` is then converted into an array so that what you get back is already parsed and ready for you to manipulate in PHP. You can review the code if you want, but it is extremely unlikely (virtually impossible) that you will need to change it.

Regardless of the internal differences, in both PHP 4 and PHP 5, the parameters are taken care of for you, and the resulting XML is converted into an array or other immediately usable data structure. In Chapter 10, you will see how to use the major API calls through their Facebook REST interfaces.

Chapter 9

Use Facebook Markup Language (FBML)

How to...

- Use the FBML test tool

- Use FBML data elements

- Use FBML control elements

- Use the FBML the share element

- Use FBML forms

- Use FBML dialogs

Now that you have seen the overall architecture of Facebook, you will find in this chapter and the two that follow a description of the major components of that architecture: FBML (Chapter 10), the Facebook API (Chapter 11), and then, in Chapter 11, Facebook Query Language (FQL), Mock- AJAX, and Facebook JavaScript implementation.

FBML is used to help specify your Facebook pages. In fact, all of your Facebook pages consist entirely of FBML, whether you realize it or not. As described in the previous chapter, Facebook reads your pages, parses the HTML and FBML, and regenerates it for transmission back to the user. As the Facebook documentation makes clear, FBML can include a wide variety of HTML elements, so from that standpoint, as well as the standpoint of what actually happens, it is only FBML (possibly including HTML) that is sent to Facebook by your application.

NOTE   *In markup languages such as HTML, XML, and FBML,* elements *are composed of* tags—*an opening and closing tag, as well as* content *that may appear within the tag. A tag can be its own opening and closing tag, and, in languages such as HTML that are not strict, a closing tag can sometimes be omitted. The element is the entire structure. People often talk about tags when they mean elements, as in "the* div *tag" or the "*fb:name*" tag. It is clear what is being talked about. In this book, every attempt has been made to identify elements as elements and tags as tags.*

FBML elements serve several purposes. Some of them retrieve data from Facebook's database—typically, these elements are self-closing. The attributes specify the data to be retrieved, and, when Facebook parses the FBML element, it returns the appropriate text. You often have a choice of using FBML elements or API calls. For example, if you use an FBML element to display a person's name, Facebook takes care of retrieving the data and formatting it. You can also use an

API call to retrieve information about a user which you can then format yourself. Where there is a choice, some people are more comfortable with one structure rather than the other.

Other FBML elements serve to control processing. A variety of if elements let you check to see if a condition is true or not; depending on the result, one or another section of FBML is then parsed and returned.

In addition, there are sets of FBML elements that implement forms, dialogs, and other traditional HTML features using the Facebook look and feel.

Finally, FBML elements implement Facebook-specific interactions, such as selecting one or more of the user's friends, wrapping media for a Facebook page, or sending requests and invitations to friends.

Many FBML elements are created dynamically in your PHP (or other language) code, where you can dynamically fill in attributes of the element such as a specific user id, a specific URL to be shared, and so forth.

Beginning at the end of 2007, it is possible for people to view Facebook applications' Canvas pages without being logged in to Facebook. This allows people to place links to pages of Facebook applications on any Web page or to discover them in a search engine. If you allow people who are not logged in to Facebook to view your pages, some FBML elements will automatically behave differently in order to enforce privacy. For example, the fb:profile-pic element will only show a question mark if the user has marked the picture as private. The automatic behaviors for logged-out users are noted in this chapter. Chapter 12 shows you how to make your page available (or not) to non-logged in users.

Did you know?

Find More Information about FBML

Find more information about FBML and lists of the current elements at http://wiki.developers.facebook.com/index.php/FBML. This chapter provides an overview of the types of elements you can expect to find and how to use them. Facebook is always refining the interface, so browse through this URL to see what is available. Also look at the discussions in the Developer application to find new features and changes. As always, keep an eye out for notices of items that have been or are about to be deprecated.

Use the FBML Test Tool

The indispensable tool for working with FBML is the test tool, located at http://developers.facebook.com/tools.php. As you can see in Figure 9-1, this tool lets you enter FBML code and test it. The user id (yours) is filled in, along with an API key. You can use the Position menu to choose how the FBML should be evaluated: sometimes the result is different, depending on whether or not it is a Canvas page, a wide or narrow Profile page column, or other specific positions.

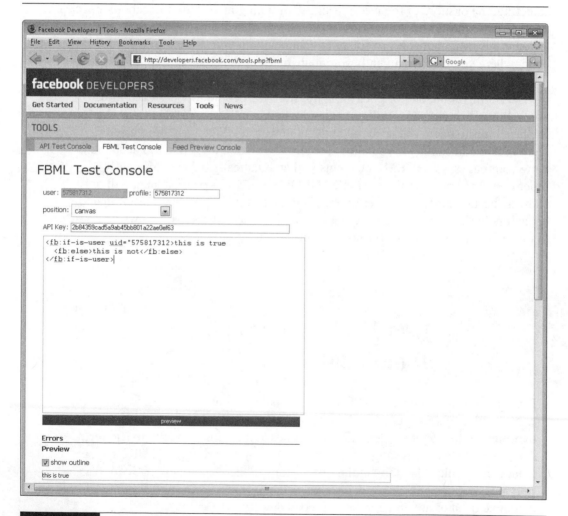

FIGURE 9-1 Use the FBML test tool.

You type your code into the large box, then click the Preview button (the blue bar below the box) to have the code evaluated.

> **TIP**   *In the case of complex FBML, copy the code that works and paste it into your application rather than retyping it.*

Use FBML Data Elements

FBML data elements are those with a self-closing element that are translated into data. They typically have an identifier of the data to be retrieved (such as a user id); other attributes specify how the retrieved data is processed.

For example, the `fb:name` element requires a `uid` attribute, which specifies the user id of the person in which you are interested. Then a variety of Boolean attributes can be specified to determine exactly what is returned. Table 9-1 shows those attributes as well as their meanings (unless they are self-evident).

> **NOTE**   *If some who is not logged in to Facebook views your page, the `fb:name` element will only return the first name. Once someone has logged in to Facebook, the other attributes may be used. You do not have to worry about this: Facebook does it automatically.*

Attribute	Default Value	Meaning
firstnameonly	false	
lastnameonly	false	
linked	true	The returned name is placed in a link to the user's Profile page.
shownetwork	false	User's primary network.
useyou	true	Instead of a name, returns "you" if the current user is the `uid` specified in the element.
possessive	false	Make the name (first, last, or full) possessive, as in Roger's instead of Roger.
reflexive	false	If the current user is the `uid` specified in the element and `useyou` is true, returns "yourself."
capitalize	false	If the current user is the `uid` specified in the element and `useyou` is true, capitalizes the returned text's first word.

TABLE 9-1   fb:name Attributes

Two other attributes can be specified for fb:name:

- ifcantsee is an FBML string to be displayed if the current user cannot see the target user's data because of privacy settings.

- subjectid is used when you are constructing a sentence with both subject and object (as in "Subject made dinner for Object"). If you specify subjectid (which is a uid), you receive the appropriate name for that user when used as a sentence subject; the uid attribute is assumed to be the name of the user who is the object of the sentence if subjectid is present. All appropriate conversions (such as using "you") are observed.

This is just one example of a number of tags such as fb:pronoun (which gives you "his" or "hers" as necessary) that help you convert Facebook data into meaningful and grammatical text. Similarly, fb:profile-pic, which returns the profile photo, helps you further construct useful information for your application's interface.

Use FBML Control Elements

These are elements that almost always contain data—frequently other elements. The basic elements are shown in Table 9-2.

Between the opening and closing tags, you place the text or other elements to be displayed if the condition is true.

You can use the fb:else element to encase the alternate text for any of these elements. (A sample of this code has been shown previously in Figure 9-1 as an example of using the FBML test tool.)

Control Elements
fb:is-in-network
fb:if-can-see
fb:if-can-see-photo
fb:if-is-app-user
fb:if-is-friends-with-viewer
fb:if-is-group-member
fb:if-is-user
fb:if-user-has-added-app
fb:is-logged-out

TABLE 9-2   FBML Control Elements

NOTE   *If someone who is viewing your page is not logged in to Facebook, all* `fb:if` *elements are false and an* `fb:else` *element is used (if it exists). You do not have to do anything for this behavior to occur. If you want to test whether the user is logged in or out, use* `fb:is-logged-out` *which is true when someone has not logged in to Facebook.*

Use the FBML Share Element

Sometimes, an FBML element implements specific Facebook functionality. One example of this is the Share button that appears throughout the Facebook site. The Share button is one of the Facebook features that you should implement whenever possible: Users know what it is, and it takes advantage of the social graph and friends networks to let people interact not just with Facebook and your content, but also with their friends.

When you click a Share button, the dialog shown in Figure 9-2 appears so that you can select whether to email the information or post it to your profile. In either

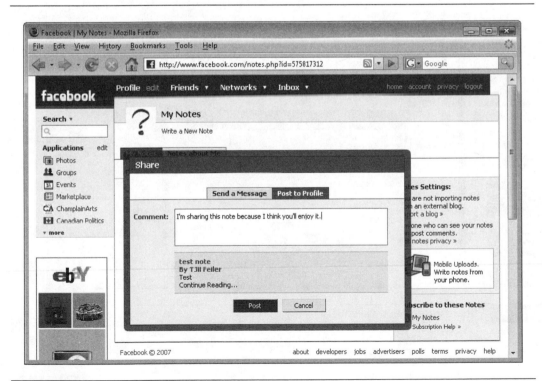

FIGURE 9-2   Share information via your Profile page.

case, you get to enter a comment for the information. Figure 9-2 shows the posting dialog.

In Figure 9-3, you can see how to send the shared information to a friend via email.

Although the user interface is the same, behind the scenes, there are two types of sharing involved: one shares just a URL, and the other shares structured information with the user (either via the Profile page or email). Thus, there are two forms of the `fb:share-button` element.

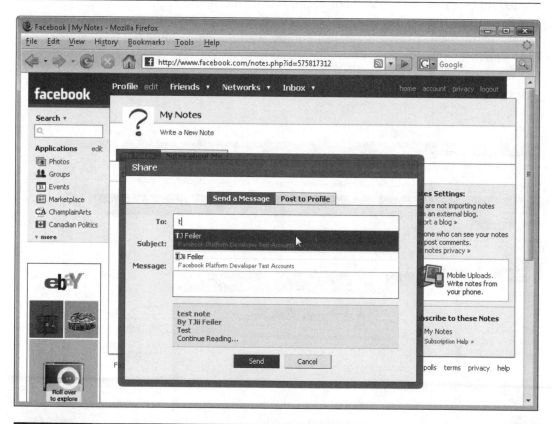

FIGURE 9-3   Share information via email.

Sharing a URL

If you share a URL, the syntax is quite simple. You use the `class` attribute to indicate that you are sharing a URL, and then you provide it, as in this example:

```
<fb:share-button
  class="url"
  href="http://www.yourWebSite.com?caeid=12345"
/>
```

This is the type of code that might be used to share an event, as the example application in Part III does.

Sharing Data

If you are sharing data, you set the `class` attribute to `meta`, and you provide a number of `meta` and `link` elements within the `fb:share-button` element.

```
<fb:share-button class="meta">
  <!-- link and meta elements here-->
</fb:share-button>
```

Meta Elements

This is the ordinary HTML `meta` element; it must contain a `name` and a `content` attribute, as, for example:

```
<meta name="title" content="Greyhounds in Concert"/>
<meta name="video_type" content="application/x-shockwave-flash"/>
```

Link Elements

These, too, are standard HTML. Each link element normally has an `href` attribute, specifying where the resource is, and a `rel` attribute that specifies the relationship of that resource. Thus, to specify a target document as well as an image to be used in displaying the link, you could use this syntax:

```
<link rel="image_src" href="http://www.yourWebSite.com/caeid14.jpg"/>
<link rel="target_url" href="www.yourWebSite.com?caeid=14"/>
```

Use FBML Forms

You can use the FBML form elements to construct a form that behaves like an ordinary HTML form. Figure 9-4 shows a form from a page in the example that will be constructed in Part III.

Here is the code that produces that form. Key parts of it are underlined and discussed following the code:

```
<fb:editor
  action="http://www.yourWebSite.com/add user.php"
  labelwidth="100">

  <fb:editor-text label="First Name" name="firstName" value="<?php
echo $firstName; ?>"/>
  <fb:editor-text label="Last Name" name="lastName" value=""/>
```

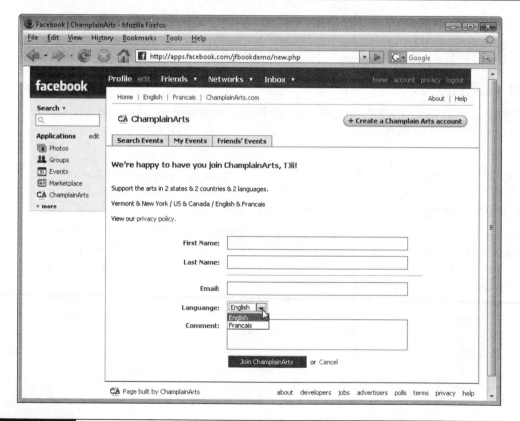

FIGURE 9-4   FBML form

```
<fb:editor-divider/>
<fb:editor-text label="Email" name="email" value=""/>
<fb:editor-custom name="language" label="Language">
  <select name="language">
    <option value="english" selected>English</option>
    <option value="french">Francais</option>
  </select>
</fb:editor-custom>
<fb:editor-textarea label="Comment" name="comment."/>
<fb:editor-buttonset>
  <fb:editor-button value="Join ChamplainArts"/>
  <fb:editor-cancel value="Cancel"/>
</fb:editor-buttonset>
</fb:editor>
```

You are basically constructing a form here, just as you would in HTML. The `action` of the HTML form that is generated will be set to the `action` attribute specified at the beginning. `fb:editor-text` elements are like HTML `input` elements. The Facebook-defined elements that can be used are shown in Table 9-3. They have similar functionality to HTML constructs, but they will be rendered using the Facebook look and feel. In addition to these elements, you can specify not only the `action`, but the total width of the `fb:editor` object, as well as the width of the left-hand (label) column using its `width` and `labelwidth` attributes, as you can see in the preceding code. Custom Facebook interface elements let you provide date and time inputs.

Elements for fb:editor
fb:editor-text
fb:editor-textarea
fb:editor-time
fb:editor-month
fb:editor-date
fb:editor-divider
fb:editor-buttonset
fb:editor-button
fb:editor-cancel
fb:editor-custom

TABLE 9-3   fb:editor Elements

The `fb:editor-custom` element lets you enclose standard HTML (such as a `select` element) inside it; it will be rendered appropriately. But you must always check to see that happens because sometimes there is a disparity between the wrapped HTML and the Facebook look and feel.

The `fb:buttonset` element lets you enclose buttons, as you see in Figure 9-4. The `value` of the clicked button will be sent through, and you can test to see what it is.

Use FBML Dialogs

You can create your own dialogs with the Facebook look and feel. Figure 9-5 shows a dialog from the example that will be built in Part III.

The dialog shown in Figure 9-5 is used to allow users to report on problems with database items. Rather than taking space on the standard layout to allow users to report problems, the problem reporting mechanism is triggered by a link on a single word: Report. Here is the link.

```
<a href="#" clicktoshowdialog="report dialog">Report</a>
```

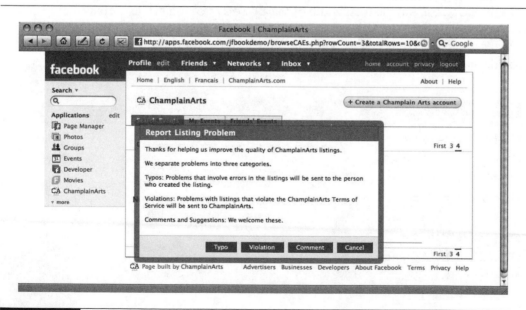

FIGURE 9-5   Create a Facebook dialog.

Because it is hoped that most database items will not have problems, it makes sense to move the information and action buttons to a dialog that only appears when necessary.

Here is the code to create the dialog.

Listing 9-1

```
<fb:dialog id="report_dialog" cancel_button=1>
  <fb:dialog-title>Report Listing Problem</fb:dialog-title>
  <fb:dialog-content>
    <form id="report_form">
      Thanks for helping us improve the quality of
      ChamplainArts listings. <br /> <br />
      We separate problems into three categories.
      <br /> <br />
      Typos: Problems that involve errors in the listings
      will be sent to the person who created the listing.
      <br /> <br />
      Violations: Problems with listings that violate the
      ChamplainArts Terms of Service will be sent to
      ChamplainArts.
      <br /> <br />
      Comments and Suggestions: We welcome these.
      <br />  <br />
    </form>
  </fb:dialog-content>
  <fb:dialog-button type="button" value="Typo"
    href="http://www.yourWebSite.com/receive_report?
    type=typo"/>
  <fb:dialog-button type="button" value="Violation"
    href="http://www.yourWebSite.com/receive_report?
    type=violation"/>
  <fb:dialog-button type="button" value="Comment"
    href="http://www.yourWebSite.com/receive_report?
    type=comment"/>
</fb:dialog>
```

The fb:dialog element must contain an fb:dialog_content element. It may also contain an fb:dialog-title element and one or more fb:dialog-button elements. The id of the fb:dialog must match the value of the clicktoshowdialog attribute in the link as indicated with the underlining. Note that you do not create a Cancel button; rather, you add cancel_button="1" to the opening tag of the fb:dialog element.

Chapter 10

Use the Facebook API

How to...

- Use the User API
- Use the Profile API
- Use the Events API
- Use the Feed API
- Use the Friends API
- Use the Groups API
- Use the Notifications API
- Use the Photos API
- Use the Marketplace API

In Chapter 8, you saw how the Facebook REST object wraps the basic API calls for you, executes the call, and then unwraps the result. This chapter shows you the most commonly used API calls as they are implemented in the Facebook REST object (which is where you most commonly will use them). Full documentation is provided in the Facebook developer wiki, but that documentation also includes parameters such as the session key, signature, and call id that are common to most API calls. In this chapter, you will find the calls and parameters that you need to actually worry about if you are using the objects. As described in the previous two chapters, you will use them most often to retrieve data that you then use in Facebook Markup Language (FBML) elements.

If you create a Facebook object using this common code:

```
$facebook = new Facebook($api_key, $secret);
```

You can then call a method in the REST object using the following code (assuming the name of the method is users_getInfo):

```
$facebook->api_client->users_getInfo($uids, $fields)
```

NOTE   *The Facebook Query Language (FQL) API is discussed in Chapter 11.*

Use the User API

These are the calls that you use to find out the basic information about a user (usually the logged-in session user).

users_getInfo

For a given list of users, this method returns the values of fields as specified in an input array. The names for the fields are shown in Table 10-1, along with the Profile tab from which they come (or the notation that they are calculated or come from the user's account information). The result is an array with one row for each user; the row consists of the user id and the values for each of the fields.

Fields	Contents	Profile Tab or Account
about_me	About Me	Personal
activities	Activities	Personal
affiliations		
birthday	Birthday (with the option to not show; show month and day only; or show month, day and year)	Basic
books	Favorite Books	Personal
current_location	State and Country	Basic
education_history	College/University and Class/Year	Personal
first_name		Account
hometown_location	Hometown	Basic
hs_info	High School and Class/Year	Education
interests	Interests	Personal
is_app_user		Calculated
last_name		Account
meeting_for	Looking For	Relationships
meeting_sex	Interest in (Men/Women)	Relationships
movies	Favorite Movies	Personal
music	Favorite Music	Personal

TABLE 10-1   Field Names from Profile

Fields	Contents	Profile Tab or Account
name		Account
notes_count		Calculated
pic		Picture
pic_big		Picture
pic_small		Picture
political	Political Views	Basic
profile_update_time		Calculated
quotes	Favorite Quotes	Personal
relationship_status	Relationship Status	Relationships
religion	Religious Views	Basic
sex	Sex	Basic
significant_other_id		Relationships
status		
timezone		
tv	Favorite TV Shows	Personal
wall_count		Calculated
work_history	Employer/Position/Description/City, State, Country/Time Period	Work

TABLE 10-1   Field Names from Profile (*Continued*)

Here is the method's header:

```
public function users_getInfo($uids, $fields)
```

users_getLoggedInUser

This method returns the current session user:

```
public function users_getLoggedInUser()
```

NOTE   *If you have public Canvas pages which can be accessed by people who are not logged in to Facebook, you can test if the result of this call is null to find a user who is not logged in.*

users_isAppAdded

This method returns a Boolean value indicating whether the current session user has added the application that makes the call:

```
public function users_isAppAdded()
```

Use the Profile API

The first pair of methods lets you get and set the user's FBML on the Profile page. The remaining three pairs let you set or change the references to your application's data that are used in preparing the user's FBML for the Profile page.

set_FBML

This method sets the markup for the current user or the one specified by $uid. Its result is a list of strings describing any errors that have been found in the markup.

```
public function profile_setFBML($markup, $uid = null)
```

get_FBML

This method gets the existing FBML. One reason for using this is that if you provide a mechanism for users to post quotes or pithy sayings to their Profile boxes, you can retrieve the current values from there, rather than having to implement a storage mechanism of your own. Here is the header:

```
public function profile_getFBML($uid)
```

fbml_refreshImgSrc

This changes the application's image for Profile pages. Here is the header:

```
public function fbml_refreshImgSrc($url)
```

fbml_refreshRefURL

This function changes a set of FBML code that has been pushed up for all of the application's users (not a specific user). Here is the header:

```
public function fbml_refreshRefUrl($url)
```

fbml_setRefHandle

This function does the initial setting of the application's FBML code:

```
public function fbml_setRefHandle($handle, $fbml)
```

Use Events API

There are two methods in the Events API, as described in the following sections.

events_get

The first, `events_get`, returns an array of `eids` for all events that fulfill the optional filtering requirements. Table 10-2 shows the parameters. Note that UTC is an integer representing a specific date and time in epoch seconds—the number of seconds since the Unix Epoch (January 1 1970 00:00:00 GMT); PHP and other languages have conversion routines to set values for specific dates, times, and time zones.

Here is the header:

```
public function events_get(
  $uid, $eids, $start_time, $end_time, $rsvp_status)
```

Parameter	Required	Meaning
uid	Required if `rsvp_status` is set	If null, the session user
eids		If null, all the user's events
start_time		UTC for lower bound to search; null means no lower bound, retrieve all events from the beginning for the user
end_time		UTC for upper bound; null means no upper bound, retrieve all events to the end of time for the user
rsvp_status		'attending,' 'unsure,' 'declined,' 'not_replied'
result		array of `eids`

TABLE 10-2   Parameters for `events_get`

events_getMembers

The `events_getMembers` method returns the members of a specific event. Here is the header:

```
public function events_getMembers($eid)
```

The result is an array, which itself is an array consisting of four associative arrays, each of which contains a list of the relevant ids identified by the values of `rsvp_status` in Table 10-2. You can access them by using syntax such as:

```
$theResult = $facebook->api_client->events_getMembers ($eid);
$attendees = $theResult ['attending'];
$unsures = $theResult ['unsure'];
```

... and so forth

The `eid` passed into this method may be one that was found by a previous call to `events_get`.

Use the Feed API

There are three methods in the Feed API. They differ in the feeds to which they are published, as well as in their usage limits.

feed_publishStoryToUser

This method publishes stories to the user's News Feed. It can be used once every 12 hours per user. The `title` and `body` parameters contain FBML.

In `title`, only the a element is allowed.

In `body`, you can use a, b, and i elements. `body` can also contain up to four image/link pairs.

```
public function feed_publishStoryToUser (
  $title,
  $body,
  $image_1=null, $image_1_link=null,
  $image_2=null, $image_2_link=null,
  $image_3=null, $image_3_link=null,
  $image_4=null, $image_4_link=null)
```

feed_publishActionOfUser

This method publishes an action to the user's Mini-Feed and, depending on settings, may publish it for friends' News Feeds. It can be used up to ten times per user in a 48-hour period.

In `title`, a and `fb:userlink` elements can be used, at most, once each. The only other element allowed is `fb:name`. If `fb:userlink` is not used in `title`, the user's named is appended to the front of the title.

In `body`, there are no limits on the number of times you can use specific elements. The same elements are allowed as in `title`, with the addition of b and i. The body can also contain up to four image/link pairs:

```
public function feed_publishActionOfUser (
  $title,
  $body,
  $image_1=null, $image_1_link=null,
  $image_2=null, $image_2_link=null,
  $image_3=null, $image_3_link=null,
  $image_4=null, $image_4_link=null)
```

feed_publishTemplatizedAction

This method publishes an action in much the same way as the previous method. However, JavaScript Object Notation (JSON) associative arrays are used to specify data. This allows Facebook to potentially aggregate stories across a number of users. Aggregation is very important because by constructing an aggregated story, Facebook can construct a story that is more interesting to most people. Because of this, aggregated stories are more likely to appear in News Feeds. An example of the use of this method is given in Chapter 15.

```
public function feed_publishTemplatizedAction(
  $actor_id,
  $title_template,
  $title_data,
  $body_template,
  $body_data,
  $body_general,
  $image_1=null, $image_1_link=null,
  $image_2=null, $image_2_link=null,
  $image_3=null, $image_3_link=null,
  $image_4=null, $image_4_link=null,
  $target_ids='')
```

Use the Friends API

There are three methods in this API, as the following sections explain.

friends_areFriends

You send two equal-length arrays of uids into this method. The result consists of an array, each element of which is an array with three associative elements: uid1, uid2, and are_friends. The results array will be the same length as the two arrays sent into the method, with a 0/1 value indicating if the combination of the nth elements of the two input arrays are friends.

This is the header:

```
public function friends_areFriends($uids1, $uids2)
```

friends_get

This method and the one that follows simply return a list of uids in the result. In this case, it is a list of uids of friends for the current session user.

This is the header:

```
public function friends_get()
```

friends_getAppUsers

This method returns the session user's friends who are also users of the calling application.

Here is the header:

```
public function friends_getAppUsers()
```

Use the Groups API

The two methods in this API are analogous to the methods in the Events API. The first filters groups, and the second gets members of a specified group (which may have been found by using the first method).

groups_get

This method filters groups based on a specific uid and a list of groups. If the uid is not specified, the session user is used; if the list of groups is not provided, all of the user's groups are used as the list.

Here is the header:

```
public function groups_get($uid, $gids)
```

groups_getMembers

For a given group, this method returns its members:

```
public function groups_getMembers($gid)
```

Use the Notifications API

These two methods implement the notifications and requests API, as explained in the following sections.

notifications_get

This method gets outstanding notifications for the session user. It returns an associative array of counts and invitations. The six arrays, which are contained within the result, are shown with their associative names and their contents, as outlined in Table 10-3.

Here is the header:

```
public function notifications_get()
```

notifications_send

Notifications are an important part of Facebook; they play off of the social graph and networks of friends, adding value to everyone. They are also subject to controls on how they are sent to avoid turning the notification system into spam. Table 10-4 shows the conditions under which notifications can be sent.

Array Name	Meaning
messages	count of outstanding messages
pokes	count of outstanding pokes
shares	count of outstanding shares
friend_requests	uid list of friend requests (the data)
group_invites	gid list of group invitations (the data)
event_invites	eid list of event invitations (the data)

TABLE 10-3   Results of notifications_get

Notification Recipient	Method	Method Condition
User	Send to user's Notifications page	None
Users of the application	Use notification system to send a URL for user to click	Up to 40 per day
Non-users of the application	Send to user's Notifications page	
User	Shown on user's Notifications page as "sent notification"	

TABLE 10-4   Conditions for Sending Notifications

This is the basic method for sending notifications. Table 10-5 shows the parameters.

Here is the method header:

```
public function notifications_send($to_ids, $notification)
```

notifications_sendEmail

This method replaces an email option in notifications_send that has since been deprecated. You can send up to five email messages to a user per day, with a maximum of 100 messages per call.

Table 10-6 shows the parameters.

Here is the method header:

```
public function notifications_sendEmail
  ($recipients, $subject, $text, $fbml)
```

Parameter	Required	Daily Limit	Meaning
to_ids	Required	40	Comma-separated list of recipients; they must be friends of the user or people who have added the calling application. If empty, send to the user's Notifications page.
notification	Required	10	FBML containing only text and links.

TABLE 10-5   Parameters for notifications.send

Parameter	Required	Meaning
recipients	Required	Comma-separated list of recipients. They must be people who have added your application.
subject	Required	Email subject.
text	Either text or FBML or both is required.	Plain text for the message.
fbml	Either text or FBML or both is required.	FBML that will be parsed into HTML for the message.

TABLE 10-6   Parameters for notifications.sendEmail

Use the Photos API

Facebook is one of the largest photo-sharing sites on the Web, in part, because it is easy to share and manipulate photos and albums. These three methods implement the basic functionality.

photos_get

Like other filtering methods (such as events_get), this one lets you quickly retrieve the items you are interested in. The parameters are listed in Table 10-7; at least one of them is required, but it does not matter which one you use.

Here is the method header:

```
public function photos_get($subj_id, $aid, $pids)
```

photos_getAlbums

This method gets the albums for a specified user or, if no user is specified, the current session user. An optional list of album ids can be used to restrict the search. At least one of the parameters is required.

Parameter	Meaning
subj_id	uid of a user tagged in photos
aid	An album id
pids	List of pids

TABLE 10-7   Parameters for photos_get

Here is the method header:

```
public function photos_getAlbums($uid, $aids)
```

photos_getTags

Finally, this method returns the tags for an array of photos. Each element of the result consists of a `pid` and then x- and y-coordinates of the tag (these are floating-point values).

Here is the method header:

```
public function photos_getTags($pids)
```

Use the Marketplace API

Finally, the Marketplace API lets you interact with the built-in Marketplace functionality.

marketplace_createListing

This method lets you create or modify a listing for the current user. The listing itself is provided in an associative array with the elements:

```
category
subcategory
title
description
```

NOTE   *The current values for listing attributes can be found on the Facebook developers wiki. Search for "Marketplace Listing Attributes."*

If this is a modification, the `listing_id` of the original listing is provided in the first parameter; otherwise, set it to zero. You also can specify (0/1)—whether or not this listing should appear on the user's Profile page.

The result of the method call (if it succeeds) is the `listing_id` of the new or modified listing. In the case of a new listing, you may want to store that number if you need to interact with the listing in the future (for example, if the listing is linked to an item in an external database).

Here is the header:

```
function marketplace_createListing(
  $listing_id, $show_on_profile, $attrs)
```

marketplace_removeListing

With a `listing_id` for a listing belonging to the current user, you can remove that listing if you want. You need both the `listing_id` and an indication of why it is being removed. The following status strings are defined: SUCCESS, NOT_SUCCESS, or DEFAULT.

```
function marketplace_removeListing($listing_id, $status='DEFAULT')
```

marketplace_getCategories

This method returns a list of the category names:

```
function marketplace_getCategories()
```

marketplace_getSubCategories

This method returns the subcategories for a category from the previous method's list:

```
function marketplace_getSubCategories($category)
```

marketplace_getListings

Listings in the Marketplace are identified by a `listing_id` as well as by the `uid` of the user who created the listing. You can retrieve listings based on either or both of these values, as shown in this method's header. (Note that both parameters are lists of identifiers.)

```
function marketplace_getListings($listing_ids, $uids)
```

marketplace_search

Like all the filtering methods, none of these arguments is required, but at least one must be present.

```
function marketplace_search($category, $subcategory, $query)
```

The query parameter lets you further refine your search.

Chapter 11

Use Facebook Query Language (FQL), Mock-AJAX, FBJS, and Facebook Mobile

How to...

- Use Facebook Query Language (FQL)
- Use dynamic FBML action attributes
- Use Mock-AJAX
- Use FBJS
- Use Facebook mobile
- Watch for further developments

This chapter completes this part of the book in which you have seen the basic technologies on which Facebook is built—both the open technologies—XML, XHTML, CSS, and PHP—and the Facebook technologies of Facebook Markup Language (FBML), the API, and the overall architecture. There are many more parts of Facebook for you to explore on the Developers section of Facebook and in the discussions and news in the Developer application. In this chapter, you will find some of the features of Facebook that have not yet been discussed and that may be useful to you in developing your applications.

> **TIP** *Remember to use the test tools at http://developers.facebook.com/ tools.php to experiment with Facebook Platform.*

Use Facebook Query Language (FQL)

As you have seen, Facebook has several layers that you as a developer can access. You can make REST calls to the Facebook REST server using the parameters defined in the API; these calls can be constructed in any language that is capable of creating them (many people tend to use PHP). And further, instead of constructing the raw REST API calls, you can use the wrappers in a Facebook class that simplify their use if you are using PHP. Likewise, you can parse the XML or JSON that is returned in your own code, or you can use the automatic parsing in the Facebook class to parse the XML and return PHP arrays to you.

The API calls themselves often have a further level of detail. When they retrieve data from Facebook, they abstract the Facebook Query Language (FQL), which is a custom-built query language. Using the Facebook class is the simplest way of communicating with Facebook if you are using PHP; constructing your own REST calls to the API is more complex, but provides language-independence; and constructing FQL calls that you place via the REST interface or through the API lets you customize the actual Facebook database calls that you make.

For example, some of the API calls automatically retrieve data that is specified in the API; others let you choose what is retrieved. If you want to totally customize what is retrieved without retrieving anything you do not want, FQL may be for you.

> **NOTE** *Whether or not FQL is more complex than the API and the Facebook class methods is a debatable point. The API and Facebook class methods are customized for each call; thus, there is a multitude of calls you can make, each with its own syntax (which is, nevertheless, quite similar across calls). With FQL, you need only learn the basics to construct all of your calls. Whether the multitude of calls with prepared parameters is easier for you to use, or the single FQL calls with the do-it-yourself query is simpler, is up to you. There also may be performance differences between the two strategies; as is always the case (and particularly so with a distributed component-based platform such as Facebook), the only way to truly evaluate the performance differences is to test in real life with a real workload. Variables such as network availability, the responsiveness of your server and Facebook's servers, and more all contribute to performance. You can hypothesize about what may slow down or speed up your application, but you must prove it in solid testing before deciding that it is worthwhile to choose one road or another.*

FQL is based on SQL, with a basic syntax like this:

```
SELECT data FROM table WHERE condition
```

Unlike SQL, you are limited to retrieving data from a single table, but you can use subqueries so that you can access multiple tables (such as you do in SQL with a subquery for selecting which rows to retrieve), although the actual data can only be retrieved from a single table. (The description of SQL and MySQL in Chapter 14 contains information about these database concepts that may be useful to you at this point.)

Furthermore, some of the columns of Facebook data that you retrieve are themselves structures of data. In a fanatically normalized world, they would possibly be related tables. For example, in the users table, there are columns such as `education_history` and `hometown_location`. You can retrieve columns such as these, but you can also retrieve particular elements of those columns, such as `education_history.name` or `hometown_location.zip`. Using such specific data descriptions in the SELECT clause of an FQL query can drastically reduce the bandwidth that would otherwise be wasted in retrieving all of the fields of `hometown_location` when you only care about `hometown_location.zip`.

You construct your query in the same way in which you construct an SQL query. Generally, you construct it in PHP code that inserts specific data values into it to determine exactly what is retrieved. Here is the header of the method of the Facebook class that you would use to make the call:

```
public function fql_query($myQuery)
```

For more information on FQL, see the overview at http:/developers.facebook .com/documentation.php.

Use Dynamic FBML Action Attributes

There are several dynamic FBML attributes that you can use within FBML elements. These attributes make the particular FBML element responsive to clicks in a variety of ways. Table 11-1 shows the dynamic FBML attributes, what values they take, and what the consequences are.

Use Mock-AJAX

Asynchronous JavaScript and XML (AJAX) is the set of technologies that enables Web page developers to load (or reload) parts of pages instead of the entire page. This can drastically reduce bandwidth, not just because less data needs to be transmitted, but also because the amounts of data that are transmitted are much smaller and, therefore, the transmission is completed faster.

Dynamic Attribute	Values	Consequence
clicktoshow	Comma-separated list of `id` attributes (typically of `div` elements)	Makes the elements visible
clicktohide	Same	Makes the elements invisible
clicktotoggle	Same	Makes the elements visible if invisible and invisible if visible
clickthrough	`true` or `false`	If `false`, clicks are not passed through to the element (e.g., buttons are disabled)
clicktoenable	Comma-separated list of id attributes within a form	In a form, enables the elements
clicktodisable	Same	In a form, disables the elements

TABLE 11-1   Dynamic FBML Action Attributes

Facebook uses dynamic FBML action attributes to implement Mock-AJAX functionality in which you can achieve the same results. There are two dynamic FBML action attributes that you use:

- `clickrewriteid` is the `id` of the `div` that the returned data will placed in.

- `clickrewriteurl` is the address—on your site, not a Facebook URL—from which the replacement data will be retrieved.

You can create a form and attach these two attributes to its Submit button. Alternatively, you can create a form and place an `a` link in it, setting these attributes in the link element. If you take this route, you must add a third attribute to the link—`clickrewriteform`—and it is set to the name of the form. In either case, the user's click will cause the data to be fetched from the `clickrewriteurl` and placed in the `div` identified by `clickrewriteid`. And in either case, what is visible on the page need be nothing more than the link or a submit button; the form containing these items need have no visible components.

Use FBJS

You can use JavaScript on Facebook pages (both Canvas pages and Profile pages), but there are some issues to consider. JavaScript runs on the client side in the browser; at that point, it may be able to accidentally do some mischief to JavaScript that has been downloaded from Facebook and that was created by the FBML parser. The solution to this is that the FBML parser will prepend your application ID to every identifier, such as a variable or function. Thus, your JavaScript code can never use an identifier that Facebook has already created.

> TIP
>
> *You write the JavaScript code as usual, but the parser, at this point, requires that you place the code inside a comment. This was a standard practice in the old days, when JavaScript was not available on all browsers. Placing the code in a comment meant that a browser that did not understand it had no problems, but the JavaScript-enabled browsers could strip the comments out from within script elements. It is worthwhile checking to see if Facebook has modified this restriction (they have announced their intention to do so).*

Because Facebook is parsing your JavaScript code (to prepend the application ID and to make the other necessary changes), there are some differences between JavaScript and FBJS. Perhaps the most important changes are in the

FBJS Document Object Model (DOM) object. The basic calls are as they are in JavaScript, but JavaScript properties have been transformed into more object-oriented routines. Thus, the standard JavaScript `scrollTop` property becomes `getScrollTop` and `setScrollTop`. These differences from standard JavaScript are described in the documentation.

> **NOTE**   *If you are using the DOM model, you can also use the FBJS Events and Dialog classes along with the AJAX class. These are described in the documentation previously mentioned. This part of Facebook Platform is evolving rapidly.*

If you are using JavaScript for basic page scripting, you will probably find that you do not need to worry about any of the differences: They are irrelevant to what you are doing.

Here, for example, is a bare-bones example of the use of FBJS:

```
<div id="test">Before Test</div>
<a href="#"
  id="hello"
  onclick="do_test(document.getElementById('test'))">
  Do Test
</a>
```

A `div` element is created and some text ("Before Test") is placed into it. Because you will be using the DOM and will be locating this via the `id`, it must be identified, and it is: `test`.

Next comes a standard `a` link; it links to this document (#), and it includes an `onclick` handler. The `onclick` handler calls a script in this document called `do_test`; it passes in the element identified as `test`.

> **NOTE**   *You can attach the `onclick` handler to other types of elements, but by using the `a` link, you inherit the default Facebook behavior for links (such as the light blue color), and it makes it easier for users to understand that the text is clickable. You also increase usability by providing text that itself makes it clear that it will cause an action to occur.*

Here is the script that is invoked by the `onclick` handler. The `onclick` handler's invocation has taken care of locating the appropriate object in the document, so this function is totally generic, and it can be used to apply the same process to any of several clicked items on the page.

Remember that you are producing the JavaScript (as well as the entire page) dynamically. Thus, your PHP code might follow one of three patterns. The first would be to generate the script as it is shown here:

```
<script>
<!--
  function do_test(obj) {
    obj.setTextValue('test value');
  }
-->
</script>
```

A variation on this might be to dynamically calculate the text value. Thus, within your PHP code, you might set a variable, $userName, to the user's name. You could then produce the substring shown here:

```
$subString = "$userName has clicked on this page";
```

That string could replace the quoted string in obj.setTextValue. Yet another variation would be to not use the same function everywhere, but instead to customize the functions for specific objects on the page. You might then have half a dozen separate functions, each with its own name, of course. The key line of code might vary:

```
$subString = "$userName has clicked in the X location on the page";
```

or

```
$subString = "$userName has clicked in the Y location on the page";
```

You could also implement this functionality by passing $subString into do_test as a second parameter.

Use Facebook Mobile

Facebook is available on Web-equipped mobile phones at http://m.facebook.com. (Note that this URL may not work on a device other than a mobile device.) Your application may be used by a user from that site. If so, there are two pieces of information that you should know about.

First, one of the parameters that is sent to your application is now fb_sig_ mobile, which has a value of 1 if the request comes from what Facebook thinks is a mobile phone browser. This does not require you to do anything, but it may influence you to provide mobile-specific Canvas pages.

You do this by wrapping your code in an `fb:mobile` element (this must be the outermost element of the page). It will be rendered if your page has been reached through http://m.facebook.com, and you do not have to worry about testing the parameter.

> **TIP**
>
> *When you are testing, you can ignore the* `fb_sig_mobile` *parameter and* `fb:mobile` *so as to view the mobile page in your computer's browser. But be certain to conduct final testing on the mobile devices you will be using.*

You should be aware that FBJS and Mock-AJAX are not available within `fb:mobile` elements (this is for performance reasons). Writing for a mobile device is very different from writing for a larger screened device with (usually) faster connections. Images, tables, and some styles can slow things down. Basically, what you have to do is rethink your application's interface: Just making things smaller is not going to provide a satisfactory user experience.

As part of its mobile API, Facebook is now exposing its Short Message Service (SMS) functionality to send and receive messages.

> **CAUTION**
>
> *Before using this API, make certain that you read the policies at http:// wiki.developers.facebook.com/index.php?title=Mobile. Also look at the guidelines from the Mobile Marketing Association (www.mmaglobal.com). Violating the terms of service of the best practices can cause you to be terminated from the Facebook Platform.*

Watch for Further Developments

The topics discussed briefly in this chapter provide you with some additional functionality for your Facebook applications. More importantly, they open doors to very powerful parts of the Facebook Platform.

It cannot be said too often: Keep up with the discussions surrounding the Developer application as Facebook Platform evolves. Although the architecture is settling down, there still are a few areas in which existing parts of Facebook Platform are deprecated and sometimes even broken. Usually warning is given, and, if something accidentally breaks, the code can be quickly rolled back. What this means, however, is that you must keep on your toes, watching not only the Developer News Feed, but also watching your application to see if something has broken. (In all fairness, many of the recent "breakages" have to do with legacy aspects of Facebook Platform, some of which predate its opening to all developers. These are gradually going away.)

TIP

There is little to compare with the excitement of working on an evolving platform. It was just over a decade ago (1995, to be precise) when a number of developers in various places started working on something called a Web browser. There was one (Netscape) and another one on the horizon (Internet Explorer), but the dominant players on the Internet (America On Line, Prodigy, and CompuServe) were building browsers into their software. Facebook is just as exciting today (and, in some ways, more so, because it is less of a technical marvel than a social one and people are generally more interesting than computers). If the pace of change makes you nervous, consider programming in a terminally stable environment, such as COBOL.

Now it is time to start putting it all together—to first build the most basic application (Chapter 12) and then, in Chapters 13 through 15, to build a more complex Facebook application.

Part III

Build Facebook Applications

Chapter 12

Get Started as a Facebook Developer

How to...

- Add the Facebook Developer application
- Create a new application
- Create a test account

This chapter describes the process of becoming a Facebook developer and creating your first minimal application. It is the type of task that is often difficult to do: The individual steps are simple, but you normally only do it once in your entire life, which makes it difficult to learn from experience. Thus, each step in the simple process is described and shown here. Of course, while you only do this once, Facebook does it many times (over 100,000 times by late 2007), and it can learn from the process and make changes. If the pages you encounter differ from the figures in this chapter that may be the reason why.

Anyone with a Facebook account can become a developer; there is no charge. The only prerequisite is that you have a Facebook account, so if you do not have one, create one now.

Add the Facebook Developer Application

There are two related parts of Facebook for developers. Clicking on the Developers link at the bottom of a Facebook page will take you to http://developer.facebook.com, as shown in Figure 12-1.

It should not surprise you that the next step is to click Get Started, which opens the page shown in Figure 12-2. As you see from that page, the next step is to add the Facebook Developer application; just click the link on this page to do so. This is a regular Facebook application; it will appear in the Left Nav list, and you go through the same privacy settings that you do for any application.

The Developer application will be added to your account. It will be in the left-hand menu, and the application will open as shown in Figure 12-3.

The Developer application provides you with the tools to begin to create your application. It also serves as a demonstration of Facebook Platform. On the

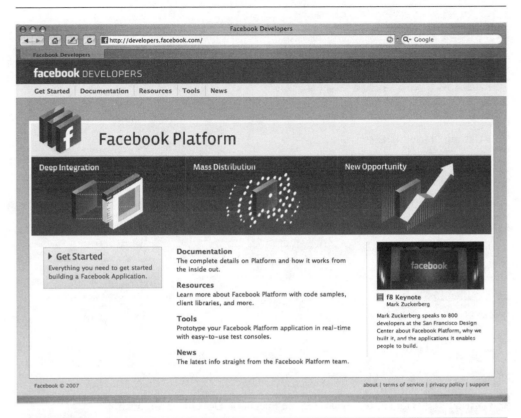

FIGURE 12-1   The Facebook Developers page

Facebook Developer Application page, shown in Figure 12-3, you will find the following boxes:

- **Discussion Board**   In the Developer page, you see only the first few topics. You can click the title bar or See All to open the discussion board. It is a typical list of topics and responses that you can browse. It provides valuable insight, and it is a good tool to use, not only to answer your own questions, but also to help others with their Facebook Platform issues.

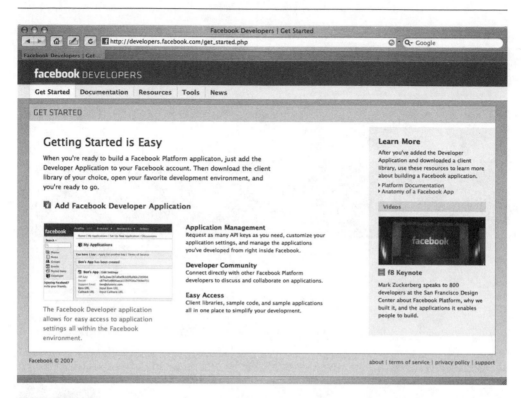

FIGURE 12-2   Get started by adding the Facebook Developer application.

■ **Latest News**   Beneath the discussion board is a newsfeed for developers from Facebook. You can choose to subscribe to this news feed or share it.

■ **My Applications**   At the top of the right-hand column is a list of your applications. It starts out empty, of course, and then grows as you add applications. In Figure 12-3, one application has been created.

■ **Platform Status**   You will find Platform Status to be an essential tool in tracking down issues that your users may raise and in following the development of Facebook.

■ **Members**   At the bottom of the right-hand column (just scroll down the window shown in Figure 12-3) is a sample of the members of the Facebook Developers group. If you click See All, you can browse through the members, if you have enough time.

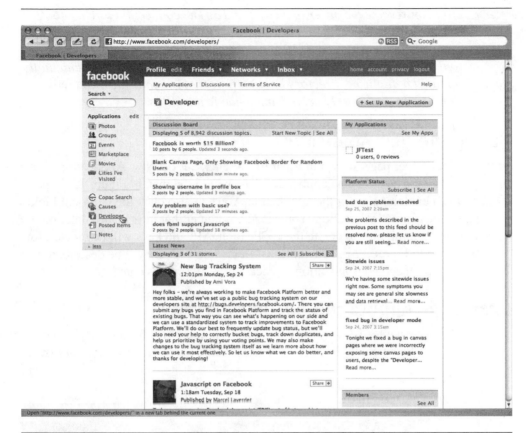

FIGURE 12-3   Developer is now one of your applications.

Create a New Application

The process of creating a new application has five initial steps:

1. Set up the new application and get your API keys.

2. Create the application on the server that you will be using.

3. Connect the application to Facebook.

4. Test.

5. Update the About page.

NOTE *You can reverse the order of steps 2 and 3. The connection to Facebook requires the URLs of the directories you create in step 2, but you can enter the information into Facebook before you have created them. The only reason for proceeding in this order is so that if you have accidentally created a duplicate directory or need to rearrange your files, you will not have to go back into Facebook and change the URLs.*

Set Up the New Application

From the Developer page, shown in Figure 12-3, click Set Up New Application in the upper-right area to create a new application. The window shown in Figure 12-4 opens.

You must enter a name for the application. You can also click the Optional Fields triangle to enter other information. You can always enter that information later on, so you can click Submit now to create the application. API and keys will be created for you, as shown in Figure 12-5. (The optional fields information will be described in the section, "Connect the Application to Facebook" later in this chapter.)

Create the Application on Your Server

As described in Chapter 10, your Facebook application runs on your own server with links from Facebook to it. So you need to create the application on your own server next.

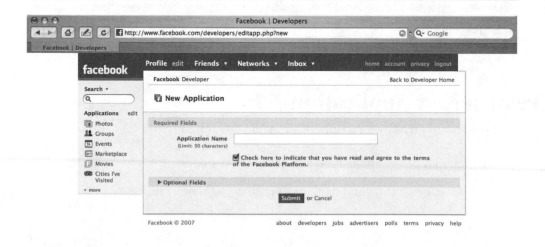

FIGURE 12-4   Create a new application.

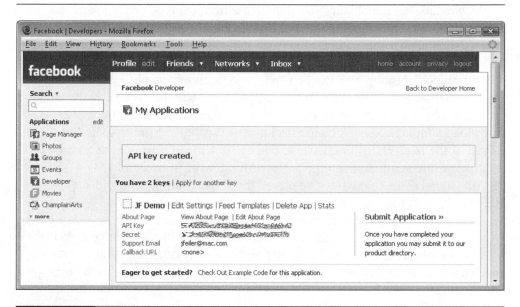

FIGURE 12-5   Create the API keys.

TIP   *When you create your application, as shown in Figure 12-5, you can download example code by clicking the link towards the bottom of the box. This example code will include your keys; there also are instructions for downloading and installing the client libraries. The process is the same as that described in this section.*

Download and Install the Client Libraries

The most common programming language for Facebook applications is PHP. You can use other programming languages, because all that matters is that you return the appropriate Facebook Markup Language (FBML) code to Facebook so that it can show it to the user. You will also need to make calls to the Facebook API routines, but you can accomplish this from a variety of languages. Facebook provides client libraries for PHP 5, PHP 4, and Java. On the Resources page at http://developers.facebook.com/resources.php, you will find download links to client libraries in ActionScript, Cocoa, ColdFusion, .NET, Perl, PHP4, Python, Ruby, and VB.NET. Whatever language you choose, make certain that it runs on your server.

NOTE   *The code in this chapter has been tested with both PHP 4 and PHP 5. No differences have been encountered when the libraries are installed as directed.*

Download the client library you want to use from the Resources link on the Developers page shown in Figure 12-1. The PHP client libraries will be in an archive that will contain a sample application, such as Footprints, a READ ME document, and possibly other files. For PHP 5, look for the client folder; it will contain three files: facebook_desktop.php, facebook.php, and facebookapi_php5_restlib.php.

For PHP 4, a separate php4client folder in the download archive will contain facebook.php and facebookapi_php4_restlip.php. For PHP 4, you must also download simplexml44, which is a backport of the PHP 5 SimpleXML API; it is part of the Ister PHP 4 Framework. You can download it from SourceForge at http://prdownloads.sourceforge.net/ister4framework/simplexml44-0_4_4.tar .gz?download. This folder must be placed inside your php4client folder. (The READ ME document describes the installation process.)

In order to keep your Facebook code organized on your server, you may want to create a high-level folder called FB into which you will place all your code for all your Facebook applications. Into that folder (or any other that you want to use), place the appropriate client folder. You do not have to do anything to the files; just use them as is.

Build Your Client Application

The next step is to build your client application. Next to the client folder and within the FB folder, create a new folder for your application. In the case of the application used in this chapter, that folder is called Chapter12. (The folder and the application files are available for download, as described in the Introduction.)

There are some common files and naming conventions that many Facebook applications written in PHP use. The main application file is index.php; a separate file containing API keys and other information is config.php. Although there is a minimal amount of code in this bare-bones application, it still makes sense to use separate files. They will grow as your application grows.

The first file, config.php, contains environmental information. It will be loaded once for each page; its information is available to that page and, as globals, to any files that are included in that page. For now, it contains only the keys that you received when you set up your application, as shown previously in Figure 12-5. There are two of them. One of them is the API key; it is shown in URLs as Facebook navigates to your application. The second one is a secret key. You hard-code it in your application (in the config.php file), and it is passed back to Facebook as validation.

Here is the entire config.php file needed for this basic application. It contains defines for each of the keys; you should replace them with the ones you received:

```php
<?php
  $api_key = 'yourAPIKeyHere';
  $secret = 'yourSecretKeyHere';
?>
```

The index.php file is the file that will be called by Facebook. It consists of three sections: includes of config.php and facebook.php from the client folder, standard initialization code that calls some routines in facebook.php, and code that actually draws on the Canvas.

The includes and standard initialization code are PHP code; here is the beginning of index.php:

Listing 12-1

```
<?php
  // the facebook client library
  include_once '../client/facebook.php';
  // for PHP 4 use include_once '../client/facebook.php';

  // keys and other setup
  include_once 'config.php';

  $facebook = new Facebook($api_key, $secret);
  $facebook->require_frame();
  // $user = $facebook->require_login();
  // $user = $facebook->require_add();
?>
```

Following this is some ordinary HTML:

```
<div style="padding: 10px;">
  <p>Hello.</p>
</div>
```

And that is all that you need for a very basic application.

NOTE
This is a public Canvas page. The two commented-out lines let you require a login to the application (and Facebook) or to require that the application be added. In general, public is best, requiring a login is next-best, and requiring an add is the most restrictive (and least inviting to new users). There is more on this in Chapter 15.

Connect the Application to Facebook

From the Developer application page, shown previously in Figure 12-3, you can click My Applications in the upper-right area to open My Applications page, shown previously in Figure 12-5. From there, click Edit Settings for the application you are setting up to open the page shown in Figure 12-6.

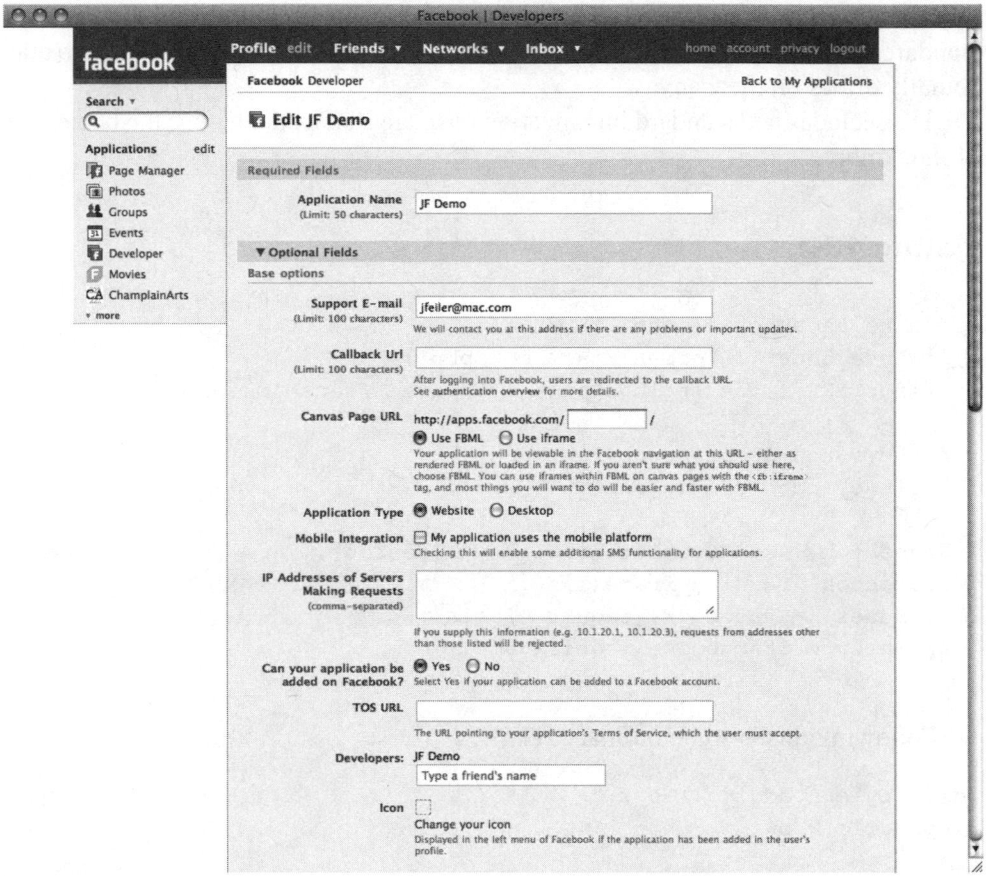

FIGURE 12-6   Set the optional fields for the application.

Default settings should be already set; if not, set these as follows:

- **Support Email:** The support email address is taken from your profile.
- **Canvas Page:** Use FBML rather than iFrame
- **Application Type:** Website rather than Desktop
- **Can Application Be Added:** Yes

Now forge the connections to Facebook.

Callback URL: This is the URL of the directory into which you placed the files in the previous step. If you put everything in an FB folder, this address might be http://www.yoursite.com/FB/ see Chapter 12.

Canvas Page URL: This is a URL through Facebook that will point to your callback URL. You can only enter the last part of the URL (the beginning is always http://apps.facebook.com/. Your name is limited to letters and underscores—numbers are not allowed. It also must be at least seven characters long. This is used internally, but it is a URL that you can use to link to your application through Facebook from the outside world. If you enter a name that has already been used, Facebook will let you know. This name is visible to users in links to your application from outside Facebook.

Once you have answered Yes to "Can your applications be added?," additional fields are available to you. The Installation Options page is shown in Figure 12-7.

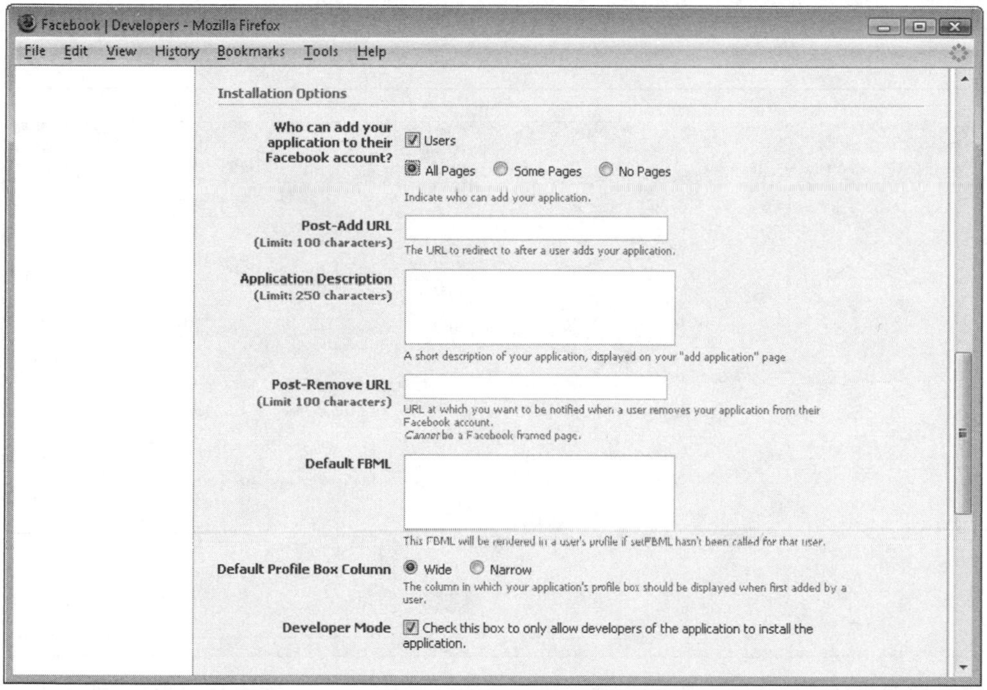

FIGURE 12-7   Sct installation options.

The most important one to set here at this time is Developer Mode. By choosing this option, only you and any other developers you have specified on the first page shown in Figure 12-6 can install the application. This means that your testing can be done in private. You also need to indicate that users can add the application.

Integration points, shown in Figure 12-8, are further down the page. Here you should select Private Installation for now. This will disable the News Feed and Mini-Feed so that other people will not see what is happening.

Test

If everything is configured properly, you should be able to open the page shown in Figure 12-9 by typing either of the URLs you set in Figure 12-6.

You can type your callback URL, such as:

```
http://www.yourserver.com/FB/Chapter12/
```

You also could type your Canvas page URL, such as:

```
http://apps.facebook.com/jfdemo
```

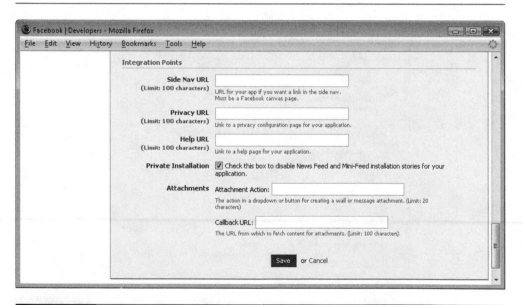

FIGURE 12-8   Set integration points.

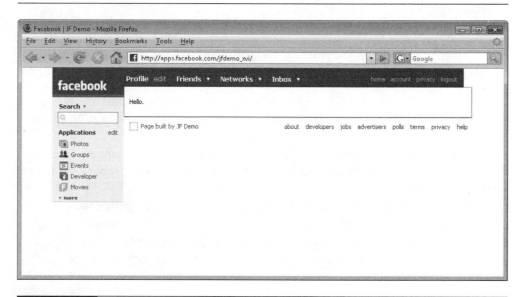

Your application page

Both should work. If they don't, retrace your steps. If nothing is immediately clear, check your PHP installation. Begin by placing an ordinary HTML page in your directory, and attempt to open your equivalent of the first URL. Here is what you might be trying to open:

```
http://www.yourserver.com/FB/Chapter12/index.html
```

This will verify if your directory is okay. If it is, replace index.html with a PHP script that does very little—perhaps this standard testing script. You might call it phpinfo.php.

```
<!DOCTYPE html PUBLIC "-//W3C//DTD XHTML 1.0 Transitional//EN"
  "http://www.w3.org/TR/xhtml1/DTD/xhtml1-transitional.dtd">.
<html xmlns="http://www.w3.org/1999/xhtml">
  <head>
    <title>Untitled Document</title>
    <meta http-equiv="Content-Type" content="text/html;
      charset=iso-8859-1" />
  </head>
```

```
  <body>
<?php
  phpinfo();
?>
  </body>
</html>
```

This will display a page with information about the PHP configuration file on your server. This will confirm that PHP is working properly.

If this does not work, then check and recheck the URLs. Remember—they are directories, not files. And if that does not work, recheck that the proper keys are set in the config.php file.

When it all works, you will see that Facebook has built the frame, the application list, and put your application name at the bottom. The small rectangle to the left of your application name will eventually be your application's icon. Experiment by requiring a login: You should see the login page shown in Figure 12-10.

FIGURE 12-10   Your login page

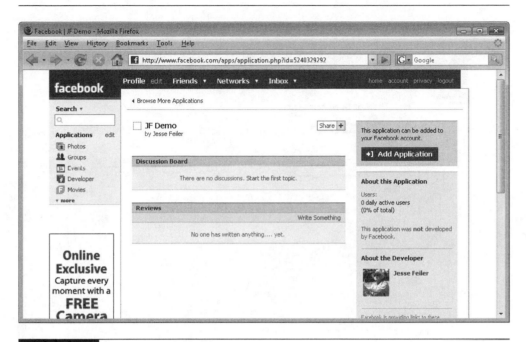

FIGURE 12-11   View the About page.

Update the About Page

From your My Applications page (see Figure 12-5), you can view your new application's About page, as shown in Figure 12-11.

If you choose the Edit the About page link on the My Application page, you will see the page shown in Figure 12-12. From here, you can also add an icon to the application (4 megabytes, or MB, or smaller).

Add the Application

So far, you have only run the application by typing one of the two URLs. You can now try to add the application. To do so, you need to update your settings. For now, set both the Post-Add URL (see Figure 12-7) and the Side Nav URL (see Figure 12-8) to the Canvas page URL (the one that begins with http://apps.facebook.com/).

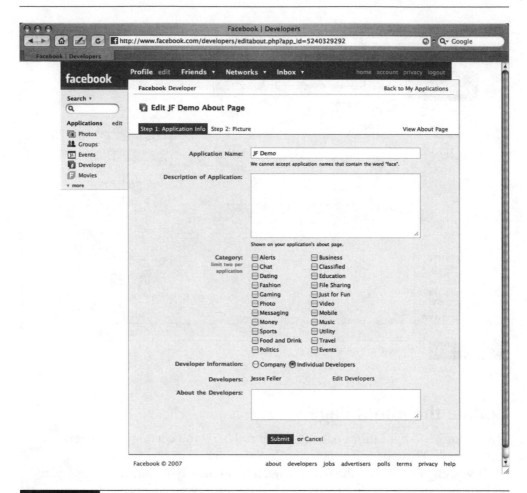

FIGURE 12-12   Edit the settings.

NOTE

This is only for testing. Each of these URLs can be a different one and usually is in a Facebook application.

The easiest way to add the application is from the About page. You can click View About Page from the application list shown previously in Figure 12-5. When you click Add This Application on the About page, you open the confirmation page shown in Figure 12-13.

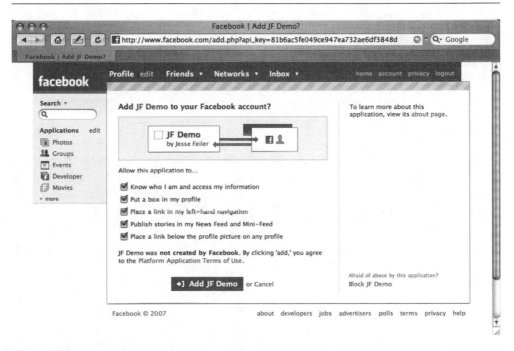

Confirm the addition of the application and its privileges.

TIP   *If the About page does not let you add the application, go back to the settings and recheck. If you have checked that people should be able to add the application but the option reverts to their not being able to add it, check all of the file names and then check all of the other options.*

The application should be added. You will go to the Post-Add URL (the basic Canvas page), and the application will be added in the Applications list, as shown in Figure 12-14.

Congratulations! You have created your first basic Facebook application. It is as basic as possible, but you have navigated the various settings and gotten your server talking to Facebook and vice versa. This is not to be sneezed at. From now on, you can create other applications in the same way. You also can build on this sample application.

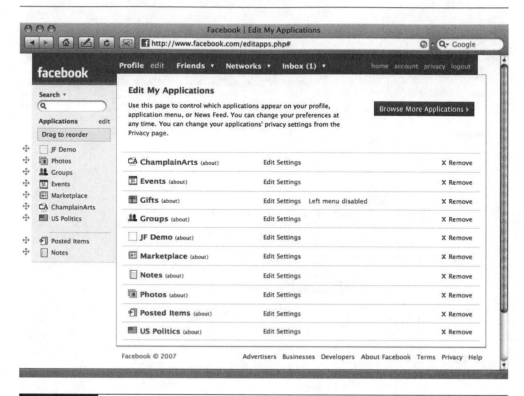

FIGURE 12-14   The application is added.

Create a Test Account

There is one other step to take to get started as a Facebook developer. As you
have read, it is a violation of the Terms of Service to open more than one account.
That has made it difficult to test certain conditions. You should create an alter ego
with another account that does not violate the Terms of Service. Do so by creating
another account, as shown in Figure 12-15.

Log in as this new user, and convert it to a test account. Click on this URL
to open the page shown in Figure 12-16: http://www.facebook.com/developers/
become_test_account.php.

FIGURE 12-15   Create a new account.

Test accounts can only see one another, and real accounts cannot see test accounts. Also, test accounts cannot be application owners or developers. You develop under your own account (although, as you have seen, you can do so privately), but you can create additional test accounts that can add your account for testing.

Note that although test accounts let you have multiple accounts without them being disabled, test accounts can be disabled for any other reason that a real account could be disabled for.

FIGURE 12-16   Make the new account a test account.

Chapter 13

Build a Basic Interface

How to...

- Decide what you want to do
- Design the application
- Set up the application parameters
- Implement the basic page and navigation
- Implement utilities
- Implement the pages
- Begin to test

In the previous chapter, you saw how to create a bare-bones Facebook application and set up the parameters so that you can access it. In this chapter, you will start to develop a more usable Facebook application that will be added to in the following chapters. You can download the code as described in the Introduction. Make certain that you download the Chapter 13 version.

> **TIP**
> *Before beginning to build your own application, make certain that you really understand what it means to use Facebook and Facebook applications. If you do not have an account, sign up. The Facebook experience is heavily dependent on your friends—without friends, your News Feed is much less interesting. Reach out to people who use Facebook in different ways from you, and observe how you act and react with Facebook. Become sensitive to the applications that you are using: Watch yourself as you do something that satisfies you or frustrates you. The easiest way to set up a user interface research lab is to learn how to watch yourself. And be sure to watch for errors and mistakes—these point up tricky aspects of user interfaces.*

Decide What You Want to Do

Facebook has an enormous user base. It is distributed around the world, and it represents all ages. (In the United States, where Facebook started in universities, the user base skews younger; this is not true in other areas.) More than half the users visit at least once each day. With that in mind, here are some of the things you could do with your application.

■ Do you want to build an application to market to these people? If so what are you marketing? Your Web site? A service you provide? Products for sale?

■ Perhaps you want to provide an application for people to use for fun or other purposes. That application can include advertising, either for your own products or for other peoples'. In this way, your application is much like a magazine or newspaper; it is in many ways a vehicle for the advertisements.

■ The massive numbers of Facebook users represent marketing and advertising opportunities for many people. But looked at another way, they may be a way for you to reach a subgroup of a subgroup of a subgroup that, because of Facebook's large size, is a significant number of people.

■ Another possibility is to write an application that ignores the large numbers of Facebook users. It might be just for your friends to use, and it might be full of in-jokes or jargon. If it winds up with half a dozen users and provides entertainment to half of them for a month, it may have achieved its purpose.

■ Private applications like this can be developed for an organization, not just for a group of friends. The social graph (the structure of friends and the News Feed) provides a simple yet sophisticated way for people to keep in touch with one another and share information. Organizations large and small can profit from this functionality, which comes for free in Facebook (indeed, it is the heart and soul of Facebook).

■ Finally, you may be building an application primarily for yourself. You may want to learn how to build Facebook applications so that you can go out and build them for others, whether as part of your job or volunteer work or on a freelance basis. Or you may want to learn the technologies and design principles simply to learn them.

Any and all of these are valid reasons for building Facebook applications. Make certain you know what you are trying to do before you start. (And if you decide to change course in the middle, make it a conscious decision.)

TIP   *What you want to do should be able to be expressed in a single declarative sentence. If you can't do so, your objective is not yet clear enough in your own mind. The details will come in the next step, designing the application.*

Design the Application

Designing a Facebook application is often more interesting and challenging than building a stand-alone application or Web site. The reason is that a Facebook application lives within the Facebook frame and becomes part of the pages people receive from Facebook. From a technical point of view, designing a Facebook application is like designing a single piece of a jigsaw puzzle: It must be part of the finished picture, but in the best jigsaw puzzles, each piece is interesting and different.

When you start to think about a Facebook application, you generally have some kind of idea in mind. Before going much further, think about the design considerations described in this section. (If you do not have a basic idea for an application, the design considerations in this section may start you thinking of one.)

| TIP | *Facebook applications are still relatively new—as is Facebook. Design criteria are still emerging. However, these basic principles seem to be used by many successful Facebook applications. They have their roots in the design principles of many other applications.* |

Add Value to Facebook

Facebook is a wonderful tool; the built-in applications, such as Events, Photos, and Groups, are extraordinarily powerful. If you are going to build a Facebook application, make certain that you add value—do not reinvent a Facebook wheel.

The most obvious value to add to Facebook is information that you have. External databases and Web sites that are integrated with Facebook provide information and content in the worlds of music, news, entertainment, books, and more. If you are adding value with information, consider how that information is relevant to Facebook users. It is perfectly simple to build an application that is nothing but a front end to a public search engine, but is that really what people are looking for in Facebook?

Another value to add to Facebook is your imagination, your take on a different way to do something that Facebook users want to do. A number of applications expand on Facebook pokes to let people have a variety of poke-like actions. Other applications replace the Wall with a new object that can receive more types of media than the Facebook Wall.

When you extend Facebook applications and metaphors, make certain that you truly are adding value to them, not complicating them. The simplicity of Facebook applications (both applications from Facebook and from third-party developers) is a major part of what attracts people to them.

NOTE *Because Facebook has so many members, and because groups of friends can find one another so easily on Facebook, an application that appeals only to a minuscule percent of Facebook users can still have substantial numbers of users. If the purpose of your application is to make money in a mass-marketing environment, that is not a good choice. However, if your objective is to work with a selective audience (either to accomplish some objective other than earning money or to be able to sell advertising at a premium rate to your highly selected users), such a minuscule user base can be to your advantage.*

Become Facebook-ish

Why are you in the Facebook world—just because of the numbers? Barging into Facebook with your own interface and ideas is not a good idea. People use Facebook—often more than once a day—and they know what to expect from it. They know what it looks like, and they know what interface elements do what.

Although this is news to some developers, almost all people (except close relatives of developers) are not interested in applications. What they are interested in is what the applications *do*. If you want to redesign the Facebook interface, the best way to do it is to work for them (www.facebook.com/jobs).

Use the Social Graph, News Feed, and Mini-Feed

For most people, the key to Facebook is the social graph (friends, in other words). People generally start by bringing their real-world friends and social network to Facebook; from there, they frequently expand it to friends of friends and new friends.

You use the social graph in a variety of ways. Here are four of the most powerful:

- If you store a list of items as favorites for a user (photos, music, events, etc.), you can get the user's friends and see what their favorites are. This is how many applications create tabs for My Things and My Friends' Things. You will need to use a join table in your database (as described in Chapter 14), as well as the list of friends which you can get with the Facebook object's `$facebook->api_client->friends_get()` method.

- When a user performs an action, such as adding an item to favorites, selecting something, or otherwise doing something with your application, post it to the News Feed so that friends will see it. As you build your application, look for actions that will generate succinct News Feed items. (Use `feed.publishTemplatizedAction` to allow these stories to be aggregated rather than just becoming a drip-drip-drip of unrelated events.) Your users will not need to do anything special for this to happen.

- Let users tell their friends about things they do in your application or information they find. Implement a Let My Friends Know link with an `fb:request-form` and a `fb:multi-friend-selector`. After you write the code, users will need only two mouse clicks to spread the news.

- Add a Share button with an `fb:share-button` so that users can post information about what they have seen to their profile or share it with friends on or off Facebook.

All of these will be implemented in the sample application and described in this book.

Use the Profile Box Properly

The Profile page is primarily for information about a user. When you create a Profile box, it is best to use it for information about the user and your application. It is not the best place (nor even a good place) to present content. The News Feed on the Home page and the Mini-Feed on the Profile page summarize recent interactions with your application and should provide links back to the application for deeper interaction.

> **TIP**   *You may want to use the Profile box to post reminders of actions taken in your application. You could certainly do that, but you would be reinventing the Facebook wheel. The Share button lets you post items of any sort to your profile, and that's how this type of profile update should take place.*

Use FBML

Facebook Markup Language (FBML) provides the look and feel of Facebook. You can often produce the same functionality with handwritten HTML, but in almost all cases, you should avoid that. If you are doing something that can be done with FBML and the Facebook look and feel, do so. Even if you can exactly duplicate the Facebook look and feel, use FBML, because if there are changes to the Facebook interface, the FBML tags will incorporate those changes, while your HTML code will not.

Whatever you do, do not redefine the Facebook interface. While you can place the Share button on your page as an image and attach a different type of action to it, this is just out-and-out wrong.

Draw the Facebook Line

When you create pages for your Facebook application, you live within the Facebook frame. If you are integrating external data or functionality, you frequently will provide links from your Facebook pages to your own Web site. Draw the line very distinctly so that you and your users know what is where.

Make certain that there is a logic to what is on which side of the line. (You will see in the next section how this line is drawn and justified for the sample application.) Once you have drawn this line, many interface questions will be resolved. On the Facebook side of the line, everything should be Facebook-ish. On your side of the line, you may well be fitting into an existing Web site with different colors and graphics, and you can construct an environment that is distinct from Facebook, perhaps by picking up graphical elements (and colors—other than blue) from your own Web site).

NOTE   *On Help pages, you may need to show parts of both the Facebook interface to your application and your native interface. When providing help of this kind, make certain that images of the interfaces are framed with a distinctive border or otherwise distinguished from a live interface. One of the most common problems people have with Help pages is that they click on the illustrations thinking that they are, in fact, the live interface.*

Obey the Rules

When you are on the Facebook side of the line, you must play by the Facebook rules. These are available from the Developer application pages, and are technically advanced in the developer documentation. Perhaps the most important rule has to do with the storability of Facebook information. You must use the API or other tools to request Facebook data when you need it. You may cache it for no more than 24 hours, but in practice, it is generally easiest to request it on an as-needed basis rather than figure out how long you have had it. (One critical argument for getting data as you need it is that if it has changed on Facebook, you want the changed data. This argument applies not just to Facebook, but to any system with which you interact.) The exceptions to this are the items shown in Table 13-1 that you can store indefinitely.

You can store only the basic user information: Nothing about the social graph is storable. If you are integrating Facebook with another Web site or database, this means that the only thing that you can store is the information shown in Table 13-1.

CAUTION   *The last two items in the table, notes_count and profile_update_time, are storable, but in general, if you want this information, you need to retrieve it when you want it to get the latest data. The main reason for storing these items is so that you can check if they have changed since the last time you checked; you do so by retrieving the current values and comparing them to the stored values.*

Identifier	Meaning
uid	User ID
nid	Primary network ID
eid	Event ID
gid	Group ID
pid	Photo ID
aid	Photo album ID
notes_count	Total number of notes written by the user
profile_update_time	Time that the user's profile was last updated

TABLE 13-1 Storable Facebook Data

Iterate

Building Facebook applications is a fascinating process, and it is one that often has a number of iterations. At this time, Facebook itself is still growing and Facebook Platform is evolving. If only for that reason, you will probably find that your application changes as new features are implemented and new ways of implementing old features are developed.

Also, your Facebook application is living in a complex world. It lives within the Facebook environment of frame, Left Nav, and the footer links; it may also integrate with other Web pages. Any change to any element that the Facebook application touches may require the Facebook application to change. And, most exciting of all, this is such a new area of development that people are still exploring how to use Facebook and the social graph; those adventures and explorations also can inspire you to go back and rethink parts of your application. But at each step, remember the basics. Know when to stop adding complexity; keep focused on your basic objective.

Start to Build the Sample Application

Now that you have seen the basics of application design, you can go to work designing your own application. In this and the chapters that follow, you will see the step-by-step process of implementing an application. Here is a summary of the steps involved in the design process. You may be chafing at the bit to start coding, but omitting the details of the design process will save you no time in the long run.

Decide What You Want to Do

The sample application is a real-world example. As such, it is very specific; however, it stands as a prototype for an unlimited number of other, equally specific applications.

ChamplainArts is a small Web site that lists arts and entertainment events in the area around the north of Lake Champlain (which is sometimes referred to as the "sixth Great Lake"). A beautiful area nestled between the Adirondack Mountains of New York on the west, the Green Mountains of Vermont on the east, and the Saint Lawrence River on the north, it has three major cities: Burlington, Vermont; Plattsburgh, New York; and Montreal, Quebec. Unlike major metropolitan areas, such as London, Rome, New York, and even Montreal itself, the region has no single media market and no single reliable resource of information about events. The problem is confounded by the issue expressed in the ChamplainArts slogan: "2 states and 2 countries and 2 languages."

Because there are no artificial boundaries on the Internet, it is an obvious tool for helping groups to publicize their events in a region such as this. Facebook is an ideal partner in this endeavor because of its social graph. There are numerous Facebook applications in which people share and recommend things to their friends (Goodreads Books, Causes, and Flixster Movies, among others). These applications all integrate Facebook and its social graph with an external database—exactly the goal here.

The decision of what you want to do here is simple: Integrate the ChamplainArts Web site with Facebook using a Facebook application.

NOTE *This example is an obvious prototype for any collection of items stored in an external database. Pieces of it are useful on their own, even without an external database and the use of another Web site. Some of these are pointed out in the course of developing the application.*

Decide How You Want to Do It

In Chapter 15, you will see how to create an application with public Canvas pages that can be reached from external Web sites without logging in to Facebook. Applications such as those are easier for users to use, but they are slightly more complicated for developers to create because you need to handle the case where you do know who the user is (logged in) and where you do not.

The example built in this chapter requires a login.

Design the Application

Now it is time to flesh out the application design. The four points described in the last section are a good place to start:

- Add value to Facebook
- Become Facebook-ish

■ Draw the Facebook line

■ Obey the rules

Add Value to Facebook

The immediate value that is added, of course, is the data in the external database. Beyond the data, the functionality it adds to Facebook is to provide another topic of conversation and another way in which friends can communicate, share, and observe what they are doing.

Part of adding value to Facebook is not complicating or reinventing existing Facebook features, and that point is relevant to this application. Facebook already has events built into it: Why would anyone add a new type of event?

TIP   *This is a common question at this stage of development. Argue with yourself and your friends about whether or not you really are adding value and not reinventing the wheel. Many Facebook applications successfully extend existing Facebook features without complicating them or duplicating them, but the line between the successful and unsuccessful extension of Facebook features can be remarkably hazy. Clarify exactly what you will and will not do, and your application will turn out to be clear in your mind and the minds of your users.*

In this case, the arguments for inventing a new type of event are compelling. They are centered around the difference between existing Facebook events and the cultural events in the database:

■ Facebook events arose out of parties and extend easily to meetings. They are often associated with a network.

■ A user creates a Facebook event and invites people to it. They respond.

■ In the case of cultural events, the event is scheduled and announced (in a variety of media); people who will attend make the first move. (They may receive invitations or notifications from the sponsoring organization, but in general, the attendee makes the first move rather than responding to a personal invitation.)

■ For cultural events, people can almost always bring friends. These events may require a reservation or paid admission.

■ The list of Facebook event attendees can be seen under some circumstances. The list of attendees at a cultural event is generally not public knowledge until it occurs.

■ Cultural events can be categorized (theater, dance, art show, and so forth). In fact, they must be, because the audiences often do not overlap.

■ And, perhaps most important of all: Facebook events live within Facebook. Large though the Facebook community may be, cultural events can appeal beyond its borders.

Having thought through these points, it seems to make sense not to build on the Facebook event structure, but to create a new one to handle the specific and different needs of cultural events.

NOTE *One of the ongoing challenges in this project has been the naming of cultural events. It is important to distinguish them from Facebook events. As you will see in the figures documenting the project's development, they have variously been named Performances, Shows, CAEvents, and others.*

Because of the integration with the external database, and because Facebook events are intrinsically different from the cultural events in this application, it seems that this application will add value to Facebook.

Become Facebook-ish

Perhaps the simplest way to adopt the Facebook look and feel is to look at Facebook applications that have some similarities to your application and analyze their interface. The first cut of this analysis is best done with applications developed by Facebook, because they are a bit stricter in using the interface than third-party applications are in some cases.

The social graph is one of the most important features of Facebook to most users. That is a good place to start. With an application such as this one, the ability to add events to a user's own list, to let friends know, to share them with people on and off Facebook, to update the News Feed, and to browse friends' events are all ways of using the social graph.

Now that you have some basic ideas for hooking into Facebook's functionality, it is a good opportunity to do what many people consider "real" design: consider the graphical user interface.

Many Facebook applications have a single page, but many others have multiple pages. At this stage, it seems that at least three pages will be needed. One will allow people to browse the database for events in which they are interested. For each event, users should be able to share it or to add it to their own list of events. That list is obviously a second type of page. A third page, similar to the second, will contain a list of friends' events.

In addition, many applications have a Home page and a variety of supporting pages, such as an About page. For now, the sample will focus on the four basic pages: Home, My Events, Friends' Events, and Browse Events.

Draw the Facebook Line

Drawing the Facebook line helps you make clear to yourself and your users what functionality belongs where. In practice, it is often easiest to create a table of data and functionality. In two columns, indicate which are part of the external database or Web site and which are part of Facebook. For example, Table 13-2 is the table used in the sample application to draw the Facebook line.

In this case, some of the choices are easy to make. Because you cannot save any part of the social graph, you only have access to friends' events through Facebook. Likewise, the ability to add and delete events easily is chosen as a Web-site-only feature. It must be implemented there, because not all users of the system are Facebook members. It could be implemented as well on the Facebook side, but because of the security mechanism that is used to protect the database, it is easier to limit updates simply to the Web site.

Despite the fact that drawing the line clearly helps you develop the application, sometimes there will be questions, as is the case with See My Events and the Web site. During the iterations of the application's development and subsequent life, any of these decisions may be revisited; this one, in particular, is open for further discussion.

Obey the Rules

The last step in starting to build the sample application is to remember to obey the rules. If you have made the decisions in the previous steps, you are far along the path.

Functionality	Facebook	Web Site
Browse events	X	X
Add/delete events		X
Add to My Events	X	
See My Events	X	?
See my friends' events	X	
Share events	X	
Receive weekly list of events via email		X

TABLE 13-2   Draw the Facebook Line

Set Up the Application Parameters

At last you are ready to begin building your application. The first step is to create the application or reuse another application, such as the one from the previous chapter. (You can always change an application's name.)

Using the Developer application in Facebook, create or edit an application, as described in the previous chapter. You can always come back to it, so you may want to enter only the minimal information. The first settings are on the Optional Fields page:

- Application name (required; maximum of 50 characters)

- Callback URL and Canvas Page URL. The callback URL is in the form http://www.<yourServerName>.<com or org or whatever>/<yourDirectoryOnYourServer>/. The Canvas Page URL is in the form http://apps.facebook.com/<yourInternalAppName>/, where yourInternalAppName is the name you have created for your application in the Developer application (not the application name that is shown to users). Each URL is limited to 100 characters, and each ends with a slash.

- Set the application type to Website.

- Make certain that the application can be added on Facebook and that the checkbox for users to add it is checked. If you do not do this, the Installation Options and Integration Points areas will not be visible.

- You do not have to create an icon, but if you do, it should be 16 × 16. It can be useful to create at least a dummy icon so that as you lay out your pages you are reminded of where it will be.

- For now, select the Developer Mode check box in the Installation Options section. This means that only you and developers you specify can install the application.

- At this point, you should probably select Private Installation in the Integration Points area. This means that the News Feed and Mini-Feed are disabled for application adds.

TIP *The application settings fit neatly on two pages of paper (or on both sides of a single page). Print them out as you begin, and refer to them during development as you add new settings or change old ones.*

Implement the Basic Page and Navigation

At last: It is time to begin laying out pages and writing some code. Step one is to decide what your pages should look like. In a multipage Facebook application, consistency and predictability are essential. Begin by looking at existing Facebook applications to get an idea of what you might want to do.

Choose the Basic Design

The US Politics application, shown in Figure 13-1, has a good, basic, bare-bones interface. (It has evolved over time and is a little more complex today.)

There is not much to the interface, but when you start to browse or add your choices, the interface recedes and the content takes center stage, which should be what you want. Figure 13-2 shows a page of politicians you can browse.

If you compare Figures 13-1 and 13-2, you will immediately see a choice that you have to make: How should navigation be accomplished in your application? The general answer is as simply as possible. If a user has to stop and think about it, there is something wrong.

In Figure 13-1, you see an action in the dashboard at the top of the Canvas (Browse Politicians); the Help action at the right should be an almost-always present action. Beneath the dashboard, there are two tabs for two similar lists: Politicians You Support and Politicians Your Friends Support. This is as simple as it gets, and it will serve as the basis for navigation in the sample application.

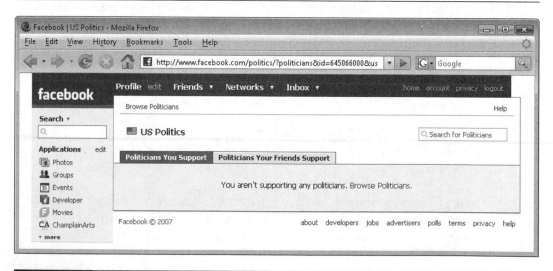

FIGURE 13-1   US Politics application

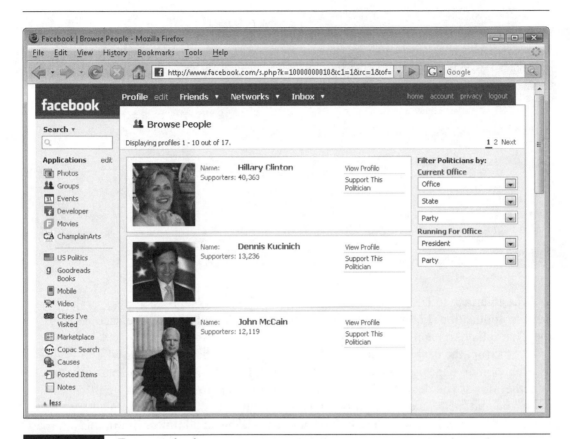

FIGURE 13-2   Focus on the data.

NOTE *This is the same basic paradigm as the example application and many, many other applications: a list of your items and a list of your friends' items—politicians, events, music, books, philosophies, and so forth.*

Figure 13-2, the browseable list of politicians, does not provide a way to get back to the first page (other than through your browser's back button). If you choose to view a politician's profile or to support the politician, you move on to the profile and whatever you want to do. (If you support the politician, the profile will now indicate your support and allow you to remove the support if you want by changing Support This Politician to Remove Support. And, of course, your Mini-Feed and News Feed properly reflect these events.)

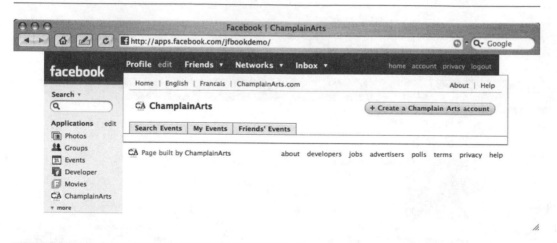

FIGURE 13-3   Basic page layout

The interface to US Politics shown in Figure 13-1 is a good basis to use for the sample application. Figure 13-3 shows the basic page layout that will be used for the ChamplainArts application.

At the top, the dashboard provides basic navigation and controls that will be available on all pages. About and Help, located at the right, are self-explanatory. Whether or not you decide to have a Home page or a link to it on each page is up to you and the type of application you are building. If you are linking to an external Web site, it makes sense to have a link available at all times. But in this case, the choice has been made to move the link to ChamplainArts.com away from the Home link; if you accidentally click ChamplainArts.com, you will be out of Facebook and on another site, so keeping the physical separation makes an accidental click less likely.

Between these two actions are the choices to flip the interface between French and English, a feature that eventually will be added to the application.

NOTE   *You may think that the choice of language should be a preference—and it is. But it is also a command. The logic is two-fold. First, many people never bother to set preferences, and in this case, many users are bilingual, so the language choice is a true preference, not a barrier to understanding or using the application. Second, preferences need to be stored, and part of drawing the Facebook line is deciding that preferences are stored for people who create an account explicitly; they are not stored for casual users, such as people who do not have an account or do not add the application.*

A Create button is often present on Home pages and other Facebook application pages. It is essential if you need to create something (such as a photo album) before you can get to work (uploading photos). It also is a good location to implement a link to an external site.

Finally, three tabs let you browse events, view your own events, and view your friends' events.

The design of event displays will be one of the next steps in the design process; at this point, it is a good idea simply to think about what navigation will be presented as part of the data interface. Two choices are made now:

■ All events that are displayed will have a Share button and a Let My Friends Know link

■ Events displayed in the browse list or the friends' list will have an Add to My Events action; events displayed in your own list will have a Remove from My Events action.

TIP   *Spelling out the actions as you go helps you develop a better interface. For example, you may have started out thinking that it would be unnecessary to have an Add to My Events action on an event that is already in your events list. As you think about making certain that action is* not *there, you may realize that you need to implement the Remove from My Events action in that place. The earlier you think about features and interface items, the easier it is to implement them.*

Implement the Basic Design

This application will start out with the same two files that many applications use: config.php and index.php. Soon, another file, lib.php (sometimes named util.php), will be added. The names are up to you, of course.

config.php

For now, this file contains two PHP variables $api_key and $secret. It is also useful to assign your Canvas page URL to a variable so that if you move it, you need only change it in this file; this also means that when you download the

sample code, this is the only file you will need to customize. Later on, this file will
contain the MySQL login information.

```php
<?php
  $api_key = 'yourAPIKey';
  $secret = 'yourSecretKey';

  $canvas_page = 'apps.facebook.com/yourInternalAppName/';
?>
```

index.php

At this point, this file will contain the basic navigational features shown in Figure 13-3.
It makes sense to implement them once and then copy the file to make changes to it
(for example, to change the highlighted tab). The facebook.php client library will
be included (either PHP 4 or PHP 5, depending on your server). Listing 13-1 shows
the basic code.

NOTE   *The dashboard actions and tabs will need file names. You can use dummy
filenames (in this case, all of the actions link back to index.php), or
you can name the files. For the tabs, this example assumes that when
they are created, the files will be myCAEs.php, friendsCAEs.php, and
browseCAEs.php. They need not exist yet: If you click on a tab, you will
get an error, but as soon as you create the file, that error will go away
when you click on a tab. Also, make certain to use your own Canvas page
URL to replace the underlined application name.*

Listing 13-1

```php
<?php
  // the facebook client library
  include_once '../php4client/facebook.php';
  // OR the PHP 5 version
  // ONLY USE ONE OF THESE
  include_once '../client/facebook.php';

  // keys and other setup
  include_once 'config.php';

  $facebook = new Facebook($api_key, $secret);
  $facebook->require_frame();
  $user = $facebook->require_login();
?>
```

```
  <fb:dashboard>
    <fb:action href="index.php">Home</fb:action>
    <fb:action href="index.php">English</fb:action>
    <fb:action href="index.php">Francais</fb:action>
    <fb:action href="index.php">ChamplainArts.com</fb:action>
    <fb:help href="about.php">About</fb:help>
    <fb:help href="help.php">Help</fb:help>
    <fb:create-button href="new.php">
      Create a Champlain Arts account
    </fb:create-button>
  </fb:dashboard>

  <fb:tabs>
    <fb:tab-item href=
      "http://<?php echo $canvas_page;?>browseCAEs.php"
      title="Browse Events"/>
    <fb:tab-item href=
      "http://<?php echo $canvas_page;?>myCAEs.php"
      title="My Events" />
    <fb:tab-item href=
      "http://<?php echo $canvas_page;?>friendsCAEs.php"
      title="Friends' Events" />
  </fb:tabs>
?>
```

If you upload the files and run the application using the Canvas Page URL (http://apps.facebook.com/<yourInternalAppName>/), you should see the page shown previously in Figure 13-3. The links and actions will not work, because the other pages are not present, but you have something to look at and start to work with.

If you do not, backtrack to the bare-bones application in the previous chapter. Remove the dashboard and the tabs. See if things work for you. If so, add the dashboard element back in, then the tabs.

Once this page works, save it. You will copy it for the various other pages.

TIP   *At every step of the way, reevaluate your choices. You are certainly entitled to take pride in your achievement (and creating your first Facebook application is a major achievement—congratulations!). But then start questioning it and trying it out on friends. As you will see in the figures that accompany the text, ongoing discussions about whether events should be browseable or searcheable have occurred through the development process. This is normal and a good thing, as long as the final interface is consistent.*

Implement the Pages

You have the basic shell of your pages, but what goes into them? As you browse Facebook applications and think about your own application, it should be clear that many of your pages will be lists of events. There are several ways in which you can present lists in Facebook: The Groups application uses two of them.

In Figure 13-4, you can see the first Groups page. Two columns present two lists of groups.

Figure 13-5 shows the single-column format for a list of groups; it is what you see when you look at My Groups.

In the sample, you can use both formats for different purposes (and to get experience with various formatting techniques).

The design for this site is highly dependent on lists, and they use the Facebook styles. Because they are used on most of the pages, it makes sense to add them to the template page you have created. The easiest way is to create a separate file, such as list_styles.php, and include it at the top of the template. Here is the code for that file (it is from the Facebook Wiki Facebook Styles entry):

Listing 13-2

```
<!-- styles for lists from Facebook-->
<style>
  .lists th {
```

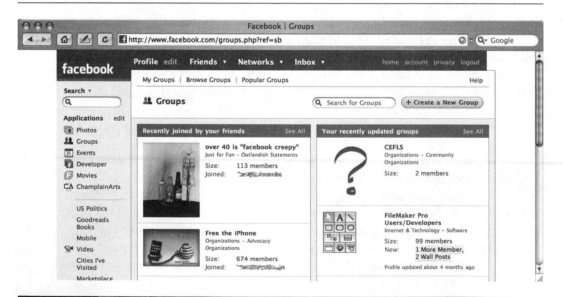

FIGURE 13-4   The two-column Groups page

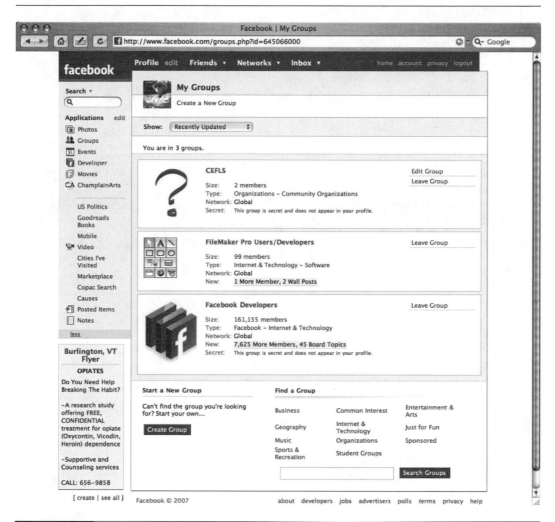

FIGURE 13-5   The one-column Groups page

```
      text-align: left;
      padding: 5px 10px;
      background: #6d84b4;
}

.lists .spacer {
   background: none;
   border: none;
```

```css
    padding: 0px;
    margin: 0px;
    width: 10px;
}

.lists th h4 {
  float: left;
  color: white;
}

.lists th a {
  float: right;
  font-weight: normal;
  color: #d9dfea;
}

.lists th a:hover {
  color: white;
}

.lists td {
  margin:0px 10px;
  padding:0px;
  vertical-align:top;
  width:306px;
}

.lists .list {
  background:white none repeat scroll 0%;
  border-color:-moz-use-text-color #BBBBBB;
  border-style:none solid;
  border-width:medium 1px;
}

.lists .list .list_item {
  border-top:1px solid #E5E5E5;
  padding: 10px;
}

.lists .list .list_item.first {
  border-top: none;
}
```

```
.lists .see_all {
  background:white none repeat scroll 0%;
  border-color:-moz-use-text-color #BBBBBB rgb(187, 187, 187);
  border-style:none solid solid;
  border-width:medium 1px 1px;
  text-align:left;
}

.lists .see_all div {
  border-top:1px solid #E5E5E5; padding:5px 10px;
}
</style>
```

If you have named the file list_styles.php, the include statement for the type of your template file is:

```
// Facebook lists styles
include_once 'list_styles.php';
```

To improve readability, all of the include statements are normally placed at the top of the PHP file.

That completes the basic template; save the file in a safe place and be careful not to accidentally update it.

Home Page

You can use the two-column format for your Home page, as shown in Figure 13-6.

This format can be a good choice for a landing page in an application that people may browse. The left-hand column can contain news or other non-specific data (or sponsored material), and the right-hand column is well suited to displaying a single highlighted event or other item. (This is because the column's narrow width means that the data takes a good deal of vertical space, and that makes it difficult to have several of them easily on a single page.)

> TIP
>
> *To you, this may be a Home page or a landing page, but that may not be the case for your users. Any of your Canvas pages may be the first page someone sees. As people share links to your application and its data, they may wind up following a link that sends them to your My Events page or another one. Avoid creating forced marches through the sequence of pages that makes sense to you. Making everything available to your users through any entry point helps your application be integrated fully into Facebook.*

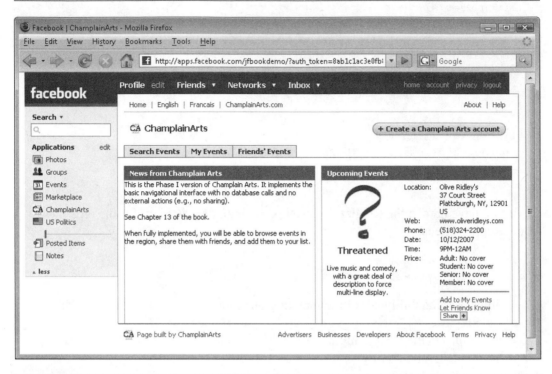

FIGURE 13-6 Two-column Home page

Copy the code shown previously in Listing 13-1 to index.php. Here is a schematic outline of what the index.php file will look like at this point:

```php
<?php
  // the facebook client library
   include_once '../php4client/facebook.php';
  // keys and other setup
  // other includes for lib.php, list_styles.php

  $facebook = new Facebook($api_key, $secret);
  $facebook->require_frame();
  $user = $facebook->require_login();
 ?>
<fb:dashboard>
  // code removed
</fb:dashboard>
```

```
<fb:tabs>
  // code removed
</fb:tabs>
?>
```

Now that you have the basic functionality implemented, all that remains is to hard-code the data to be displayed in the two columns. For initial testing, you can type in some dummy text just so that you can see the layout and make any adjustments that are necessary. (If you have used the Facebook styles and not made any typographical errors in them, there should not be any adjustments necessary.)

The code for the two lists is ordinary HTML constructing a table. Here it is. It goes right after the `fb:tabs` element. It starts with a blank line and then consists of a single `div` element containing a table that uses the Facebook list styles:

Listing 13-3

```
<br/>
<div class="two_column profile clearfix">
  <table class="lists" align="center" cellspacing="0" border="0">
    <tr>
      <th>
         <h4>News from Champlain Arts</h4>
      </th>
      <th class="spacer"></th>
      <th>
        <h4>Upcoming Events</h4>
      </th>
    </tr>

    <tr>
      <td class="list">
        <div class="list_item_first clearfix">
          This is the Phase I version of Champlain Arts.
          It implements the basic navigational interface
          with no database calls and no external actions
          (e.g., no sharing).
          <br />
          <br />
          See Chapter 13 of the book.
          <br/>
          <br />
```

```
        When fully implemented, you will be able to browse
        events in the region, share them with friends, and
        add them to your list.
      </div>
    </td>
    <td class="spacer"></td>
    <td class="list">
      <div class="list_item_first clearfix">
        Sample database text here.
      </div>
    </td>
  </tr>
</table>
</div>
```

There is one other adjustment to make; it is one that you will need to make each time you copy the template for a new page. In the tabs, make certain that the appropriate tab is selected. In this case, none of the three should be selected. If you have been testing with the template, you may have left one selected, as in this line of code. The `selected` attribute (see the underlined segment) needs to be set appropriately for each page.

```
<fb:tab-item href="http://<?php echo $canvas_page;?>myCAEs.php"
  title="My Events" selected="true"/>
```

You should now be able to launch your application by using the URL to the Canvas page. When it works, add one more feature to it. Instead of hard-coding the text in the right-hand list, call a function to create the text. This is a function that can live in the lib.php file. In the code shown previously, replace

```
Sample database text here.
```

with a call to the new function. It will be called `get_from_database_and_render`; this reflects its ultimate functionality of interacting with the database and rendering the results.

This will be a function that will retrieve an event (`cae`—ChamplainArts event). It will be described more fully later, but for now, it is sufficient to implement it in lib.php to simply return the sample text. One feature will be added that will soon become necessary: the number of columns in which to render the data. By passing that parameter into the function, you can have a single function that will handle database access and any necessary massaging of data and then format it for a one- or two-column display. You can build the most basic FBML code here; later on, it will be more complex. It is returned and echoed in your main page.

```
function get_from_database_and_render (
  $nColumns)
  {
    $fbml = 'Sample database text here.';
    return $fbml;
})
```

Thus, you replace the text in the index.php file with this code. It will display the data in a single column (the right-hand one in Figure 13-6).

```
<?php
  echo get_from_database_and_render ( 1 );
?>
```

What this means is that the page should function properly and that from now on, you need only work in lib.php to implement further functionality. (To be fair, some parameters will be added to the function later, but that is a minor change.)

> **TIP** *This is a good time to check the progress so far by running your application with the revised index.php and lib.php files. If you have implemented the tabs as described here, you will get errors if you click on tabs such as Search Events where the underlying files have not yet been created.*

My Events

The work you have done in creating the template starts to pay off now. The My Events tab will use the one-column format, as shown in Figure 13-7.

Make a copy of your template, and make two changes to it. First, check that no other tab is selected and make certain that My Events is selected:

```
<fb:tab-item href="http://<?php echo $canvas_page;?>myCAEs.php"
  title="My Events" selected="true"/>.
```

Then, instead of creating a one-column data table, you will just be able to call the utility function to display data in a double width column:

```
<? php.
  echo get_from_database_and_render ( 2 );
?>
```

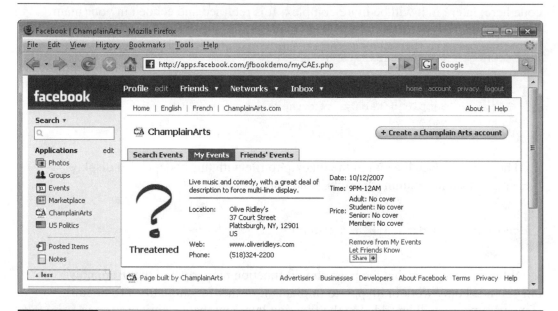

FIGURE 13-7   My Events uses a single column.

Friends' Events

The layout for friends' events is almost always the same as for your own events, so you can follow the steps in the previous section exactly.

As you do so, something may seem wrong to you, and it is. The display of friends' events is almost exactly the same as your events, but not quite. Although only dummy text is displayed now, when you start to add real events, remember that each one will have a Share button. Events other than your own will also have an Add to My Events action; your own events will have a Remove From My Events Action.

This means that the utility function `get_from_database_and_render` will need to know whether or not these are your own events so that it knows how to render them. That means a second parameter must be added to the function. It will be called `$owner`; a value `mine` will generate the Remove From My Events link, while any other value (or null) will generate Add to My Events.

Browse Events

There will be yet another page, the Browse Events page. It will require direct interaction with the database, so it will be implemented in the next chapter, which adds the MySQL database to the application.

Now is a good time to take another pass at `get_from_database_and_ render`.

Implement Utilities

Think for a few moments about the kinds of utilities you will need to display events. It is obvious that you will have to get data from the database and display it. You may not have thought much about the database that will contain your data, but you will need to consider one aspect of it now.

The data for the events (or whatever you store in the database) will probably have its own structure, and you may not be able to change it. However, each record in the database should have a *primary key*—a unique value in the database table that applies to only this record. If you know the primary key, you can always retrieve a record from a database.

In Facebook, a user id (`uid`) is a primary key—it uniquely identifies one user. Given the `uid` (which is one of the few items that you can store), you can access Facebook's database at runtime to retrieve the user's name and other information.

In order to implement a list of a user's events, you will need to store records in a database table that has two values: a `uid` and an event id. Each is a primary key that uniquely identifies a user or an event). A single record—the `uid`/event id combination—identifies one item in a given user's My Events list.

If you search on the `uid`s of a user's friends, you wind up with the `uid`/event combinations for those friends—that is, the My Friends' Events list. You can construct this table of `uid`s and event ids without knowing anything about the data structure of the Facebook data or the data structure of the event data. (This is called a *join table*, and there is much more about it in the following chapter.)

Event Retrieval

At various points as your application is running, you will need to retrieve events—either to browse them or for the My Events list or My Friends' Events list. Right now, you can implement a basic function to retrieve a single event. This function will probably wind up being called in a loop to retrieve multiple events, but it is safe to create it now, without the database calls, to retrieve a single event. The data for that event will be hard-coded, and in the next chapter, as the database is added, it will be replaced with actual database calls.

For now, the function will take two arguments: the number of columns to format the data in and the owner (so that you know whether to render Add to My Events or Remove from My Events).

In addition to retrieving the needed data, this function will call another function that will format the data. The function with a single line of text was created previously. Now you can expand on it and call another utility function, render_ cae, which will be described in the next section. Note that the $ncolumns and $owner parameters are passed through to the subsidiary function. The standard Facebook "unknown" image (the question mark) is used for now. In practice, you will probably find it easiest to implement render_cae with one or two parameters first and then add more and more to it. The only thing to remember is that the parameter list in get_from_database_and_render must match that in render_cae as you bounce back and forth between the two functions.

NOTE
This iterative process of starting from the high-level function and providing more and more detail is a common development process. It may seem more tedious than writing everything at once, but in the long run, it is much more efficient to proceed in this step-by-step manner.

Listing 13-4

```
function get_from_database_and_render (
  $ncolumns,
  $owner )
{
  // this will perform a database access later on
  $fbml = render_cae (
    $ncolumns,
    $owner,
    'http://static.ak.facebook.com//pics/s_default.jpg',
    'Threatened', //name
    "Olive Ridley's", // venue name
    '37 Court Street', //address
    'Plattsburgh', //city
    'NY', //state
    '12901', //postal code
    'US', //country
    'www.oliveridleys.com', //web site
    '(518)324-2200', //phone
    '10', //month
    '12', //day
    '2007', //year
    '9PM-12AM', //time
    'No cover', //price - regular
    'No cover', //price - student
```

```
    'No cover', //price - senior
    'No cover', //price - member
    'Live music and comedy, with a great deal of description
    to force multi-line display.' // description
  );
  return $fbml;
}
```

> **NOTE**
>
> *In this dummy data, the description is deliberately created to be lengthy.
> As you test with dummy data, make certain that you test things such as
> line breaks and long text runs. When you start testing with live data, you
> may not stress your code as much as you can when you create artificial
> data that deliberately poses potential problems.*

Event Display

You can write the retrieval function without knowing the details of the database.
You will have two opportunities to massage the data from the database: You can
massage it after you retrieve it in this function, and you can massage it in the
function that actually renders the data.

   This function will need at least the shell of the other function. You can create its
shell for now as follows. It will receive the data that you send in, but do nothing yet:

Listing 13-5

```
function render_cae (
  $ncolumns,
  $owner,
  $image,
  $caeName,
  $venue,
  $address,
  $city,
  $state,
  $postal,
  $country,
  $emailOrWeb,
  $phone,
  $dateMonth,
  $dateDay,
  $dateYear,
```

```
    $time,
    $costAdult,
    $costStudent,
    $costSenior,
    $costMember,
    $details)
{
}
```

As you can see, there is no body for this function yet. The code for it is lengthy, but not particularly complex. You have already built the pages that will display it, so as soon as this function is completed, the dummy data will be displayed properly on the pages you have already created.

The logic is to fill a variable (`$fbmlhd`) using heredoc coding with all of the code that is needed to display the data. The heredoc syntax will be interrupted at several points to handle the columns and the ownership issue.

Here is a walkthrough of the code structure. You may want to refer back to Figures 13-6 and 13-7 to see what is being produced.

Set the Owner Text

The variable text and link for whether or not this is the owner's event can be set in a variable. This function uses both this technique as well as if statements interspersed in heredoc code. You can choose one method or the other, or use them both. The add_remove_myCAE code may not exist yet, but you can plan ahead for it (just do not click the links yet). As you can see, the assumption is that a single routine will handle both events. Parameters will be added to it later; for now, it will work to display the text, and you can then implement it later.

> **NOTE** *Because this file is included in several of the main files, remember that you will need the* $GLOBALS *syntax to access the globals declared in* config.php.

```
if ($owner == 'mine') {
  $addRemoveHref = "<a href=\"http://"
    .$GLOBALS['canvas_page']
    ."add_remove_myCAE.php\">Remove from My Events</a>";
} else {
  $addRemoveHref = "<a href=\"http://"
    .$GLOBALS['canvas_page']
    ."add_remove_myCAE.php\">Add to My Events</a>";
}
```

It is also a good idea to prepare the Let My Friends Know link here.

```
$letFriendsKnow = "<a href=\"http://"
  .$GLOBALS['canvas_page']
  ."invite_friends.php\">Let Friends Know</a>";
```

Create the Table

The body of the data will be displayed in a table. The table will have one row. The first cell (`td`) contains the image for the event and, below it, the name. In the case of the one-column display, the description then appears below the name.

The second cell in the row contains another table. For the one-column display (as in Figure 13-6), that table contains a number of rows, each of which contains two cells. One cell has a label (such as Location:), and the next contains data.

The last two rows have no labels; the contents are "Add To My Events," "Let Friends Know," and the Share button.

In the two-column display (Figure 13-7), two cells follow the image and title. Each of them contains a table, just as the single-column display did. The only additional variation is that in the two-column display, the description spans both cells in the first row of the left-hand column. Make certain that you can map these components to Figures 13-6 and 13-7 so that you do not get lost.

Here is the code to start creating the overall table. It creates the table, the first row, and a 100-pixel `td` element with the event image and its name:

```
$myString = <<<fbmlhd
<table>
  <tr>
    <td style = "text-align: center" width="100">
      <img  src=$image alt="event_image" class=""/>
      />
      <H1>$caeName</H1>
fbmlhd;
```

Handle the First Column Break

In the one-column display, you need to place the details beneath the image and title:

```
if ($nColumns == 1 )
$myString .= <<<fbmlhd
      <br/>
      $details
fbmlhd;
```

Then, for both, you need to close the `td` element:

```
$myString .= <<<fbmlhd
    </td>
fbmlhd;
```

Now you need to open a new `td` element. If it is for a two-column display, it will be 223 pixels wide; otherwise, it will be the full width, 446 pixels.

```
if ($nColumns == 1) {
  $myString .= '<td width="446" valign="top">';
} else {
  $myString .= '<td width="223">';
}
```

Create the Inner Table

Whether you are in the two-column or one-column `td`, you now need to create an inner table for the data. This is the code to begin the table:

```
$myString .= <<<fbmlhd
    <table  valign="top">
      <tbody valign="top">
fbmlhd;
```

In the case of the two-column display, the first row of the table contains a two-cell span with the `$details` data:

```
if ($nColumns == 2 )
$myString .= <<<fbmlhd
        <tr>
          <td colspan="2">
            $details
            <hr/>
          </td>
        </tr>
fbmlhd;
```

Insert the Common Data

You now have the inner table created inside either a wide or narrow `td`. The next chunk of code is ordinary HTML to create the various rows with labels and data. This code generates the entire left-hand side of the two-column display:

Listing 13-6

```
$myString .= <<<fbmlhd
        <tr>
```

```
      <td>
        Location:
      </td>
      <td>
        $venue
        <br/>
        $address
        <br/>
        $city, $state, $postal
        <br/>
        $country
      </td>
    </tr>
    <tr>
      <td>
        Web:
      </td>
      <td>
        $emailOrWeb
      </td>
    </tr>
    <tr>
      <td>
        Phone:
      </td>
      <td>
        $phone
      </td>
    </tr>
fbmlhd;
```

Handle the Inner Column Break

If this is a two-column display, you now need to create the second column. You do this by closing the tbody, table, and td elements and opening new ones. In a single-column display, you just keep on adding to the existing column you are working with in the existing tbody, table, and td elements.

```
if ($nColumns == 2) {
  $myString .= '</tbody>';
  $myString .= '</table>';
  $myString .= '</td>';
  $myString .= '<td width="223">';
```

```
  $myString .= '<table>';
  $myString .= '<tbody>';
}
```

Finish the Data

The last section of code completes the data in either the one- or two-column table. This is exactly like the previous code, except the $addRemoveHref variable that was filled based on the value of $owner is used here:

Listing 13-7

```
$myString .= <<<fbmlhd
        <tr>
          <td>
            Date:
          </td>
          <td>
            $dateMonth/$dateDay/$dateYear
            <br/>
          </td>
        </tr>
        <tr>              <td>
            Time:
          </td>
          <td>
            $time
            <br/>
          </td>
        </tr>
        <tr>
          <td>
            Price:
          </td>
          <td>
            Adult: $costAdult
            <br/>
            Student: $costStudent
            <br/>
            Senior: $costSenior
```

```
            <br/>
            Member: $costMember
          </td>
        </tr>
        <tr>
          <td/> <!--blank cell, no label for link-->
          <td>
            <hr/>
            $addRemoveHref <br/>
            $letFriendsKnow <br/>
            <fb:share-button class="url" href="#" />
          </td>
        </tr>
      </tbody>
    </table>
  </td>
 </tr>
</table>
fbmlhd;
```

Finish Up and Return the FBML

That completes the function.

```
return $myString;
```

All of this code goes into the body of the `render_cae` function (remember you can download the full code).

Begin to Test

That completes the basic interface of the application. You have the three tabs on a Home page. You can see the Add to/Remove from My Events link as well as the Let Friends Know link and the Share button, although none of them is wired up yet.

In lib.php, you should have `get_from_database_and_render` and `render_cae` created. If you have followed the steps in this chapter, in index.php, you have created the two-column table as shown in Figure 13-6, with the data for the second column generated by a call to

```
get_from_database_and_render ( 1, null ); //not 'mine'
```

You can now copy that file to myCAEs.php and create a one-column table that spans the display shown in Figure 13-7. That is even simpler. Start from the basic template code described previously:

```php
<?php
  // the facebook client library
   include_once './php4client/facebook.php';
  // keys and other setup
  // other includes for lib.php, list_styles.php

  $facebook = new Facebook($api_key, $secret);
  $facebook->require_frame();
  $user = $facebook->require_login();
 ?>
<fb:dashboard>
  // code removed
</fb:dashboard>

<fb:tabs>
  // code removed
</fb:tabs>
```

Now, just add a line break and a call to the new function:

```php
<br />
<?php
  echo get_from_database_and_render ( 1, mine );
?>
```

Make certain that the tabs for My Events now link to this file.

Experiment and start to test. There is enough functionality there that you can begin to allow other people to try the application. On your application settings (in the Developer application) you can clear the Developer Mode checkbox if you want to allow other people to try the application. For now, you may want to leave Developer Mode selected and continue with a private installation so that the News Feed and Mini-Feed are disabled. You and your friends should start to get a sense of how the application will run.

Now it is time for the database.

Chapter 14

Integrate MySQL Data

How to...

- Understand SQL basics
- Use MySQL
- Build the example database
- Construct and test the first query
- Use PHP to run the first query
- Finish the PHP work

In the previous chapter, you saw how to flesh out the interface of a bare-bones application into something that starts to look like a real Facebook application that might actually be usable. One advantage of starting from the interface with dummy data is that you can test it on yourself and others. Another advantage is what will become obvious in this chapter: When the interface is complete (or nearly so), adding the database is something that you can do in the supporting files without revisiting the interface.

The example that is used here is very specific, but, as noted previously, the architecture is applicable to any Facebook application that lets you browse items (music, images, information), display them, select some for further interest, browse your selected items, and browse your friends' items. In this chapter, because you are dealing with the database that manages the items involved, the applicability to other purposes is even clearer—except for the figures and the names of database variables, everything here can be reused for other projects.

You do not need to use a database to implement your Facebook application, but unless you are dealing totally with Facebook data, you will need some place to store your information. Because the volume of data may become large (either because it is intrinsically large or because your application serves many users), a database is practically almost indispensable.

NOTE   *Facebook is now working on a data store API (http://wiki.developers .facebook.com/index.php/Data_Store_API_documentation). It has been designed to be scalable and generalizable to many types of data. The architecture is also optimized for a distributed environment (which is what Facebook Platform is). Much of what you know about optimizing databases on a single computer or network is not directly applicable to a distributed environment (and may, in fact, be incorrect in that context). One issue that affects many suddenly popular Facebook applications is the rapid need for more and more storage; the data store API may help deal with that issue.*

Furthermore, many Facebook applications start not from the Facebook side, but from a database or Web site. The Facebook application may be nothing more than a portal to an external Web site, but it may also be a fully featured Facebook application, like the example used here.

So it is highly likely that you will need to know a bit about databases. Have no fear: There is not much that you will need to know.

> NOTE   *Remember that you can download this chapter's code as described in the Introduction.*

Understand SQL Basics

Today, almost all databases use SQL, the basic language for relational databases. SQL started life as the Structured English Query Language—SEQUEL, but morphed from an acronym that was actually a term copyrighted by others into the three letters. Whether you pronounce it "s-q-l" or "sequel" is up to you.

The idea behind databases is the storage and retrieval of structured information without the programmer having to worry about reading and writing the data. The database itself takes care of the storage. Over decades of experience, databases have become remarkably efficient at their processing. Today, not only are they fast, but they also can handle redundant disks, distributed databases across a network, and many other features.

Did you know?

Find More Information about SQL

The classic references on SQL and relational databases are the books by C. J. Date. Online tutorials and references about SQL are available from a number of sites, including a tutorial at www.w3schools.com, and documentation from specific database vendors, such as MySQL (www.mysql.org), Oracle (www.oracle.com), IBM (DB2) (www.ibm.com), and Microsoft (SQL Server) (www.microsoft.com). From each of those sites, you can search for "SQL" to find where the current documentation is located. The standard itself is published by American National Standards Institute (ANSI) and International Standards Organization (ISO), and is available for purchase from those organizations.

Relational databases store data that can be related to other data in the database to form dynamic, complex, but logical structures. SQL is not a requirement for relational databases, but it is commonly used to implement the concepts of relational databases.

The basics of SQL are simple:

- A *table* is a collection of data that has some common characteristics.

- The data is placed in *columns* or *fields* (the terms are interchangeable in most cases). A column might contain address information, a salary value, an image, or even a movie. All of the data in a column is of the same type (all numeric, all text, all binary data such as images, and so forth), and all of the data in a column represents the same thing (address, salary, user photo).

- The table consists of *rows* or *records* (again, interchangeable terms). Each row has a value for each of the table columns (null is a value). Thus, the fifth record might contain the address, salary, and image of a single individual.

- Some columns are *keys* to the database: Their values can be used to retrieve information quickly. If salary is a key, you can retrieve all of the rows with certain values for salary, and in doing so, you can retrieve non-key data (such as images). A *primary key* is a key that has a unique value for each row in the database. The fifth record in the database may vary, depending on how the database is sorted and what other records are inserted or deleted from it, but the record with a primary key value of 93893 is always the same record.

- A *database* consists of tables.

There are two additional aspects of SQL that are important to know. Indexes contain values for keys; they are stored along with the actual data in the database, but the index contains copies of the key values. To retrieve all salaries in a certain range, the database can read a salary index, which is much smaller than the entire database, to find out which records are in the given range. Having identified the records (with their primary keys from the index), the database can then read the full data from those records.

Because your Facebook application database may become large, and because you want it to be as responsive as possible in the online environment, indexes are a matter of some concern to you. In general, indexes can slow down database updates, but they can significantly improve retrieval time. This is because when you update key data, the data must be written into the database itself as well as into any relevant indexes. If your database application is update-intensive, you may have a different approach to indexes than if your database is read-intensive.

The last point to know is how relationships are implemented. In SQL, they are implemented at runtime, when you ask the database to combine rows from one or more tables with one another based on certain values. For example, if you retrieve the records from a table for individuals with a given salary range, you can create a relationship at that point to combine each individual's salary data with address data from another table; to do this, some column in each table must be related to (often equal to) a column in the other table. They may have different names, but their data must be relatable.

NOTE *You may notice that you can combine rows from one or more tables in the previous description. That is correct: You can implement what is called a self-join, in which a table is related to itself.*

Use MySQL

MySQL is one of the most commonly used SQL products. For many purposes, you can use it under the free software/open-source GNU General Public License which you can find at www.gnu.org. You can run it on your own computer, or you

How to ...   Get MySQL

Log on to www.mysql.com to download MySQL. Several versions are available, but you almost always want *MySQL Community Server - Generally Available Release*. Look for the Download button on the Home page, and follow the links. (One way of determining if you are downloading the right product is to see if you can download it for free. For learning, testing, and small development projects, that is all you need.)

Separate installers are available for various operating systems. Use the appropriate installer and, if you are installing MySQL for the first time, do not customize it until you are familiar with its use.

In the Downloads section, you will find graphical user interface (GUI) tools in the GUI section (http://dev.mysql.com/downloads/gui-tools/5.0.html). The primary tools are MySQL Administrator and MySQL Query Browser. You can use MySQL with a command-line interface, but these tools are much easier to use, so you should download them when you download MySQL. If you are using MySQL on an ISP's Web server, there may be server-specific tools that you can use to access your account and your MySQL databases.

can run it on an external server. If you are building your Facebook application to run on a server that you do not control—such as your ISP's server—you may have access to a copy of MySQL that is already installed there. If not, the How To box will show you how to download and install MySQL.

PHP has excellent support for MySQL, so the combination of the two is an efficient and easy way to implement the database needs of Facebook applications (and others).

> **TIP** *MySQL implements data types much the same as other SQL databases do. There are a very few subtle differences in some of the data types. If you move beyond the basic data types, you may want to consult the documentation at http://dev.mysql.com/doc/refman/5.1/en/data-type-overview.html.*

Explore the Example Database

You may or may not want to build your own database. In the case of the downloadable example, an existing database is used, which stores data for events. That database preceded the Facebook example, and that may be the case for you. You may wind up adding tables to an existing database (in the example, the database implementation of favorite events required a new table). You also may discover that you would like to tweak some of the existing database fields. This may or may not be possible. In building a Facebook application that will be integrated with an existing database and applications (and possibly Web sites) that also use that database, your ground rules may indicate that nothing in the existing database will change (although you probably will need permission from the database administrator to build a Facebook application-only table inside the database).

Work with the Schema

The database structure is called a *schema*. Whether you are designing the database, redesigning the database, or using an existing database without changes, you need to understand its schema.

In this example, the existing database stores information about events and the locations at which they are held. A separate table allows visitors to the Web site to enter information to become users. With the Facebook application, people will be able to browse the events and they will be able to create database user accounts directly from Facebook.

Because the events typically take place at a limited number of locations, information about the locations is stored separately from the events. Thus, both event A and event B may take place in location Z, and the location information only needs to be stored once.

> **CAUTION** *This structure is common and efficient, but it contains a potential trap. If information about a location changes, the revised information will be displayed for any event linked to that location. By separating the location information from the event information, you can save space, but you may run into this problem. The simplest way of handling it is never to change location information. Instead, copy the location and make the change in the copy. Events that need to retain the old information (such as events in the past) will be unchanged, but new events will use the revised location information. This applies to many database designs; for example, on an invoice, the price of an item should be the price that was in effect at the time the invoice was created, even if the price subsequently changes.*

In the next section, you will see how to browse or create the three tables. For now, you can explore them conceptually. Pencil and paper are the best tools for doing initial database design. You can easily modify SQL databases, but nothing is quite as easy as an eraser. Here is the logical structure of the tables; remember that the structure will hold true for whatever types of information you store.

All Tables

Three fields are implemented for each of the tables (and for many tables throughout the SQL world). You may give them other names, but here is the meaning of the three fields:

- **Primary key**   You must implement a primary key with a unique value. A common name for this field is *id*. You can set the default value for this field to be an auto-incremented value. This relies on the database to do the numbering, which is the safest way.

> **TIP** *This field should be unique and meaningless. Particularly in conversions from manual systems, you will find keys that combine pieces of data, such as name-date hired-location. Such a key may temporarily be unique, but is not guaranteed to be so. Furthermore, the value of the key changes when the data it contains changes (or it should). Any references to the prior value will now break. In this case, meaningless data is your friend.*

■ **Modification timestamp** A second common field is also generated automatically by the database. It is a field containing the timestamp of the last modification of the record. This can help in debugging, and it does not take any effort on your part, other than creating it. The database will update it as needed.

■ **Name** A third common field is the name of the item. It will make your life a little simpler on the PHP side if that name includes what it is— eventName, locationName, imageName, and so forth.

Events Table

The heart of the database will be a table containing the items that you want to track. It will have the three common fields (id, last modification, and name) in almost every case. Then you will have fields that are specific to the item being described. Some of these fields are very specific, such as these items in the Events table, but they should give you an idea of the types of data you may store or any type of items. (Note that these are not individual fields in all cases, but descriptions of the type of data you may need.)

■ **category** dance, festival, music, etc.

■ **public contact information** person, phone, email, Web

■ **private contact information** person, phone, email, Web—this information is for management purposes, such as verifying data, but it is not publishable

■ **descriptions** often a short and a long description; you can choose which to display, depending on the format you are using

■ **prices** normal, student, child, senior, member; consider making these text fields, rather than numeric so that phrases such as "under 12 not admitted" or "requires membership card" can be added

■ **time** an actual time field or a text field that can accommodate something like "Tuesday-Saturday 8 PM; Saturday, Sunday 2 PM"

■ **date** stored separately for month/day/year in one scenario; free-format text to allow inputs such as "February 20—March 3"

■ **display information** visibility, dates, status

■ **public notes** information that does not fit anywhere else

- **private notes**   information that does not fit anywhere else but that should not be published

- **location**

A few of these items are worth discussing in some detail, because you may encounter issues in your own data that are similar to these.

When you have a database that drives a Web site and/or a Facebook application, you may need several fields that let you know what information you can display. A useful field is a simple yes/no field that indicates if the data can be displayed. You may choose to mark the data as not displayable for any number of reasons—it is not complete, it is inaccurate, or whatever. If you have a do-not-display flag, you can leave the data in the database until you do want to display it.

Also, note in this structure that display information contains visibility dates. For an event on a given date, you may want to display it for one week prior to and for no days after the event. By using the date range, you can control whether or not it is shown, even if its visibility suggests that it is publishable.

Finally, note the status information. Depending on how your database is updated, you may allow users to enter data directly, but until it is confirmed, it will not be displayed. The confirmation process may be manual, or it may be automated. Although not implemented in this table, you may also have advertising information in your database. Perhaps the size or placement of data on your Web site or Facebook application depends on an advertising contract; you can store that information in the table so you know how to render the data.

Note, too, that some of the information comes in pairs of public and private information. Database storage is relatively cheap, and it is much more efficient to have extra fields than half a page of notes information telling you which phone number or email address to use when.

Another useful field in this table is the location. That is a *foreign key,* the identifier of a unique record in another table (in this case, Locations). The actual name of the field in Events is `locationID`; the name of the matching field in Locations is `id`; it does not matter that they have different names as long as the values match.

TIP   *The more information you can place in the database that controls how, when, and where the data will be displayed, the more effective your Facebook application will be. Users like to have direct access to very specific portions of very large databases.*

Locations Table

The Locations table contains the three basic fields (id, modification timestamp, and name). It also contains the location-specific information, such as address, city, and so forth. The set of contact information is repeated for the location, both in public and private versions. (The contact information for a concert hall may be different from the contact information for a band.)

Users

The Users table contains the three basic fields as well as the names and email addresses of users.

Build the Database (if necessary)

If you need to install MySQL, do so as described previously. Once you have access to MySQL on your own or another computer, you can get to work if you need to build the database. The first step is to gain access to your MySQL account. You can use the MySQL command-line interface, but it is much easier to download the GUI tools and use MySQL Query Browser. That software should be installed on the computer where you are doing your work—it may or may not be the same computer on which the MySQL database is running.

> **TIP**   *If you are using MySQL on a remote host, other tools may be installed there to help you build and maintain your databases. Explore your hosting account to see what is provided. It may be easier to use a Web-based tool that runs on the MySQL server; in any event, the syntax will be the same no matter where you are working or what you are working with.*

Log in to your MySQL account from MySQL Query Browser, as shown in Figure 14-1. (The address, user name, and password are assigned by your ISP, database administrator, or yourself, if you are managing your own database and Web server.)

The main window will open, as shown in Figure 14-2. This is where you do your work.

The routine will be quite simple: Type in a MySQL command at the top and then click Execute. The results will be displayed in the central part of the window; in the bottom of the window, you will either see an error message or the result of the successful query.

SQL queries can interrogate the database or manipulate it. In this case, you need to create a database and then create tables within it.

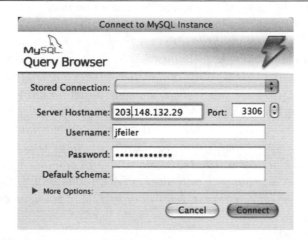

Log in to MySQL Query Browser.

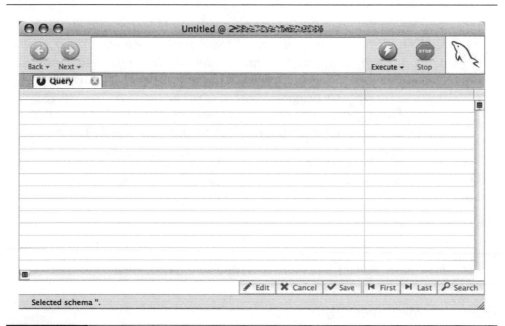

MySQL Query Browser main window

NOTE

You need the correct permissions to create and modify the database. If you are the owner of the MySQL account, you probably already have the appropriate permissions to do everything. As you continue development, you will add additional accounts that have fewer permissions so that users cannot undo all your good work. This section is a summary of SQL syntax; refer to the MySQL documentation for more details. But if you cannot access your MySQL account at all in order to get started (particularly if you have not used it before), you may have to contact your ISP or database administrator to get your initial privileges correctly set up. If you have just installed MySQL on your own computer, you probably have a root account with unlimited access, so the problem is not that you do not have enough access, but rather that there is too much access.

Create the Database

The command is simple. Choose a name for your database, type the following query at the top of the window, and click Execute:

```
CREATE DATABASE myDatabase;
```

NOTE

SQL syntax is not case-sensitive, but it frequently is shown in all capital letters to distinguish it from variables and other user syntax. You need not adopt this policy, but it can improve readability. It is important to note that spaces can matter in MySQL statements, particularly spaces before parentheses (the spaces should generally not be present). Lowercase is used for user syntax, such as—in code—events table. In the text of this and other chapters, common English capitalization is used—Events table.

You create the database once. Thereafter, when you begin to use MySQL Query Browser, the first command you execute uses the previously created database:

```
USE myDatabase;
```

NOTE

Remember that all SQL commands end with a semicolon (;).

Create or Modify a Table

To create a table within a database, you must create at least one column in it. It is generally easiest to create a single column and then add other columns. Otherwise, you wind up with a long multiline query where one typo can cause it to fail. You can always go back and fix the typo and reexecute the query, but it is often simplest to do it in a step-by-step process. (Remember to start by using the database.)

In this case, you could start with the Events table. You might want to add the `eventName` column. To do this, the query is:

```
CREATE TABLE events (eventName,VARCHAR(50));
```

Once a table is created, you can modify it. For example, to add a `phonePublic` field to the Events table, here is the syntax:

```
ALTER TABLE events ADD phonePublic VARCHAR(9);
```

To remove a column called `mistake`, use this:

```
ALTER TABLE events DROP COLUMNS mistake;
```

To change a column's type, use this (it will enlarge the column in this case):

```
ALTER TABLE events MODIFY phonePublic VARCHAR(50);
```

And to rename a column, use this code. Note that you need to specify the renamed column's type.

```
ALTER TABLE events CHANGE typophonePublic phonePublic VARCHAR(50);
```

As you go along, you can see how a table is shaping up by using the following query:

```
DESCRIBE events;
```

The results of this type of query are shown in Figure 14-3 (the table has been expanded beyond the fields listed in these commands.

The data returned from a query is the *resultset*. In the File menu, you will find an Export Resultset command that lets you export it as comma-separated values (CSV), HTML, XML, or other formats. Once you have exported it, you can open it in other applications, such as Excel, Word, FileMaker, or any application that you choose. You can then reformat the results, sort them, and otherwise manipulate them. This is a useful tool for working with the schema that is returned from the `describe` query.

Use MySQL Query Browser for Testing

MySQL Query Browser (or another tool you prefer) will be an indispensable part of your development environment. As you add database functionality to your Facebook

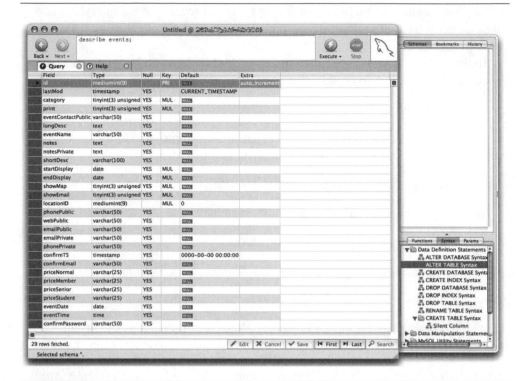

FIGURE 14-3   Describe the database.

application, you should devise each query, test it in MySQL Query Browser, and then implement it in your PHP code. This section provides a step-by-step process of developing a query for your Facebook application. It addresses the issue of adding an event to your Events list. From the user's point of view, this is implemented in the Add To My Events link shown in the lower-right area of Figure 14-4.

To implement this, you need a table that links events and users. If you are building off an existing database, you will probably have the tables you need to store events (or photos or music or whatever), but you likely will not have a table that lets users store their favorites. And if you do, because you do not yet have a Facebook application, that table will be storing the information for your users, not your Facebook users.

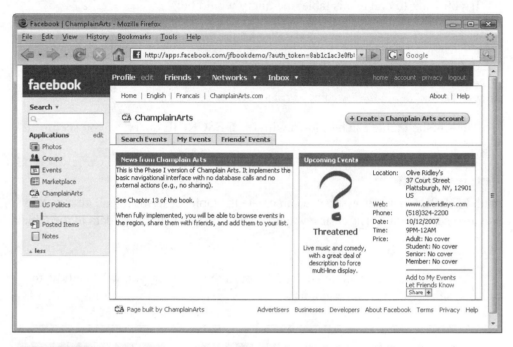

FIGURE 14-4 Users can add events to their lists.

Create a Join Table for Users and Events

In order to implement a table like this, you need to store only two pieces of information:

- You need the Facebook `uid` (it will be named `fbuid` in this table).

- You need an identifier of the event (it will be named `caeid`).

Two other columns will be created. One is an `id` column that is auto-incremented and provides a unique key; the other is a timestamp of last modification of the record. These two columns are automatically maintained by MySQL.

This is called a *join* table. It is used to join together two other tables and implements a *many-to-many* relationship. A user can have many events in a list, and a single event can be in many users' lists.

If you want to create this table, the query would be:

```
CREATE TABLE userevents (fbuid BIGINT(20),
  caeidINT(12),
  id INT(1) PRIMARY KEY AUTO_INCREMENT,
  lastMod TIMESTAMP);
ALTER TABLE userevents ADD PRIMARY KEY (id);
```

The finished table can be shown with the DESCRIBE query, as you see in Figure 14-5.

Retrieve Data

With MySQL Query Browser, you can create the table, describe it, and alter it. You can also edit the data. The easiest way to begin is to show all of the data in the table:

```
SELECT * FROM userevents;
```

At this point, there will be no data. Later in this chapter, you will see how to retrieve selected rows and columns.

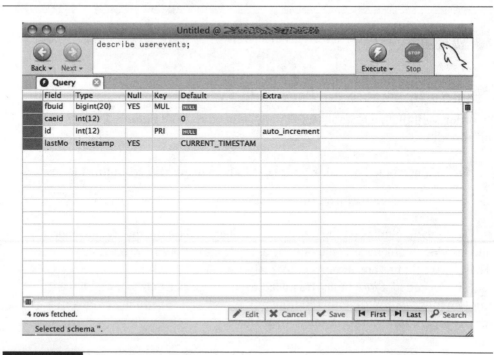

FIGURE 14-5   Describe userevents.

> TIP   *This is a good table to experiment with, because if you already have a database that is driving a Web site or other applications, you may not want to experiment with live data. Because this table is designed just for your Facebook application, you can do what you want.*

Edit Data

At the bottom of the window, you will see buttons that let you manipulate the data. If you click Edit, you can edit the data in the table. There is no data at this point, but clicking Edit will give you a blank row. You can now enter values. It does not matter what the values are because this is just for background testing. The only values you should be able to enter without an error are `fbuid` and `caeid`. When you have entered values for them, click Save. The `id` value will be auto-entered, and the timestamp will be filled in.

As you will see, the SELECT query is the basic query for retrieving data from a table. It can have many options and parameters, but it will not be hard to work with it, because you do not need to use many of them to get started.

Insert Data

The companion query to SELECT inserts data into the database. Instead of using the Edit and Save buttons, you can add a row to this table with the following query:

```
INSERT INTO userevents set fbuid=123, caeid=456;
```

> TIP   *If you are working with an existing database that has data in it, it will be easy for you to move forward. If not, you either need to construct an interface to add data to events (or whatever you are managing), or you can use MySQL Query Browser to manually add the data to test with. It may be a bit tedious, but you only need a few records. When your application goes live, presumably you will have a Web site or other interface to update your database.*

Construct and Test the First Query (Adding/Removing Favorites)

In the last chapter, you saw how to build the basics of the user interface. The links to add and remove events were there, but they did nothing. You can build on those to implement their functionality. This is the simplest part of the database, and it is a good place to start. You need to create a new PHP script. You can call it whatever you want; in this example, it is called add_remove_myCAEs.php. It will be a script that is called from the links to add or remove events. All that it will do is either insert a new row into the join table or delete the appropriate row. You can check on its progress by using MySQL Query Browser to watch the table as it is updated.

Connect to the Database

This is the first time you will have linked your database to your PHP scripts. To do so, you need the equivalent login information that you used to get into MySQL Query Browser. If your database is part of an existing database, you may already have this information in a file. For example, Listing 14-1 is the file that Dreamweaver has built for a Web site that accesses the databases used in this example:

Listing 14-1

```php
<?php
# FileName="Connection_php_mysql.htm"
# Type="MYSQL"
# HTTP="true"
$hostname_ChamplainArtsNetSol = "123.456.789.01";
$database_ChamplainArtsNetSol = "yourDatabaseName";
$username_ChamplainArtsNetSol = "yourUserName";
$password_ChamplainArtsNetSol = "yourPassword";
$ChamplainArtsNetSol = mysql_connect(
  $hostname_ChamplainArtsNetSol,
  $username_ChamplainArtsNetSol,
  $password_ChamplainArtsNetSol) or
  trigger_error(mysql_error(),E_USER_ERROR);
?>
```

You can reuse the Dreamweaver file as is (or use any other file that may have been created). In fact, depending on your file structure, you can reference the exact Dreamweaver file that is created for your main Web site. The advantage to doing this, of course, is that if anything changes, you need only change it in one place, and your Facebook application, as well as your Web site, will use the updated password, IP address, or other information. This information is normally placed in your config.php file. If you are reusing a file, here is what config.php will look like:

```php
<?php
  $api_key = 'your api key';
  $secret = 'your secret key';
  $canvas_page = 'apps.facebook.com/yourInternalAppName/';
  require_once('../path/yourConnectionFile.php');
?>
```

Instead of the require_once statement, you can type in the information shown in Listing 14-1.

> **TIP** *To access the globals defined in config.php, you can reference them by name in the* $GLOBALS *array that is automatically maintained for you in PHP. For a variable named* $myVariable, *the correct syntax for its use in another file is* $GLOBALS['myVariable']. *Note that the* $ *precedes GLOBALS, not the name of the variable.*

Send Parameters to the Script

Next, you have to get the information into the script. This consists of the fbuid and the caeid, as well as an indicator on whether the data is to be added or removed. You can send that information in a form, but you can also send it directly in the http request. That request could look like Listing 14-2 (with spacing added for readability):

Listing 14-2

```
http://www.champlainarts.com/CA/add_remove_myCAE.php
  ?fbuid=1234
  &caeid=5432
  &action=add
```

The parameters are sent in name/value pairs. If you choose to use these names, you can then retrieve the data in your script by querying the $PHP_REQUEST array that always contains the parameters sent in the http request. Here is some sample code (the internal PHP variables happen to have the same names as the names of the parameters in the http request, but that is not necessary):

> **NOTE** *The PHP* isset *function tests to see if a variable has a value other than* null. *This is the safest function to use to test if any value—including zero or an empty string—has been assigned to a variable.*

Here is the code (remember to substitute your own file name):

Listing 14-3

```php
<?php
include_once 'config.php';
if (isset($_REQUEST['fbuid'])) {
  $fbuid = $_REQUEST['fbuid'];
}
```

```
if (isset($_REQUEST['caeid'])) {
  $caeid = $_REQUEST['caeid'];
}
if (isset($_REQUEST['action'])) {
  $action = $_REQUEST['action'];
}
?>
```

If you run this script (using the code in Listing 14-3), it should connect to the database and retrieve the values from the http request. (The URL you use will be your Web site, and the name of the file, as well as its path, is up to you.)

> **TIP** *If the script fails now, go back and check carefully that there are no missing commas or other typos. If you find nothing amiss, remove the database code from config.php—you do not need it yet. If you cannot run the script from an http request, and if the script consists only of the code to retrieve the parameters, you have a basic configuration issue. Sometimes another pair of eyes will see an obvious error.*

Add to the Table

You have now unloaded the data from the parameters. All you need to do now is insert a row into the database. Because this is your first database connection, it makes sense to proceed step by step.

The basic sequence of MySQL/PHP code is as follows:

1. **Create a query.** To begin with, this should be a query that you have typed into MySQL Browser and tested. After you have tested the query, copy and paste it into your PHP code, setting a variable to the query. In this case, a variable called $insertSQL is set to the tested query:

```
$insertSQL = "INSERT INTO userevents set fbuid=1234, caeid=5432;";
```

This query ignores the parameters that have been passed in; instead, it uses hard-coded values. The advantage of this is that you can test it, copy it, and paste it in without making any changes that might annoy it. (Note the semicolon that ends the query is within the quoted string.)

2. **Connect to the database.** The next line of code uses the defines that you included to connect to the database:

```
mysql_select_db(
    $GLOBALS['database_ChamplainArtsNetSol'],
    $GLOBALS['ChamplainArtsNetSol']);
```

3. **Execute the query and store the result.** There is always a result to a query. It may be data, or it may be a result value. The result of processing the query can be manipulated in your PHP script. For now, just store it as this code shows:

```
$result = mysql_query($insertSQL,
$GLOBALS['ChamplainArtsNetSol'])
        or die(mysql_error());
```

Most database calls include the or die *clause that catches errors and terminates the script.*

Making certain that you have a closing ?> at the end of your script, you should be able to run it now using the code shown in this section. You should see a new line in the userevents table when you view it.

If you have successfully updated the table, you are well on your way. (If not, back up and retest the query, retest the database connection, and check each line of code.)

You can add that http request to the link that is shown in the lower-right area of Figure 14-4. But before you go ahead, there is a bit more to do.

First of all, when you execute the script by typing in that URL, the script executes and updates the database, and then it stops. You need to have another script step to display another page. The easiest way to do this is to redirect the script to another page. You can do that with a line of PHP code (substituting your Canvas URL, of course). It will redirect to a specific page, much like the header PHP function. Because this code uses the Facebook object you will need to add the Facebook libraries and instantiate the Facebook object in $facebook just as you have done previously (the full code is shown later in this chapter). Add the redirect call at the end of the script.

```
$facebook->redirect("http://$canvas_page"."myCAEs.php;
```

The logic here is that after you have added an item to the favorites list, you may want to see that list. It is a logical page to display.

Compared to stand-alone Web pages or other applications, you may find that a Facebook application needs to be a bit more self-sufficient than others. Whereas in other environments, you might choose a confirmation page, allowing the user to then choose where to go, it makes sense in an environment such as Facebook to choose a simple and logical place to go and then to go there.

With the redirect line added, you now have a script that works at a basic level. The next step is to use the variables that have been passed in. Remember that in PHP double-quoted strings, variables are expanded. This means that you can change the query to the following line, using the parameters that have been passed in:

```
$insertSQL = "INSERT INTO userevents set fbuid=$fbuid,
     caeid=$caeid;";
```

Test again, and review the results in the table.

You may find that you can run this over and over again... and create multiple identical rows in the table. This could result in the same item being shown multiple times in the user's list. To prevent this, you need another query.

The new query uses the SQL COUNT function to count the number of values that are present in a certain condition (COUNT is a fast operation):

```
SELECT COUNT(id) FROM userevents WHERE fbuid=1234 AND caeid=5432;
```

The result of the query should be the number of records with those values. You can now add a test to see if the record already exists. If it does not, you can add it.

Construct the query exactly as you did before:

1. **Create a query.** You can create a separate query variable (or reuse an old one, but this is more readable). Here is what the query would look like. (If you want to be methodical, repeat the process of first hard-coding the values and then using the variables.)

   ```
   $countSQL =
       "SELECT COUNT(id) FROM userevents WHERE fbuid=$fbuid
         AND caeid=$caeid;";
   ```

2. **Connect to the database.** This code is identical. (It is always identical for your specific database.)

   ```
   mysql_select_db(
       $GLOBALS['database_ChamplainArtsNetSol'],
       $GLOBALS['ChamplainArtsNetSol']);
   ```

3. **Execute the query and store the result.** This is the same as.

   ```
   $result = mysql_query ($countSQL,
   $GLOBALS['ChamplainArtsNetSol'])
     or die(mysql_error());
   ```

   Because you are retrieving data (not just inserting it), there are now two additional steps.

4. **Fetch the actual data.** The `result` variable contains internal information. To extract the data, you need to call `mysql_fetch_array`. You pass in the `$result` variable, and you can pass a second parameter in to specify how you will access the data. In this case, you are accessing it by a zero-relative index. You can also access it by name, as you will see later in this chapter.

```
$row = mysql_fetch_array ( $result, MYSQL_NUM );
```

5. **Extract the value.** Because you only selected a single value from the database (the result of the COUNT function), you can take the first item of the row that was returned (zero-relative) and store it in a variable:

```
$theCount = $row [0];
```

Finally, you have all the pieces. All you need to do now is add an if test to see if you should insert the data.

Remove Items from the Table

You will need code to remove items from the table. The process is almost identical to adding items. Create the query, connect to the database, and execute the query. Here is the query for deletion:

```
$deleteSQL = "DELETE FROM userevents WHERE fbuid=$fbuid
      AND caeid=$caeid;";
```

You can safely ignore the result because if you somehow try to remove something that is not there, the error message does not matter.

Putting It Together

Here is the entire script:

Listing 14-4

```php
<?php

// the facebook client library
include_once '../php4client/facebook.php';

// keys and other setup
include_once 'config.php';
// utils
include_once 'lib.php';
```

```php
$facebook = new Facebook($api_key, $secret);
$facebook->require_frame();
$user = $facebook->require_login();

if (isset($_REQUEST['fbuid'])) {
 $fbuid = $_REQUEST['fbuid'];
}
if (isset($_REQUEST['caeid'])) {
  $caeid = $_REQUEST['caeid'];
}
if (isset($_REQUEST['action'])) {
  $action = $_REQUEST['action'];
}


if ( $action == 'add' ) {
  $countSQL =
    "SELECT COUNT(id) FROM userevents WHERE fbuid=$fbuidGLOBALS['
      AND caeid=$caeid;";
    mysql_select_db(
      $database_ChamplainArtsNetSol, $GLOBALS['ChamplainArtsNetSol'] );
    $result = mysql_query ($countSQL, $GChamplainArtsNetSol'])
      or die(mysql_error());
    $row = mysql_fetch_array ( $result, MYSQL_NUM );
    $theCount = $row [0] ;
    if ( $theCount == 0 ) {
      $insertSQL = "INSERT INTO userevents SET fbuid=$fbuid,
        caeid=$caeid;";
      mysql_select_db(
        $database_ChamplainArtsNetSol, $GLOBALS['ChamplainArtsNetSol']);
      $result = mysql_query($insertSQL, $GLOBALS['ChamplainArtsNetSol'])
        or die(mysql_error());
      $facebook->redirect("http://$canvas_page"."myCAEs.php?fbuid=
$fbuid&caeid=$caeid");
      }
  } else {
    if ( $action == 'remove' ) {
      $deleteSQL = "DELETE FROM userevents WHERE fbuid=$fbuid
        AND caeid=$caeid;";
      mysql_select_db(
        $GLOBALS['database_ChamplainArtsNetSol'],
$GLOBALS['ChamplainArtsNetSol']);
      $result = mysql_query ($deleteSQL, $GLOBALS['ChamplainArtsNetSol'])
        or die(mysql_error());
  }
  $facebook->redirect("http://$canvas_page"."myCAEs.php");
  }
?>
```

Finish the PHP Work: Overview

Believe it or not, your work is almost done. You will be repeating the code to construct queries, execute them, and work with the results. To avoid making mistakes, you can work with hard-coded values for the data to be retrieved, testing the queries in MySQL Query Browser.

The remaining work is done in lib.php. In the previous chapter, two functions were used to display dummy data. They will be fleshed out to use the database data, and a third one will be added.

function get_from_database_and_render ($nColumns, $owner, $user)

This is the function that is called from several places in the code that you wrote in the last chapter. It knows how many columns it wants returned, it passes in a value (mine) if these are the user's events, and it may pass in the user id, which is set using the client library that is included in all pages (this last parameter is new).

If $user is set, events for that user are retrieved. If it is null, all events are retrieved. (The Browse Events tab is implemented in the following chapter, and there will be a change to the parameters again there.)

NOTE   *The $owner parameter is used to determine whether the link should say Add To My Events or Remove From My Events. In fact, to be foolproof, you should check whether or not a given event is already in the list. This code will work for a user's own events, but if a friend has marked an event that the user also has marked (that is, there are user records in* userevents *for both the user and the friend), this logic will put Add To My Events in the display of the record in the friends list. Because of the error-checking to avoid adding duplicate records, this does not matter much. This route is taken to avoid the database cost of checking each record in lists other than the user's favorites list.*

The primary purpose of this function is to access the database and get the results.

function render_cae ($nColumns, $owner, $user, $results)

This function is called from the previous one. The $nColumns, $owner, and $user parameters are passed through, along with the $results parameter, which is the result of the database call in the previous function.

Like the previous function, this function needs to know about the structure of the database. As you will see, it also may perform some manipulation of the data before it is sent to the final function.

In the previous chapter, this function did the formatting. Now, its functionality is split into two. The columnar formatting is moved to the next function so that render_cae serves as the bridge between the database data and the data that will be displayed.

function render_cae_columns

This function receives the $nColumns parameter and an entire list of parameters that represents the data to be displayed. (They could be sent as an array.) This function knows nothing about the database. It displays the data it is sent in the appropriate format. It is the code from render_cae in the previous chapter.

Finish the PHP Work: Details

Here are the details of the code.

function get_from_database_and_render ($nColumns, $owner, $user)

This function's primary purpose is to retrieve the data from the database. It will use a SELECT statement, as you have seen previously. Before getting into the details of the function, it is worthwhile to take a moment to look at an overview of SELECT statements and subqueries.

Use Select

You saw previously how to retrieve all the data from a table using

```
SELECT * FROM tableName;
```

There are two main extensions to this syntax. One is that rather than retrieving all columns (which is what the asterisk specifies), you can retrieve specific columns. Thus, you could write:

```
SELECT name, address, city, state FROM addressBook;
```

This would retrieve the data for those four columns from all rows in the table. You can also limit your search to specific rows, as in this example:

```
SELECT name, address, city, state FROM addressBook
  WHERE type="commercial";
```

You can join two tables together based on columns with matching values. Thus, in the case of the Events and Locations tables, you can retrieve data from both at the same time. The underlined section of the query is where the joining of the two tables takes place.

```
SELECT eventName, date, locationName FROM
   events, locations l WHERE locationID=l.id;
```

Here is where the issue of naming columns that was alluded to before comes into play. In this hypothetical example, eventName and date are part of the Events table, as is locationID. In the Locations table, the id column matches up to the locationID column in the Events table. Because both tables may contain an id column, you need some way to indicate which id column you want to use. You specify the two tables from which data is to be retrieved, and you can add an `alias` for each one (often, the first letter of the table name) that can then be used as a prefix to disambiguate columns. Many people always use this technique in a complex query (or one that may become complex with revisions). Thus, you could rewrite the previous query:

```
SELECT e.eventName, e.date, e.locationName FROM
   events e, locations l WHERE e.locationID=l.id;
```

This makes its meaning absolutely clear, and it is the heart of the query that will be created here. There will be many more fields retrieved from the two joined tables, but as long as the underlined code is there, you will be able to retrieve what you need.

NOTE *Within your database you can enforce a rule that the name of every column in every table is unique, but that does not solve the problem because you cannot control the name of every column in every table of every database you may ever access. Being able to handle duplicate column names is an essential part of the SQL developer's toolkit.*

Use Subqueries

If a user is specified, the query will select from that user's events. Recall the events are added to the user's list by clicking the Add To My Events link, running the script described at the beginning of the chapter, and adding a record to the `userevents` join table. Table 14-1 shows what the table might look like at one stage.

Remember that the purpose of this table is to join information from users and events, so the actual data lives in other tables. All this says is that user 4 has two events in the list: 17 and 20. For event 17, two users (3 and 4) have this event in their lists. You can retrieve based on either column.

User ID	Event ID
4	17
5	19
3	17
4	20

TABLE 14-1   `userevents` Join Table

Here is a simple query that will retrieve all of a given user's events:

```
SELECT caeid FROM userevents WHERE fbuid=$user;
```

You can use a subquery to use those results to process another query. You do so using another operator for the WHERE clause—IN:

```
SELECT eventName FROM events WHERE id IN
  (SELECT caeid FROM userevents WHERE fbuid=$user);
```

If you hard-code a value such as 4 for `$user` against the data in Table 14-1, the subquery (enclosed in parentheses) will return two rows, each with a value for `caeid`: 17 and 20. You can test this out for yourself using MySQL Query Browser and typing in a query like this with the hard-coded values.

Now, the outer query looks for rows from the Events table where the `id` field in the Events table matches the values returned from the subquery—17 and 20. Thus, the combined query will retrieve the `eventName` values for events 17 and 20.

Subqueries are a simple way to improve the performance of your database. If there is a subquery that can run against a compact table, such as the `userevents` table, and that will yield results to drastically limit the searching required for the main query, you are far ahead of the game. Even with a small number of users, the `userevents` table can be large. If your application has 1,000 users, each of whom has an average of five events listed, that is 5,000 rows (not really a big number for a database). If the subquery can pull out the five records for a single user in whom you are interested, you then run the main query against five records, not 5,000.

TIP   *Unless you are a careful typist and well experienced with SQL, build up your complex queries using MySQL Query Browser and then copy and paste the result into your code. At that point, replace hard-coded values with PHP variables, remembering that within quoted strings, those variables will be expanded for you.*

The Actual Code

Although it is longer than the code to add or remove items from the join table, this function has basically the same structure. Thus, the first part of the function should be familiar to you. It is the common boilerplate code you always use with the addition of a new line to create an empty string in $myResults. As the data is retrieved, it will be placed into that string and will be returned to the calling function; this will be Facebook Markup Language (FBML)—formatted data ready to be placed on the Canvas page.

```
function get_from_database_and_render ( $nColumns, $owner, $user ) {
  $myResults = '';

  mysql_select_db($GLOBALS['database_ChamplainArtsNetSol'],
    $GLOBALS['ChamplainArtsNetSol']);
```

Now the function diverges into two sections. If there is a uid passed in $user, it is used to retrieve data for that user's list in the join table. This is a fairly sophisticated piece of SQL, but it is efficient. You may want to experiment with it in MySQL Query Browser.

If there is a value for $user passed in, you need to run a subquery to find that user's events. Here is the basic query, with some lines omitted (they just add more fields to be retrieved). Note that the WHERE clause now includes two parts: the joining of the Events and Locations tables as well as the incorporation of the subquery.

```
if ( $user > 0 ) {
  //spacing for readability here//
  $query_browseResults = "SELECT
    e.id,
    e.eventName,
    e.eventDay,
    e.eventMonth,
    // lines omitted
    e.eventImageURL,
    l.locationName,
    l.address1,
    l.address2,
    l.city,
    l.state,
    l.zip,
    l.country
    FROM  events e, locations l
    WHERE e.locationID = l.id
```

```
        AND e.id IN
        (SELECT caeid FROM usereventsWHERE fbuid='$user');";
    } else {
    $query_browseResults = "SELECT e.id,
        e.eventName,
        e.eventDay,
        e.eventMonth,
        // lines omitted
        e.eventImageURL,
        l.locationName,
        l.address1,
        l.address2,
        l.city,
        l.state,
        l.zip,
        l. country
        FROM events e, locations l
        WHERE e.locationID = l.id;";
    };
```

The next line of code is the same code that you have seen before to run the query:

```
$browseResults = mysql_query(
    $query_browseResults, $GLOBALS['ChamplainArtsNetSol'])
    or die(mysql_error());
```

In the case of retrieving the count of data from the userevents table, you knew that only one row would be returned. In this case, more than one row could be returned, so the data is fetched from the results in a while loop. The underlined code retrieves one row of data and moves the pointer (called a *cursor* in SQL) to the next row of the results. What this code does is take each row of the results, place it in the variable $row_browseResults, and then call render_cae to render that data with the $nColumns, $owner, and $user parameters that were passed into this function. Within the loop, the results of render_cae are concatenated into $myResults, which is then returned.

```
while ( $row_browseResults = mysql_fetch_assoc($browseResults ) ) {
    $myResults .= render_cae ( $nColumns,
        $owner,
        $user,
        $row_browseResults );
};
```

```
return $myResults;
}
```

Previously, you saw code that was fetched with this code:

```
$row = mysql_fetch_array ( $result, MYSQL_NUM );
```

You extracted an individual value by position, starting at zero:

```
$theCount = $row [0];
```

This function lets you use an associative array to extract the data, as in:

```
$theAddress = $row['address2'];
```

The difference is whether you use `mysql_fetch_assoc` or `mysql_fetch_array` with the `MYSQL_NUM` parameter. You can also use `mysql_fetch_array` with `MYSQL_ASSOC` as the parameter instead of using `mysql_fetch_assoc`. Using the positional retrieval helps you if you have columns with the same names (but it also means that you have to count the columns in a possibly lengthy query).

function render_cae ($nColumns, $owner, $user, $results)

This function supplied the hard-coded data in the last chapter. Now, it takes the data that has been returned from the database and passes it along to `render_cae_columns`, which contains most of the formatting data that this function included in the last chapter. Note that the new parameter, `$results`, is a single row of the database result. In other words, `$results`, in this function, is `$row_browseResults` that was filled in the while loop at the end of the previous function. This function needs to know both about the database and the needs of the formatting function that it calls. That is why, for example, it concatenates the `address1` and `address2` fields, adding a line break, if necessary, between them (that is the code at the beginning of the function). After that, it calls `render_cae_columns` with the individual items from the row retrieved from the database. It does not pass on the `$results` array, because that would require `render_cae_columns` to know about the database. Only this function and the previous one know about the database, which means you can make changes to them and the database without breaking anything.

If you have a function call, such as `render_cae_columns`, *with a large number of parameters, you can space them in groups of five (or whatever number you prefer) so that you can match them up with the parameters of the function itself without having to count to see what the 17th parameter is and if it matches the 17th value passed in.*

```php
function render_cae ( $nColumns, $owner, $user, $results ) {
  $theAddress = $results['address1'];
  if ( $results['address2'] ) {
    $theAddress .= "<br>".$results['address2'];
  }

  $fbml = render_cae_columns (
    $nColumns,
    $owner,
    $results['eventImageURL'],
    $results['eventName'],
    $results['locationName'],

    $theAddress,
    $results['city'],
    $results['state'],
    $results['zip'],
    $results['country'],

    $results['webPublic'],
    $results['phonePublic'],
    $results['eventMonth'],
    $results['eventDay'],
    $results['eventYear'],

    $results['eventTime'],
    $results['priceNormal'],
    $results['priceStudent'],
    $results['priceSenior'],
    $results['priceMember'],

    $results['priceChild'],
    $results['shortDesc'],
    $user,
    $results['id']
  );
  return $fbml;
}
```

function render_cae_columns

This function takes the parameters passed into `render_cae` in the previous chapter and does the formatting. The only changes are a few more conditional statements to test for empty data values, in which case, the labels are not printed and a further implementation of the Add/Remove logic.

Here is the expansion of the Add/Remove logic.

```
if ($owner == 'mine') {
  $addRemoveHref =
    "<a href=\"$canvas_page"."add_remove_myCAE.php?fbuid=";
    $addRemoveHref .= $user;
    $addRemoveHref .= "&caeid=";
    $addRemoveHref .=$caeid;
    $addRemoveHref .="&action=remove";
    $addRemoveHref .="\">Remove from my events</a>";
} else {
  $addRemoveHref =
    "<a href=\"$canvas_page"."add_remove_myCAE.php?fbuid=";
    $addRemoveHref .= $user;
    $addRemoveHref .="&caeid=";
    $addRemoveHref .=$caeid;
    $addRemoveHref .="&action=add";
    $addRemoveHref .="\">Add to my events</a>";
}
```

For example, this code omits the label and the entire table row if no event time has been passed in:

```
if ( $time ) {
  $myString .= <<<fbmlhd
        <tr>
          <td>
            Time:
          </td>
          <td>
            $time
            <br/>
          </td>
        </tr>
fbmlhd;
  }
```

This slightly more complex code tests to see if any price has been passed in. If any price has been passed in, the Price: label is printed in a new `td`. Then the specific prices are printed.

```
if ( $costAdult or $costStudent
   or $costSenior or $costChild or $costMember ) {
   $myString .= <<<fbmlhd
           <tr>
             <td>
               Price:
             </td>
             <td>
fbmlhd;
   }
 if ( $costAdult ) {
   $myString .= "Adult: $costAdult<br/>";
 }
 if ( $costStudent ) {
   $myString .= "Student: $costStudent<br/>";
 }
```

... and so forth

At the end of the function, the FBML and HTML code that has been produced is returned and concatenated to `$myString` within the while loop at the end of the previous function:

```
   return $myString;
}
```

This chapter has shown you the basics of MySQL and SQL that you need to build your Facebook applications. If you use this architecture, remember that you can keep your database code quite separate from the display code, which makes maintaining the application much easier. If you download the code and run it, you will be able to see that the basic files in the application are untouched, except for these three functions in lib.php and the new add_remove_myCAE.php file.

Chapter 15

Add More Features

How to...

- Use Public Canvas Pages and Control Adding Applications
- Update the Profile page
- Add News Feed and Mini-Feed items
- Paginate results
- Implement Let Friends Know
- Implement a Share Button
- Add a Discussion Board
- Improve Security
- Get started with Facebook applications

Chapter 13 was devoted to building the interface, and Chapter 14 showed you how to integrate the database. This chapter wraps up the first iteration of the example application by adding support for the Profile page, as well as News and Mini-Feeds. You are not completely out of the database woods yet, though—this chapter also gives you the code you may want to use to paginate database results in long lists (the code is here because it involves both interface and database issues and thus does not fit easily into either Chapter 13 or Chapter 14).

If you have a Facebook application of any complexity, you have probably been focusing on what the application does. Beware of tunnel vision: Remember that you are living in the Facebook world. If users just wanted to use your application, they would be happy to drop by your Web site. The Facebook application's value is increased dramatically as you integrate your functionality with the Facebook world. Two of the most important aspects of that are the Profile page and the News and Mini-Feeds. They are not window dressing—in fact, for many users, they are the heart and soul of Facebook.

NOTE   *Remember that you can download this chapter's code, as described in the Introduction.*

Use Public Canvas Pages and Control Adding Applications

Among the changes made to Facebook in the fall of 2007 was the ability to have public Canvas pages. A public Canvas page is one that can be accessed from outside the Facebook environment with links from other Web sites or the results from search engines. They use the same URL you can use from inside Facebook: http://apps.facebook.com/yourInternalAppName.

Canvas pages are public by default unless they specifically require logging in to Facebook. Thus, the three lines that generally are present at the top of a Canvas page need to be reviewed. The last line, if present, means that the page is not public and is only visible to people who have logged in to Facebook.

```
$facebook = new Facebook($api_key, $secret);
$facebook->require_frame();
$user = $facebook->require_login(); //Remove for public Canvas page
```

Figure 15-1 shows a public Canvas page for a logged-out user. Note, too, the discussion board that has been added: all of the functionality is provided by an FBML element; you will see how to implement it later in this chapter.

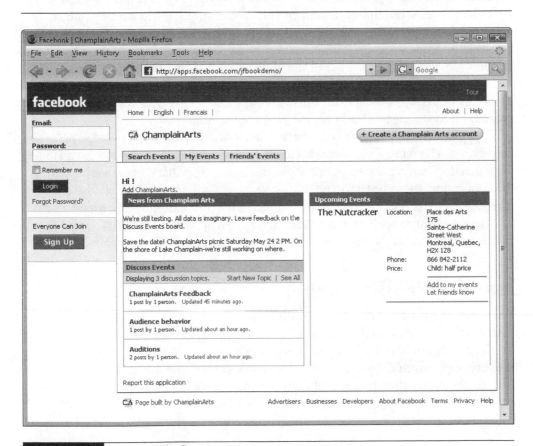

FIGURE 15-1   Use public Canvas pages

Greet the User by Name

If you remove the third line of code to make a public Canvas page, you must change any references you have to the $user variable. On a public Canvas page for a non-logged in user, there is no user information available. However, if a logged-in user accesses a public Canvas page from inside Facebook, you can find out the user's name (perhaps for use in a greeting) by using the following code:

```
<h2>Hi <fb:name firstnameonly="true" uid="loggedinuser"
  useyou="false"/>!</h2>
```

A public Canvas page can serve as an introduction or splash screen for your application. If the user is not logged in, there is no user information, and, thus, no friends' information. Depending on your application, you may choose to display some default or random information to encourage the user to log in or sign up.

In the example application, a popular event is shown (this is the standard behavior). The About link at the upper right of the page goes to another public Canvas page that can describe the application (this is separate from the About page constructed from your application settings in the Developer application). As a result, users can get a little taste of the application and find out what it does.

All other pages in the example application require logging in to Facebook. You do not have to do anything except make certain that the require_login call is present on those pages. Facebook will enforce the rule.

You also can control what is visible to users who have or have not added the application. The more accessible you can make your application with at least a Home page that does not require Facebook login and other pages that do not require adding the application, the easier it will be for people to explore it and ultimately use and add it. You need to require Facebook log in to access the user's identity and friends; you also need to require adding the application to have it appear in the Left Nav and to be able to update the user's Profile page as you can see in the following section.

Update the Profile Page

The Profile page is seen by the user and by friends of the user. It is basically a picture of that person in the context of Facebook and the Facebook applications. You certainly could put a list of all of the user's events on the Profile page, but if every application did so, the page would quickly become unwieldy. For many people, the application boxes on the Profile page work best when they succinctly provide one or two pieces of information about the user in the context of that application. If a friend wants to find out more, a mouse click can always take them to the application.

The difficult part of updating the Profile page is deciding what to put in your box. It should be short and interesting and, of course, relevant to the user and the application. In the example application, it is basically a teaser for the entire project, modeled on the status updates at the upper-right area of the Profile page.

You could use $user = $facebook->require_add() to make certain that the user has added the application, but rather than forcing the add, you can simply check to see if the user has done so. The code described here to update the profile is bracketed as follows. If the user has not added the application, a link to add it is provided.

```
<fb:if-user-has-added-app>
 // the code described below to update the profile
<fb:else> Add
  <a href="<?= $facebook->get_add_url() ?>">ChamplainArts</a>
</fb:else>
</fb:if-user-has-added-app>
```

Here is how the Profile update is done. On the page created by index.php, the user is able to make a choice (how they support the arts) and submit a form. Submitting the form causes an action to take place; most of the time, another page or script is the action, but in this case, it is the same index.php script that is the action. When a user submits the form, index.php is called with the choice selected in the form. When a user simply goes to index.php (by clicking the ChamplainArts icon, for example), there is no parameter passed in. If a parameter is passed in, it is used to update the Profile page, and the user is redirected to the updated Profile page.

> **NOTE** *This structure, in which you create a form on a Facebook page and then call the page itself to handle the process further, is shown in Facebook examples. It is a clever way of keeping functionality together in one place and not proliferating special-purpose pages.*

Update the Profile Box

As in sample Facebook code, you can now do one of two things. If text for the Profile box has been passed into the page with the `profiletext` parameter, you can simply go ahead and set it. On the other hand, you can use the interface on your page for the user to enter new text (in this case, with options, but it could also be with a freeform input field). If the parameter is set, you simply redirect the user to the Profile page after having set it. This code normally executes after the user submits the form created in the next section. You can name the parameter anything you want, but it must match in this section of code and the next one.

Listing 15-1

```php
<?php
  if (isset($_REQUEST['profiletext'])) {
    $facebook->api_client->profile_setFBML(
    '',
    $user,
    $_REQUEST['profiletext'], // FBML for Profile
    '', // FBML for Profile action
    '' // FBML for Mobile profile
    );
    $facebook->redirect(
    $facebook->get_facebook_url() . '/profile.php');
  }
```

> **NOTE**   *If the parameter is passed in, the redirect will take the user to the Profile page and the balance of this page will not be rendered. Also note that in this case, the selection from the form is passed in as a parameter and then passed on to the Profile page. You may want to modify it, add additional items, or otherwise change it before passing it along. Also note that* setFBML *allows you to set any of the profile data—Profile page, Profile action, or Mobile profile. The first, empty, parameter is a legacy from the past.*

Get the User's Text

Now you construct a form to gather the user's data. Note:

- The form's action is this very page. When the parameter is passed in from the form, the preceding section of code will execute.

- The options (implemented with a series of options, all with the same name, profiletext) select the data that will be passed back in to the previous section of code. The name of the option set (and of each option) must match the name checked for in the previous section.

This code is shown in Listing 15-2. It continues the PHP code started in Listing 15-1. It sets two variables with FBML using heredoc as well as an internal variable, $intro, to fill in the text. Then the code is echoed out.

Listing 15-2

```
    $topSupport = <<<top
How do you support the arts?
<div style="clear: both;"/>
<form action="" method="post">
top;

$intro = " I support the arts by";

$myTable = <<<theTable
<table width="100%" border="0" cellpadding="0">
  <tr>
    <td>
      <input type="radio" name="profiletext"
        value="$intro using ChamplainArts!" />
      using ChamplainArts!
    </td>
    <td>
      <input type="radio" name="profiletext"
        value="$intro attending" />
      attending
    </td>
  ... code omitted
  </tr>
</table> theTable;

echo $topSupport;
echo $myTable;
?>

<input name="submit" type="submit"
  value="Update your profile">
<br/>
<br/>
</form>
```

You can do much more with the Profile box, but this is a good way to get started. If you implement this code, Figure 15-2 shows what the Profile box will look like.

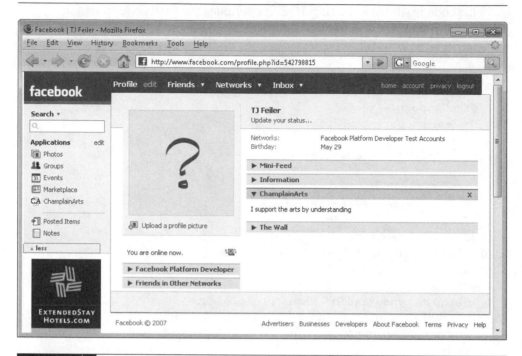

FIGURE 15-2　Updated Profile box

Add News Feed and Mini-Feed Items

Stories in the News Feed and Mini-Feed are critically important to your users; they show them what their friends are doing with your and other applications. The fact that these are people the users know gives their actions more credence (or silliness, perhaps). Create concise, meaningful stories for your users.

In the fall of 2007, Facebook began implementing a new and more powerful way of creating stories for the feeds. This method structures the data in the feeds more rigorously. This makes the stories not just a string of text, but a string of text that is consistent in its format across applications and, more importantly, a string of text with semantics that can be extracted if needed.

An important part of this structuring of stories is that Facebook can aggregate them. If X does something and Y does the same thing, these separate items can be aggregated to say that X and Y do something. The advantage of aggregation is that all of the actors' friends may receive the aggregated story, which, by virtue of its aggregation, may become more interesting. Aggregation also gets rid of the occasional multitude of almost-identical stories in your News Feed as each of your friends adds the same application or does the same thing. (And aggregated stories can be exciting when a user sees that two friends who do not know one another are doing the same thing on Facebook.) Take the time to look at stories in your News Feed. In particular, look at aggregated and updated stories and work back through the code in this section to see how they are structured.

> NOTE   `publishActionOfUser` *and* `publishStoryToUser` *are simpler methods of publishing to the News Feed and Mini-Feed. Also note that a user must have added your application and given you permission to update the News and Mini-Feed.*

The heart of this is the new `publishTemplatizedAction` function in the API. As usual, you need not bother to call the API; you can call it through the Facebook class. The key concepts are the *title* and *body* templates, as well as an *actor* or *target*.

Actor and Target

The actor is the user who initiates the action. If the story is aggregated, all of the actors' names will appear in the story. A target is just that: the object affected by the actor. For example: Roger (actor) took Carly (target) to lunch. Both actors and targets are Facebook users (or Facebook Pages, which are quasi-users). Thus, although Roger (actor) may move the sofa (target), the sofa cannot be a target in a Facebook story. The text may appear, but you would not use the {target} syntax.

Title

The title describes the action. It has two components: a template and data.

Title Template

The title template uses data elements and other parameters (both enclosed in brackets), together with text, to create the template for the title. You may also use the `fb:name` tag, and you can use the anchor (a) tag to insert a hyperlink. If there is any possibility that your stories will be aggregated, you should also include the `fb:if-multiple-actors` element so that single and plural usage is handled correctly, as in the following example:

```
<if-multiple-actors>
    are
  <fb:else>
    is
  </fb:else>
</if-multiple-actors>
```

A typical title template is simple. It uses the actor parameter that is passed in and combines it with text:

```
{actor} did something with the X application.
```

You can build up the template with components, which will be described in the data:

```
{actor} is interested in {event}.
```

Pulling the code snippets together, you could create this title template:

```
{actor}
  <if-multiple-actors>
    are
    <fb:else>
      is
    </fb:else>
  </if-multiple-actors>interested in {event} on
<a href='http://$canvas_page'>ChamplainArts</a>
```

Title Data

You use the title data to supply specific data for the template. In the case of the example, this will have to be generated by PHP—which it usually is—and will describe an event. When the data is filled in after a database access, this is what the title data could look like (note the escaped quotes):

```
{\"event\":\"$eventName\"}
```

You can have multiple pairs of names and data; separate them by commas (this is a JSON array). The combination of template and data shown here would generate the text, "X is interested in an event on ChamplainArts." ChamplainArts is a link to the Canvas page. (Note that there is no title data in this particular template.)

Body

Like the title, the body has a template and data. It also may have a general component for a comment. It provides additional information about the title.

Body Template

The structure of the body template is identical to that of the title template. The only difference is that the body template has more possible FBML tags that may be included: fb:userlink, fb:name, fb:if-multiple-actors, a, b, and i. Here is an example of a body template.

```
{event} is at {location} on {date}.
```

Body Data

Likewise, the structure of the body data is the same as that of the title template. Here is body data that would work with the body template just shown. Note the escaped quotes.

```
{ \"event\":\"$eventNameAndLink\",
  \"location\":\"$eventLocation\",
  \"date\":\"$eventDate\"
}
```

Body General

If you provide markup for the body general component, it will not be aggregated. Titles and bodies will be aggregated, but this will appear as-is and only once. (See the following Note on aggregation). This cannot contain any variable information.

Images

You can provide up to four images and their links that can be used in the story. If not provided, these are set to null if you use the $facebook->api_client >feed_publishTemplatizedAction call from PHP.

Targets

If there is a list of one or more users affected by the actor's action, you can provide such a list. You can access the list using {target} in the title or body template. If not provided, this is set to an empty string if you use the $facebook->api_client->feed_publishTemplatizedAction call from PHP.

> **NOTE** *Aggregation occurs if the title and body templates are identical and the target (if provided) is identical for all of the stories. The title and body data arrays must contain the same keys and values. One of the stories' body general data will be used—you do not know which one. You can force the body templates to be identical by not providing them. Some developers provide only a fairly generic title to make aggregation more likely; a body general complete is used to provide more details.*

Implement a Template Story

The main reason for updating a News Feed in the example application is when someone selects an event for their list. The processing is initiated by clicking on Add to My Events, and it is executed by add_remove_event.php, as described in the previous chapter. After the necessary error checking and database updates, the user is redirected to myCAEs.php, which displays the My Events tab.

You need to make a change to the redirection at the bottom of add_remove_event.php. In the case of adding an event, you will want to indicate that a story should be created by myCAEs.php. Thus, change the bottom of add_remove_event.php so as to add a doNews parameter in the case of adding an event (its value does not matter; you just want to see if it has been set).

> NOTE
>
> *Do you want to publish stories for removes? Look at other applications to make your choice. In the US Politics application from Facebook, for example, stories for supporting politicians are published; removing support is not published. It has to do with who your users are and what data you are dealing with.*

```
if ( $action == 'add' ) {
  // code removed
  $facebook->redirect ( http://$canvas_page"."myCAEs.php?
    fbuid=$fbuid&caeid=$caeid&doNews=1");
};
```

At the very bottom of the script, the default redirection should be implemented.

```
$facebook->redirect("http://$canvas_page"."myCAEs.php");
```

In order to fill the template for the story, some information from the database is needed. A new function will be added to lib.php. Called get_from_database_brief, it will retrieve the key items of a single event's data; its name suggests that at some point, another function might retrieve all of an event's data.

> NOTE
>
> *As an application starts to grow, you may consider adjusting your naming convention. For now, the database accesses in this application are all centered around events. In a different application, this function might be better named* get_event_from_database_brief. *The tradeoff is usually between longer, more complex, and more descriptive titles and shorter ones.*

Test with Hard-Coded Data

This code can be quite complex. The testing console shown in Figure 15-3 is a vital tool in getting it to work. Test with hard-coded data until you are certain each of the parameters is correct.

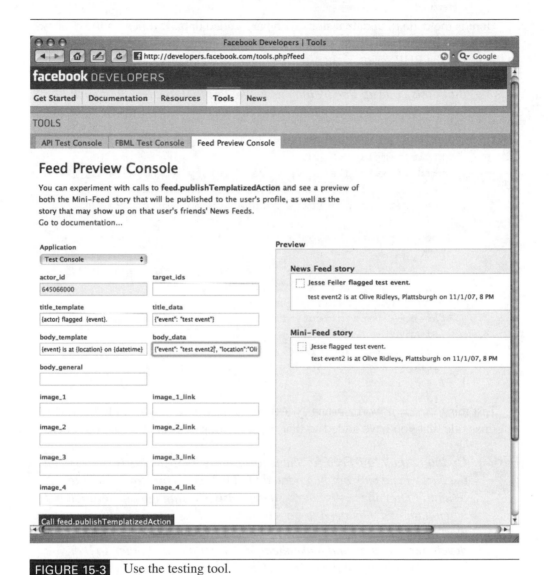

FIGURE 15-3   Use the testing tool.

Once you are satisfied that the hard-coded data is correct, you can begin to implement the same hard-coded data in your application. For all of the hard-coded data that may vary, you will need to make database calls. To begin with, you can update myCAEs.php to make the necessary call to create the story with variables containing the dummy data. Then you will pass those variables in from the new `get_from_database_brief` function.

Here is the code to update a story with hard-coded data. It relies on the doNews parameter; if it is set, this code should execute and create the story. Place this code at the top of the PHP script, right after the other isset calls.

TIP *Build this code up line by line, using the test tool to check that each line works before assembling it as shown here.*

```
if (isset($_REQUEST['doNews'])){
  $title_template="{actor}
    <fb:if-multiple-actors>are<fb:else>is</fb:else>
    </fb:if-multiple-actors> interested in an event on
    <a href='http://$canvas_page'>ChamplainArts</a>.";

  $body_template="{event} is at {location} on {datetime}";
  $body_data="{\"event\": \"test event2\",
          \"location\":\"Olive Ridleys, Plattsburgh\",
          \"datetime\":\"11/1/07, 8 PM\"}'";
  $body_general=null;
  $facebook->api_client->feed_publishTemplatizedAction(
    $fbuid,
    $title_template, $title_data,
    $body_template, $body_data, $body_general);
} // end isset
```

Test this to see if it works properly. After your test, you may want to comment out this code that you have added so that myCAEs.php can function as it did before.

TIP *Updating the Mini-Feed for the actor usually happens fairly quickly, but the News Feed may not be updated until the following day. Also, there is a limit of ten calls in 48 hours, so aggressive testing may generate too much data and may need to be repeated two days later. Finally, if you are working on a yet-unpublished application, you may need to create two developer accounts and make them friends with one another so that you can test both sides of the relationship (the action of the actor that shows up in that person's Mini-Feed and the action of the actor that shows up in the actor's friends' News Feeds).*

Retrieve Data from the Database

As noted previously, you will need a new function in lib.php to retrieve an event's data from the database. You already have code in there to retrieve events in various ways (a user's events, a user's friends' events, and so forth). Creating this new function is simple because it builds on a subset of the code you already have.

```
function get_from_database_brief ( $caeid ) {
  mysql_select_db($GLOBALS['database_ChamplainArtsNetSol'],
    $GLOBALS['ChamplainArtsNetSol']);
  $query_browseResults =
    "SELECT e.eventName, e.eventDate,
      e.eventTime, e.webPublic, l.locationName
    FROM events e, locations l
    WHERE e.id = $caeid AND e.locationID = l.id;";
  $browseResults = mysql_query($query_rsBrowseResults,
  $GLOBALS['ChamplainArtsNetSol'])
    or die(mysql_error());
  $row_browseResults = mysql_fetch_assoc($rsBrowseResults);
  return $row_browseResults;
}
```

All of this code occurs in a longer version in `get_from_database_and_render`, which was described in the previous chapter.

NOTE   *This evolution is common in Facebook applications—particularly those that use databases. The first set of code is often the most complex. As you add functionality, you reuse, extend, or otherwise build on the code that was so time-consuming to create in the first place.*

There actually is one further addition you should make to this function's code. Remember that one of the goals of this type of architecture is to keep the database code as separate as possible from the interface and other Facebook code. In order to call `get_from_database_brief` and effectively use its result, you need to know what is returned. You could read the code, which is not very lengthy, but it is better to provide an explicit comment in case someone uses this code later on and is not familiar with SQL. So the following comment at the top of the function would be a good idea:

```
/*
This function returns:
$browseResults ['eventName']
$browseResults ['locationName']
$browseResults ['eventDate']
$browseResults ['eventTime']
$browseResults [webPublic]
*/
```

Integrate the Data with the Templates

Now, all that is left is to call this function and move the data into them, replacing the hard-coded values. Here is one way to do that. This is the code that appears at the top of `myCAEs.php` to publish the story:

Listing 15-3

```
if (isset($_REQUEST['doNews'])) {
  $results = get_from_database_brief ($caeid);
  $eventName = $results['eventName'];
  $eventLocation = $results['locationName'];
  $eventDate = $results['eventDate'];
  $eventTime = $results['eventTime'];
  if ($results['webPublic'] != null) {
    $eventNameAndLink =
      "<a href='http://".$results['webPublic']."'>".
      $eventName."</a>";
  } else {
  $eventNameAndLink = $eventName;
  }
  $title_template="{actor}
    <fb:if-multiple-actors>are<fb:else>is</fb:else>
    </fb:if-multiple-actors> interested in an event on
    <a href='http://$canvas_page'>ChamplainArts</a>.";
    $body_template = '{event} is at {location} on {date}.';
    $body_data = "{\"event\":\"$eventNameAndLink\",
      \"location\":\"$eventLocation\",
      \"date\":\"$eventDate\"}";
    $body_general=null;
    $facebook->api_client->
      feed_publishTemplatizedAction($fbuid,
      $title_template, $title_data,
      $body_template, $body_data, $body_general);
}
```

Paginate Results

The final tweak to this iteration of the application is to paginate the results, as shown in Figure 15-4.

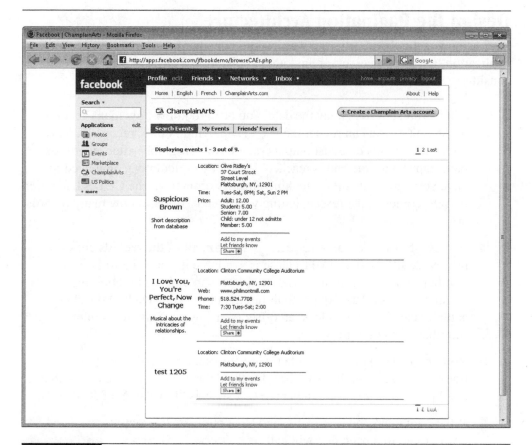

FIGURE 15-4   Paginate the results.

The pagination code implements the summary information of the records displayed, as well as the First/Last and page number links shown at the right above and below the data.

Pagination is commonly done when you are retrieving database data, but it also comes into play whenever you are displaying more data than will comfortably fit on one screen. (Scrollbars are useful, but many interface designers think carefully about using them, preferring to have some control over the data by paginating or summarizing it into a tight list, from which links go to more complex data displays.)

Design the Pagination Architecture

Pagination is actually a fairly tricky procedure, whether it is done in a Facebook application, a word processor, or any other application. Here are the main points to consider:

■ When you start to display the data, you need to know how many records there are (so you can render the text "Displaying N of X records"). Most code that outputs data just outputs record (or paragraph) after record (or paragraph) until the end is reached. In order to calculate X, you need to have some mechanism for looking ahead. Fortunately, the COUNT function in SQL comes to the rescue, letting you quickly find out how many records are to be retrieved.

■ In `get_from_database_and_render`, all of the records are retrieved, although a LIMIT clause is available if you want to limit the number of records returned. You need a way to call the function repeatedly to get chunks of data. Again, SQL has a tool for you. The LIMIT clause actually can take two values: an offset (starting row) and row count (number of rows to retrieve).

■ Row numbers in the LIMIT clause are zero-relative. You need to keep track of the zero-relative numbers for the database calls while being able to display the one-relative numbers in text such as "Display N of X records."

■ When you make the First, Last, and page number links active, you need a way to go to a page that will call `get_from_database_and_render` for the appropriate chunk and display it. Here, the solution will be parallel to the Profile page code described earlier in this chapter. The First, Last, and page number links will call the same page that called `get_from_database_and_render`, passing in the appropriate control information. Thus, the calling page (such as `myCAEs.php`) will call `get_from_database_and_render` as before, but if there are chunks to display beyond the first one, `get_from_database_and_render` will turn around and call myCAEs.php for the second chunk, and myCAEs.php, in turn, will call `get_from_database_and_render` until all of the data has been retrieved and rendered). If you are not interested in paginated data (as is the case on the Home page, where you display the single most popular event), everything should work as it has done before.

■ And finally, if you are displaying records 1 to 3 of 3, you do not want any pagination information to appear. Only if there are unseen records before or after the visible chunk do you want to get into the pagination.

If you are using database data, this method is much more effective than retrieving all of the data and then paginating the chunks of already-retrieved data. There are more database calls, but if you are retrieving a modest number of records at a time, each of the database calls should be fast. Retrieving all of the records can take a while and use large amounts of memory.

Use the Facebook Pagination Styles

If you look at the source of a paginated Facebook application, you can see the styles used. Here is the basic structure for the pagination that often appears at the top of a page. Dummy data has been inserted.

Listing 15-4

```
<div class="bar clearfix summary_bar">
  <div class="summary">
    <strong>
      Displaying profiles 21 - 30 out of over 500.
    </strong>
  </div>
  <ul class="pagerpro" id="pag_nav_links">
    <li>
      <a href="">Prev</a>
    </li>
    <li>
      <a href="">15</a>
    </li>
    <li class="current">
      <a href="">16</a>
    </li>
    <li>
      <a href="">17</a>
    </li>
    <li>
      <a href="">Next</a>
    </li>
  </ul>
</div>
```

At the bottom of a page, the summary information (total numbers of records) may not be displayed because it may only be shown at the top, as is the case in Figure 15-4. Thus, at the bottom of the page, here is how the code shown in Listing 15-4 would begin:

```
<div class="bar clearfix footer_bar">
  <ul class="pagerpro" id="pag_nav_links">
```

Note that the current page uses the `current` class for the bar above the page number in the appropriate list element.

This code, with the appropriate href and page number values, will need to be generated in `get_from_database_and_render`. It makes sense to put it there, rather than in `render_cae`, so that `render_cae` can focus entirely on displaying the data. This means that `get_from_database_and_render` will handle rendering the no-data message as well as the pagination.

Change get_from_database_and_render Parameters

You need to add new parameters to `get_from_database_and_render`. Table 15-1 shows the parameters as they will be at the end of this chapter. The four marked with asterisks are for pagination.

Parameter	Meaning
$nColumns	Number of columns to return in display
$owner	mine/null (to control Add to My Events/Remove from My Events)
$useUser	Retrieve for the uid in the next parameter
$user	user (passed through to render_cae_columns) as well as used for retrieval if $useUser is set to any value
$friends	List of friends uids to use for retrieving friends' events
$popular	If not null, the LIMIT of the number of most popular events to retrieve.
$baseURL	*The page that calls this. Can be a relative URL, as is the case with the URLs in the tabs and actions in the pages in the example application.
$offset	*Number of records to skip before retrieval. (If you skip 9 records, the first record retrieved is 10).
$rowCount	*Number of rows to retrieve for each page.
$totalRows	*Total number of rows in the query. This will initially be sent to `get_from_database_and_render` as zero; it will be returned to the calling page and then sent in subsequent calls.
$caeid	The ID of a single event to retrieve.

TABLE 15-1   New Parameters for get_from_database_and_render

Change the Page That Calls get_from_database_and_render

Instead of simply calling get_from_database_and_render once, the calling page may wind up in this back-and-forth calling to get all of the chunks (that is, of course, assuming the user wants the various chunks and uses the pagination controls rather than clicking on a tab or action to go somewhere else). If the page is called with parameters in the URL, they will need to be unloaded. If they are not present (that is, if the page is called as it is now, by clicking on a tab or other link), default values need to be set. This code can go at the top of the function for a page such as browseCAEs.php:

```
if (isset($_REQUEST['offset'])) {
  $offset = $_REQUEST['offset'];
} else {
  $offset = 0;
};
if (isset($_REQUEST['rowCount'])) {
  $rowCount = $_REQUEST['rowCount'];
} else {
  $rowCount = 3;
};
if (isset($_REQUEST['totalRows'])) {
  $totalRows = $_REQUEST['totalRows'];
} else if {
  $totalRows = 0;
};
```

This sets the parameters appropriately for starting the first chunk retrieval; chunk size is set at 3—you can vary it, depending on your data.

The other change is to the actual function call to include these parameters. Here is the call as it will be used in browseCAEs.php.

```
echo get_from_database_and_render (
  1, '', null, $user, null, null,
  "http://$canvas_page"."browseCAEs.php",
  $offset, $rowCount, $totalRows );
);
```

At this point, everything should function normally if the page is called as it is now (as from a tab). You might want to test that nothing has been broken at this point. Then you can go on to the next step.

Implement Pagination in get_from_database_and_render

Now it is just a matter of implementing the pagination. There are several sections of code to write, but they are similar to code you have already written. All of them are in `get_from_database_and_render`.

Set Default Limits

Instead of hard-coding LIMIT in the SQL calls, you can create a string that has the appropriate limit information, as passed in with the new parameters. You can use `$baseURL` as a test to see if pagination is requested. If you do, here is the code to insert at the top of the function:

```
if ( $baseURL ) {
  $limit = "LIMIT $offset, $rowCount";
} else {
  $limit = "";
};
```

In all of the queries, add `$limit` at the end of the query, just before the semicolon. For example, here is the end of the query that retrieves friends' events:

```
WHERE fbuid IN ($friends))$limit;";
```

Count the Records

The various queries you have coded all begin with code that looks like this:

Listing 15-5

```
mysql_select_db($GLOBAL['database_ChamplainArtsNetSol'],
$GLOBAL['ChamplainArtsNetSol']);
if ( $useUser ) { // My Events
  $query_browseResults = "SELECT
```

The first time through, you will need to count the total number of records. This code needs to be inserted between the second and third lines, as follows:

```
mysql_select_db($GLOBAL['database_ChamplainArtsNetSol'],
 $GLOBAL['ChamplainArtsNetSol']);
 //start of added code
 if ( $useUser ) { // My Events

   if ( $baseURL and $totalRows==0 ) {
     //want pagination and this is the first call
     $count_browseResults =
```

```
"SELECT COUNT(*) FROM events e, locations l
  WHERE e.locationID = l.id AND e.id IN
    (SELECT caeid FROM userevents WHERE fbuid=$user);";
$countResults = mysql_query($count_browseResults,
  $GLOBAL['ChamplainArtsNetSol']) or die(mysql_error());
$row_countResults =
  mysql_fetch_row($countResults );
$totalRows = $row_countResults[ 0 ];
};
//end of added code

$query_browseResults = "SELECT
```

What you do is take the query that is already there, copy and paste it, and remove all of the columns that would be retrieved, replacing them with a COUNT(*) function call. Keep subqueries, WHERE clauses, and the like. This is a fast database call that will get you the total number of rows, which you can then store in $totalRows.

Write the Pagination HTML

The pagination HTML code starts by handling the case in which there is no data to be displayed. Beyond that, it sets variables for the values of the first and last rows to be able to display the starting and ending record numbers. It then sets variables containing links to next and previous pages. Listing 15-6 shows this section of code. This code picks up after the SELECT statement shown previously in Listing 15-5.

> TIP *For the sake of clarity, if it is verbose; you can shorten it substantially if you want by removing some of the variables and simply calculating row and page numbers as needed. Also note that this code relies on the $baseURL, $offset, $rowCount, and $totalRows parameters that are passed in. These are general concepts that you can use for any code based on this architecture. There is only one thing that you will have to customize in the code shown here: change the word "Events" in the phrase "Displaying Events" so that it reflects what you are displaying. Other than that, you can use this code without modification.*

Listing 15-6

```
$browseResults = mysql_query($query_browseResults,
  $GLOBALS['ChamplainArtsNetSol']) or die(mysql_error());

if ( mysql_num_rows ( $browseResults ) < 1 ) {
  return "No data available";
};
```

```
// need to paginate
if ( $baseURL and ( $totalRows > $rowCount ) ) {

  // set row/record numbers (0-relative)
  if ( $offset >= $rowCount ) {
    $offsetPrev = $offset - $rowCount;
  } else {
    $offsetPrev = 0;
  };
  if ( $offset < $totalRows ) {
    $offsetNext = $offset + $rowCount;
  } else {
    $offsetNext = 0;
  };

  // is the last page a partial page?
  $lastPageRows = $totalRows % $rowCount;
  if ( $offset < $totalRows ) {
    if ( $lastPageRows == 0 ) {
      $offsetLast = $totalRows - $rowCount;
    } else {
      $offsetLast = $totalRows - $lastPageRows;
    }
  }

  // set 1-relative row/record numbers
  // (for UI Displaying 1-4 message)
  $firstRow1Relative = $offset + 1;
  $lastRow1Relative = min ( ( $offset + $rowCount ),
    $totalRows );

  // set page numbers (1-relative)
  $currentPageNumber =  floor ( ( $offset / $rowCount ) ) + 1;
  $totalPages = ( ceil ( $totalRows / $rowCount ) );
  if ( $currentPageNumber > 1 ) {
    $previousPageNumber = $currentPageNumber - 1;
  } else {
    $previousPageNumber = null;
  };
  if ( ( $currentPageNumber < $totalPages ) and
    ( $lastPageRows != 0 ) ) {
    $nextPageNumber = $currentPageNumber + 1;
  } else {
    $nextPageNumber = null;
  };
```

```
    // set links
    if ( $offset > 0 ) {
      $firstPageLink =
        "<li><a href=\"$baseURL?
          rowCount=$rowCount&totalRows=$totalRows&offset=0\
">First
          </a>
        </li>";
      if ( $previousPageNumber ) {
        $prevPageLink =
        "<li><a href=\"$baseURL?
          rowCount=$rowCount&totalRows=$totalRows&
          offset=$offsetPrev\">$previousPageNumber</a>
        </li>";
      }
    } else {
      $firstPageLink = null;
      $prevPageLink = null;
    }

    $currentPageLink =
      "<li class='current'><a href='#'>$currentPageNumber</
a></li>";

    if ( $lastRow1Relative < $totalRows ) {
      if ( $nextPageNumber ) {
        $nextPageLink =
          "<li><a href=\"$baseURL?
            rowCount=$rowCount&totalRows=$totalRows&
            offset=$offsetNext\">$nextPageNumber</a>
          </li>";
      }
      $lastPageLink =
        "<li><a href=\"$baseURL?
          rowCount=$rowCount&totalRows=$totalRows
          &offset=$offsetLast\">Last</a><br>
        </li>";
    } else {
      $nextPageLink = null;
      $lastPageLink = null;
    };
```

The heart of pagination is the heredoc code that uses the variables set up in Listing 15-6 to display the data. That code is shown in Listing 15-7. Notice that between the header and footer, the actual data returned is passed through to render_ cae which returns its rendered results that are added to the $myResults string. Note, too, that another variable $canvas_page is used; it has been added to config.php and is described later in this chapter.

Listing 15-7

```
// set header
$myResults = <<<header
<div class="bar clearfix summary_bar">
  <div class="summary">
    <strong>Displaying events
      $firstRow1Relative - $lastRow1Relative
      out of $totalRows.
    </strong>
  </div>
  <ul class="pagerpro" id="pag_nav_links">
    $firstPageLink
    $prevPageLink
    $currentPageLink
    $nextPageLink
    $lastPageLink
  </ul>
</div>
header;
  } else {
    // all results fit on one page, do not need pagination
    $myResults = '';
  };

  // process records
  while ( $row_browseResults =
    mysql_fetch_assoc($browseResults ) ) {
      $myResults .= render_cae ( $nColumns, $owner, $user,
        $row_browseResults, $canvas_page );
  };

  // set footer
  if ( $baseURL  and $totalRows > $rowCount  ) {
    $myResults .= <<<footer
<div class="bar clearfix footer_bar">
  <ul class="pagerpro" id="pag_nav_links">
```

```
      $firstPageLink
      $prevPageLink
      $currentPageLink
      $nextPageLink
      $lastPageLink
   </ul>
</div> footer;    }
```

Implement Let Friends Know

In order to implement Let Friends Know, you need to implement another page on your site, but do not worry, the page is almost completely written for you already. If you have a template page, make a copy, and customize it. Otherwise take any of your Canvas pages and remove the page-specific information, leaving just the dashboard and general navigation such as tabs. Name the file invite_friends.php.

It will be called with two parameters:

- `fbuid` is the Facebook uid of the user.

- `caeid` is the id of the event

Test if they are present and set local variables. Notice that if caeid is passed in, you use the brief database call to set other variables.

```php
if (isset($_REQUEST['fbuid'])) {
  $fbuid = $_REQUEST['fbuid']; }
if (isset($_REQUEST['caeid'])) {
  $caeid = $_REQUEST['caeid'];
  $results = get_from_database_brief ($caeid);
  $eventName = $results['eventName'];
  $eventLocation = $results['locationName'];
  $eventDate = $results['eventDate'];
  $eventTime = $results['eventTime'];
}
```

Implement an `fb:request-form` and use the `fb:multi-friend-selector` to invite people to add your application and to tell them about an event.

Here is the code. All that you have to change is the underlined text. This will create an invitation to a ChamplainArts event with the content you specify. You can also send requests (by setting invite to false); and you can use another page for the action, which is the page to which the user will return.

```
<fb:request-form
  action="index.php"
```

```
      method="POST"
      invite="true"
      type="ChamplainArts event"
      content="I found <?php echo $eventName; ?> on
        <?php echo $eventDate; ?> at <?php echo $eventLocation; ?>
        on the ChamplainArts app. Let me know if you're interested
        in going.<?php echo htmlentities("
          <fb:req-choice url=\"http:\/\/www.facebook.com\/add.php?
          api key=$api key\"
          label=\"Add ChamplainArts\" />
        ");?>">
  <fb:multi-friend-selector
    showborder="true"
    actiontext="Let your friends know about
      <?php echo $eventName; ?>."">
    <fb:req-choice url="htpp://<?php $canvas_page?>myCAEs.php"
      label="Yes" />
</fb:request-form>
```

Implement the Share Button

The Share button needs to be fully implemented. Facebook does almost everything for you, but you will need to supply the link as well as the title. You may choose to share a link to another environment (such as your main database), or you can share a link to your own Facebook application. It is this strategy that is implemented here. It involves a minor change to your index.php file along with some slight changes to lib.php.

The change to index.php is to allow a $caeid parameter to be passed in. If it is present, then the call to get_from_database_and_render at the bottom will pass it in as a parameter. Thus, in index.php test for the presence of the parameter:

```
if (isset($_REQUEST['caeid'])) {
  $caeid = $_REQUEST['caeid'];
else
  $caeid = null;
}
```

Add $caeid to the end of the parameters in the call.

```
echo get_from_database_and_render ( 1, '', null, $user, null,
  1, null, null, null, null, $caeid);
```

You can use the PHP option of setting right-most parameters to null in the function declaration:

```
function get_from_database_and_render ( $nColumns, $owner,
  $useUser, $user, $friends, $popular, $baseURL,
  $offset, $rowCount, $totalRows, $caeid=null) {
```

This means that at least for now, you only need to change the call in index.php: other calls need not be changed and the value of $caeid will be automatically set to null.

Add More SELECT Options

In this chapter, the SELECT code shown at the end of Listing 15-5 has been the same as described in the previous chapter. You will need to flesh that out to accommodate your various database needs. Here is what that section of code will look like now as it lets you retrieve your events, your friends' events, and other sets of events. Note that the fields retrieved are shown only in the first SELECT query so that the structure is easier to see. Likewise, the full code for counting the records to be retrieved is only shown in the first query.

Listing 15-8

```
if ( $useUser ) {
  // My Events
  if ( $baseURL and $totalRows==0 ) {
    //want pagination and this is the first call
    $count_browseResults =
      "SELECT COUNT(*) FROM events e, locations l
      WHERE e.locationID = l.id AND e.id IN
      (SELECT caeid FROM userevents WHERE fbuid=$user)$limit;";
    $countResults = mysql_query($count_browseResults,
      $GLOBALS['ChamplainArtsNetSol']) or die(mysql_error());
    $row_countResults = mysql_fetch_row($countResults );
    $totalRows = $row_countResults [ 0 ];
  };

  $query_browseResults =
    "SELECT e.id, e.eventName, e.eventDay, e.eventMonth,
      e.eventYear, e.eventDate, e.shortDesc, e.webPublic,
      e.phonePublic, e.eventTime, e.shortDesc, e.priceNormal,
      e.priceStudent, e.priceSenior, e.priceMember, e.priceChild,
      e.eventImageURL, l.locationName, l.address1, l.address2,
      l.city, l.state, l.zip, l. country
```

```
      FROM events e, locations l
      WHERE e.locationID = l.id AND e.id IN
        (SELECT caeid FROM userevents WHERE fbuid=$user)$limit;";
} elseif ( $friends ) {
  // My Friends Events
  if ( $baseURL and $totalRows==0 ) {
    //want pagination and this is the first call
    $count_browseResults = "SELECT COUNT(*) FROM events e, locations l
        WHERE e.locationID = l.id AND e.id IN
      (SELECT caeid FROM userevents
        WHERE fbuid IN ($friends) ) $limit;";
    // set $countResults, $row_countResults,
    // and $totalRows as above
  };

  $query_browseResults = "SELECT
    //fields omitted
    FROM events e, locations l
    WHERE e.locationID = l.id AND e.id IN
      (SELECT caeid FROM userevents WHERE fbuid IN ($friends))
    $limit;";
} elseif ( $popular ) {
  // Most Popular Events
  if ( $baseURL and $totalRows==0 ) {
    //want pagination and this is the first call
    $count_browseResults = "SELECT COUNT(*) FROM events e,
      locations l,
      (SELECT caeid, fbuid, count(*)as num
        FROM userevents group by caeid order by num desc) u
      WHERE u.caeid=e.id AND l.id=e.locationID LIMIT $popular";
    // set $countResults, $row_countResults,
    //and $totalRows as above
  };
  $query_browseResults = "SELECT
    //fields omitted
    FROM
      events e,
      locations l,
      (SELECT caeid, fbuid, count(*)as num
        FROM userevents group by caeid order by num desc) u
      WHERE u.caeid=e.id AND l.id=e.locationID LIMIT $popular";
} elseif ( $caeid ) {
```

```
   // One Event
   $query_browseResults = "SELECT
     //fields omitted
     FROM events e, locations l WHERE e.locationID = l.id
       AND e.id = $caeid;";
} else {
   // Browse Events
   if ( $baseURL and $totalRows==0 ) {
     //want pagination and this is the first call
     $count_browseResults = "SELECT COUNT(*) FROM events e,
       locations l WHERE e.locationID = l.id; $limit";
     // set $countResults, $row_countResults,
     //and $totalRows as above
   };
   $query_browseResults = "SELECT
     //fields omitted
     FROM events e, locations l
     WHERE e.locationID = l.id $limit;";
};

$browseResults = mysql_query($query_browseResults,
  $GLOBALS['ChamplainArtsNetSol']) or die(mysql_error());
```

Add a Discussion Board

Any features that increase the possibility of user interaction tend to make your application more popular. Adding a Discussion Board certainly is one of them. The fb:board element takes care of everything for you. All you have to do is provide an internal identifier for the board and a title to be displayed. The other settings can be adjusted as you see fit. (Obviously the introductory text will change depending on your application.) This change is made in index.php.

```
<div class="list_item_first clearfix">
   Save the date! ChamplainArts picnic Saturday May 24 2 PM.
   On the shore of Lake Champlain-we're still working on where.
   <br />
   <br />
   <fb:board xid="CA board"
     canpost="true"
     candelete="false"
     canmark="false"
     cancreatetopic="true"
```

```
   numtopics="5"
   returnurl="http://<?php echo $canvas_page;?>">
   <fb:title>Discuss Events</fb:title>
 </fb:board>
</div>
```

Improve Security

Security is something that needs to be planned from the start, particularly if your application uses non-trivial data. In general, there are few special Facebook security considerations: You need to do the same work you would do in any Web application. This book has focused on the Facebook side of things, and in order to make the architecture of the code as clear as possible, some standard security matters have been left out until now.

Perhaps the most important is to concern yourself about the potential of what are called injection attacks into SQL databases. You may be constructing a query such as that shown here where the underlined portion comes from a user.

```
SELECT * from mytable WHERE password = "mypassword";
```

You can provide a secure entry field on a Web page into which users can type their passwords, and all will be well if everyone plays by the rules.

If someone enters the following code into the password field, the database will be unlocked.

```
' OR ''='
```

The reason is that the constructed SQL would look like this, with the underlined code representing the user input.

```
SELECT * FROM myTable WHERE password='' OR ''=''
```

The solution to this weakness is to use the PHP `mysql_real_escape_string` function. This function takes two parameters: a string that is to be passed into an SQL query, and an optional link connection (the result of the previous `mysql_connect` call). Every value that a user may have entered should be passed through this function. (You can also call it in constructing the query.)

```
$safeUserInput = mysql_real_escape_string($user);
```

In addition to the possibility of injection attacks, the standard guidance for the visibility of parameters in URLs applies. Sending variables in forms is more secure than placing them in URLs, but your application may need a degree of openness that makes this impractical in some cases. (Public Canvas pages, in particular, may want to respond to parameterized URLs.) The data that you are managing will determine the degree of security you need to implement. If you are using PHP, protect data by using htmlentities and urlencode. The first function converts special characters such as a < to a string such as <. You can use it to prepare data you are about to display so that embedded characters such as < are not interpreted as HTML syntax. The second converts non-alphanumeric characters to % followed by two hexadecimal numbers. With urlencode, a < would be converted to %3C. You can use urlencode to make the URLs you generate more robust.

The only Facebook-specific security concerns you need to consider are those involving public Canvas pages and adding of applications. As long as you require a Facebook login, you have some certainty about your user. And if you require a user to add an application, you know the user has seen the privacy dialog. The choice between openness and security is age-old. Make certain that you consider the risks and benefits.

Get Started with Facebook Applications

Yes, you're back at the beginning, ready to get started with your own Facebook applications. When you reach this point in developing your own Facebook application, there are a few additional steps to take.

Most importantly, go back to the Developer application, and click See My Apps in the My Applications box at the right of the page. Edit the settings for your application one last time. If you still have Developer mode set, now is the time to change it. Revisit some of the pages, such as Post-Add URL, that you may not have implemented. If you used a placeholder page for About or Help, make certain that it is replaced by a real page.

If you have prevented updating of News Feeds and Mini-Feeds, enable those features in the application settings (and in commented-out code in your application). Gather input from friends and colleagues about what works and what doesn't.

If you are using templates for news stories, register them in your application settings. Create a new application to use for testing. Set up a parallel environment with a complete set of files in another directory and link that directory to the new Facebook application. If you are using a database, create a new database for the new application. If you use the config.php file described in this book, you will be able to switch to the new environment by simply changing that file; the coding conventions in this book rely on config.php variables such as $canvas_page so that your code will not have a hard-coded application URL in it. Read the installation instructions in the downloadable code for more tips. The process of installing the example code is precisely the set of steps that you need to do to create a test environment.

Here is the config.php file as it exists at this point.

```php
<?php
  $api_key = yourAPIKey;
  $secret  = yourSecretKey;

  $canvas_page = 'apps.facebook.com/yourInternalAppName/';

  $offsiteLink = 'http://www.yourWebSite.com/index.html';
  $offsiteLinkName = 'yourWebSite.com';

  require_once('../Connections/ChamplainArtsNetSol.php');
?>
```

And then there is one more step that is a prudent one to take, even though it may temporarily break your application. Begin by making a backup copy of everything. Then, if you have not been keeping up with new versions of the Facebook client software, download and install the current files. In general, things do not break when Facebook adds new features, but it is a good idea to make certain that you have the most current interfaces and that they work. (If they do not work, you still have your backup copy that you could install.)

TIP   *Periodically check for updates to the Facebook client files and download them so that you have as few surprises at the end as possible.*

Developing Facebook applications is an iterative process. Remember what it is that you are trying to do—adding new features that make the application more valuable is good, but adding bells and whistles can drive away users who are used to the simplicity and focus of Facebook and its applications.

Particularly at the beginning, look at the Facebook statistics from the Developer application page, as well as your own server statistics and the database statistics. (Server and database statistics may be aggregated for you by your Internet service provider, or ISP.) They will tell you how the application is performing and how people are using it. If it is linked to an external Web site, watch to see how that site's traffic rises or falls. People may be drawn to explore further after using the Facebook application; conversely, they may want the deeper involvement that your Web site may offer.

Facebook is a new environment for developers and users. Everyone is learning about it as it evolves, which is part of the excitement. What is true about Facebook today may not be true tomorrow, but chances are that anything related to its core functionality will remain. Keep up with the developer discussions, and watch for updates to this book at the URLs inside the back cover.

Index

References to figures are in italics.

A

About page, 209, 210, 211
Account button, 19
account settings
    Mobile tab, 20
    Networks tab, 19–20
    Notifications tab, 20
    Settings tab, 19
actors, 295
ad space, 52
    See also Social Ads
admins, 44
advertising. *See* Social Ads
aggregation, 294–295
aid, 82, 100
API calls, 14
    events_get, 174
    events_getMembers, 175
    events.get, 106
    events.getMembers, 106
    fbml_refreshImgSrc, 173
    fbml_refreshRefUrl, 173
    fbml_setRefHandle, 174
    fbml.refreshImgSrc, 38
    fbml.refreshRefUrl, 38
    feed_publishActionOfUser, 176

feed_publishStoryToUser, 175
feed_publishTemplatizedAction, 176
feed.publishActionOfUser, 29
feed.publishStoryToUser, 29
feed.publishTemplatizedAction, 29
friends_areFriends, 177
friends_get, 177
friends_getAppUsers, 177
friends.areFriends, 42, 151
friends.get, 42, 118
friends.getAppUsers, 42
get_FBML, 173
groups_get, 177–178
groups_getMembers, 178
groups.get, 83
groups.getMembers, 83
marketplace_createListing, 181
marketplace_getCategories, 182
marketplace_getListings, 182
marketplace_getSubCategories, 182
marketplace_removeListing, 182
marketplace_search, 182
notifications_get, 178
notifications_send, 178–179
notifications_sendEmail,
  179–180
notifications.get, 50
notifications.send, 50

API calls (*cont.*)
    pages.getInfo, 44
    pages.isAdmin, 44
    pages.isAppAdded, 44
    pages.isFan, 44
    photos_get, 180
    photos_getAlbums, 180–181
    photos_getTags, 181
    photos.addTag, 104
    photos.createAlbum, 100
    photos.get, 103
    photos.getAlbums, 100
    photos.getTags, 104
    photos.upload, 103
    profile.get FBML, 38
    profile.set FBML, 38
    PublishActionOfUser, 295
    PublishStoryToUser, 295
    publishTemplatizedAction, 295
    set_FBML, 173
    users_getInfo, 169–172
    users_getLoggedInUser, 172
    users_isAppAdded, 173
applications, 10
    About page, 93
    adding, 92, 93–95, 209–212
    building client applications,
      202–203
    choosing the basic design, 228–231
    connecting an application to
      Facebook, 203–206
    controlling information about your
      interactions, 23–25
    creating, 199–200
    creating on your server, 200–203
    designing, 218–222
    Developer, 196–199

downloading and installing client
    libraries, 201–202
Edit My Applications page, 10, *11*,
    23–25
editing, 92, 94–95, *96–97*
Events, 104–107
external, 28
Groups, 66
Groups application, 82–90
implementing pages, 234–243
implementing the basic design,
    231–233
implementing utilities, 243–251
interface design, 228–251
iterations, 222
Mobile, 189–190
Mobile application, 109–112
Notes, 107–108
Photos, 99–104
possible uses for, 216–217
privacy settings, 95–99
sample application, 222–226
searching, 10, *12*
set owner text, 246–247
setting parameters, 227
setting up a new application,
    200, *201*
test accounts, 212–214
testing, 206–208
testing the interface, 251–252
updating the About page, 209, *210*
architecture, 144–145
    pagination, 304–305
Atom feeds, 63, 108
    and XML, 117
attributes, fb:name, 159–160

B

blogs, importing from, 107–109
body data, 297
body general, 297
body template, 296–297

C

Canvas, 18
    how it works, 145–147
    public Canvas pages, 288–290
cascading style sheets. *See* CSS
classes, 148
colors for Facebook elements, 127
config.php, 231–232
Cost-Per-Click (CPC), 58
Cost-Per-View (CPM), 59
CPC, 58
CPM, 59
CSS, 125–128

D

dashboard, 18, 85
data, sharing, 163
data store API, 254
delimiters, 132
designing applications, 218–222
Developer application, 196–199
    adding applications, 209–212
    building client applications,
      202–203
    connecting an application to
      Facebook, 203–206
    creating applications on your
      server, 200–203
    creating new applications, 199–200
    discussion board, 197
    downloading and installing client
      libraries, 201–202
    iterations, 222
    members, 197
    My Applications, 197, 203
    newsfeed, 198
    Platform Status, 198
    rules, 221–222
    sample application, 222–226
    setting parameters, 227
    setting up a new application,
      200, *201*
    test accounts, 212–214
    testing applications, 206–208
    updating the About page, 209, *210*
dialogs, 166
discussion board, adding, 317–318
dynamic FBML action attributes,
  186, 187

F

Edit My Applications page, 10, *11*,
  23–25
eid, 82
email addresses, 7–8
events, 75
    browsing, 242–243
    canceling, 80, *81*
    display, 245–246
    friends' events, 242
    inviting people, 78, *79*
    managing, 78–82
    My Events, 241–242
    retrieving, 243–245
    RSVPing, 78, *79*

events (*cont.*)
setting event info, 76–77
sharing or exporting, 80–82
uploading photos, 78
Events application, 104–107
API calls, 174–175
external data, drawing the line between
Facebook Pages and, 220–221

F

Facebook Beacon, 47
Facebook Markup Language. *See* FBML
Facebook object, 147–149, 168
Facebook Pages, 42–44
creating, 53–55
drawing the line between Facebook
Pages and external data, 220–221
Platform elements for, 44
Facebook Query Language. *See* FQL
Facebook REST object, 149–153, 168
fans, 44
FBJS, 187–189
FBML, 14, 15, 156–157, 220
control elements, 160–161
dialogs, 166
dynamic FBML action attributes,
186, 187
fb_sig_mobile, 189–190
fb:action, 89
fb:attachment-preview, 49
fb:buttonset, 166
fb:comments, 49
fb:create-button, 89
fb:dashboard, 89
fb:dialog, 166

fb:editor, 90, 165–166
fb:editor-button, 90
fb:editor-buttonset, 90
fb:editor-custom, 90
fb:editor-text, 90
fb:else, 160, 161
fb:friend-selector, 42
fb:header, 89
fb:header-title, 89
fb:help, 89
fb:if, 161
fb:if-can-see-photo, 103
fb:if-is-friends-with-viewer, 42
fb:if-is-own-profile, 37
fb:is-logged-out, 161
fb:mediaheader, 89
fb:mobile, 112, 189–190
fb:multi-friend-input, 42
fb:multi-friend-selector, 42
fb:name, 38, 42, 159–160
fb:narrow, 37
fb:notif-email, 50
fb:notif-page, 50
fb:notif-subject, 50
fb:owner-action, 89
fb:page-admin-edit-header, 44
fb:photo, 103
fb:profile-action, 38
fb:profile-pic, 38, 157, 160
fb:pronoun, 38, 160
fb:ref, 38
fb:req-choice, 50
fb:request-form, 50
fb:request-form-submit, 50
fb:share-button, 162–163

fb:subtitle, 38
fb:tab-item, 89
fb:tabs, 89
fb:user-table, 38
fb:visible-to-added-app-users, 37
fb:visible-to-app-users, 37
fb:visible-to-friends, 37, 42
fb:visible-to-owner, 37
fh:visible-to-user, 37
fb:wall, 49
fb:wallpost, 49
fb:wallpost-action, 49
fb:wide, 37
forms, 164–166
link elements, 163
meta elements, 163
share element, 161–163
tags, 156
test tool, 158–159
Feed application, API calls, 175–176
Firefox browser, 128
footer links, 17
forms, 164–166, 292–293
FQL, 14, 184–186
frame, 15–17
friends
    finding, 51
    friend requests, 37–39, 50
    inviting, 51–52
    Platform elements, 42
    and search, 39–42
Friends application, API calls, 177
Friends box, 30
Friends In Other Networks box, 31
Friends list, 8–9

G

gid, 82
groups, 66
    browsing, 67–68
    creating, 68–69
    discussion board, 74
    events, 75–82
    Group Info tab, 69–71
    Members tab, 72–73
    Message All Members, 74–75
    Officers tab, 72
    Picture tab, 72
    using, 73
Groups application, 66, 82
    API calls, 82–84, 177–178
    Browse Groups page, 86–87
    FBML header elements, 87–89
    FBML page body, 90
    FBML tabs, 89
    launching, 84–85
    My Groups, 85–86
    Network page, 87, 88

H

header, 18
Help pages, 221
Home page, 21–22
    controlling your information in
        others' News Feeds, 22–25
    controlling your News Feed, 25, *27*
    controlling your status updates,
        25, *26*
    designing, 237–241
HTTP, 6

I

identifiers, 82
    namespaces, 121
images, 297
inbox, 49
index.php, 232–233
injection attacks, 318–319
instantiating classes, 148
interface design, 228–251

J

JavaScript. *See* FBJS

K

Karinthy, Frigyes, 4

L

Left Nav, 17
left-hand column. *See* Left Nav
Let Friends Know, implementing,
    313–314
links, 15
    footer links, 17
    Profile Action Links, 29

M

Marketplace application, API calls,
    181–182
mashups, 108
members, 148
messages, 37–39, 49
methods, 148
Milgrim, Stanley, 4

Mini-Feed, 9, 47, *48*
    adding items, 294–302
Mobile application, 189–190
    configuring messages, 110–111
    configuring the mobile Web,
        111–112
    using a mobile phone, 109–110
Mock-AJAX, 186–187
My Events, 241–242
My Groups, 85–86
MySQL, 257–258
    adding to the table, 272–275
    building the database, 262–264
    connecting to the database, 270–271
    constructing and testing the first
        query, 269–276
    creating or modifying a table,
        264–265
    editing data, 269
    inserting data, 269
    join tables, 267–268
    or die clause, 273
    Query Browser, 265–269
    removing items from the table, 275
    retrieving data, 268–269
    sending parameters to the script,
        271–272
    testing, 265–269
    See also SQL

N

namespaces, 121
navigation. *See* dashboard
networks, 10

News Feed, 21–22
    adding items, 294–302
    controlling your information in others' News Feeds, 22–25
    controlling your News Feed, 25, *27*
    controls for external applications, 28
    features of, 28
    Platform elements for, 28–29
nid, 82
Notes application, 107–108
notifications, 50
    API calls, 178–180

O

objects, 147–149

P

pagination, 302–303
    architecture, 304–305
    changing get_from_database_and_render parameters, 306
    changing the page that calls get_from_database_and_render, 307
    implementing in get_from_database_and_render, 308–313
    implementing Let Friends Know, 313–314
    styles, 305–306
Photos application, 99–100
    API calls, 100, 180–181
    photo albums, 100–101
    Platform elements, 103, 104
    tags, 102–104
    uploading photos, 102

PHP, 130–131
    arrays, 133
    building client applications, 202–203
    comments, 132
    concatenated strings, 134–135
    conditional statements, 135–137
    config.php, 231–232
    count, 274
    delimiters, 132
    downloading and installing client libraries, 201–202
    Facebook object, 147–149
    functions, 137–139
    get_from_database_and_render, 242, 277, 278–283, 304, 306–313
    handling exceptions, 139–141
    heredoc, 134–135, 138
    index.php, 232–233
    and MySQL, 258
    objects, 148
    render_cae, 244, 277–278, 283–285
    render_cae_columns, 278, 285–286
    strings, 133
    terminators, 133
    try/catch structures, 139–141
    using multiple files, 137
    variables, 133
pid, 82, 100
Platform elements
    for Facebook Pages, 44
    for friends, 42
    for the News Feed, 28–29
    for pokes, 49–50

Platform elements (*cont.*)
    for Profile pages, 37–38
    for the Wall, 49
pokes, 37–39, 49–50
polls, 61–63
privacy settings
    applications, 95–99
    controlling your information in
      others' News Feeds, 22–25
profile, 29
    Basic tab, 34
    Contact tab, 34–35
    Education tab, 36
    friends and search, 39–42
    information, 33–34
    Personal tab, 35
    Picture tab, 36
    Platform elements for, 37, 38
    Relationships tab, 35
    visibility for pokes, messages, and
      friend requests, 37–39
    Work tab, 36
Profile Action Links, 29
Profile box, 220
    updating, 291–294
Profile page, 7–10
    API calls, 173–174
    vs. Facebook Page, 44
    how it works, 147
    layout, 29–32
    Platform elements for, 37–38
    updating, 290–291
public Canvas pages, 288–290

R

requests. *See* friends
REST object, 149–153, 168
RSS feeds, 63, 108
    and XML, 117

S

Safari browser, 127, *128*
security, 318–319
Share button, 161–163, 314–315
    adding more SELECT options,
      315–317
signing up, 7, *8*
six degrees of separation, 4
size of Facebook, 6–7
small world experiments, 4, 6
Social Ads, 52–53
    audience, 55–56
    budget, 58–60, *61*
    creating a Facebook Page, 53–55
    creating the ad, 57–58
    reach and frequency, 57
    reviewing the ad and paying, 60, *62*
social graph, 6, 219–220
    and Facebook Pages, 44
social networking sites, 5
social utility, 5
SQL
    basics, 255–257
    building the database, 262–264
    columns or fields, 256
    constructing and testing the first
      query, 269–276

creating or modifying a table, 264–265

databases, 256

editing data, 269

Events table, 260–261

foreign keys, 261

indexes, 256

inserting data, 269

join tables, 267–268

Locations table, 262

modification timestamp, 260

MySQL, 257–258

name field, 260

primary keys, 256, 259

references, 255

relationships, 257

resultsets, 265

retrieving data, 268–269

rows or records, 256

schema, 258–259

SELECT statements, 278–279, 315–317

self-joins, 257

subqueries, 279–280

tables, 256

Users table, 262

statistics, 6–7

status updates, *26*

    controlling, 25

storable data, 221–222

style sheets, 126

    colors for Facebook elements, 127

    widths of Facebook objects, 128

    See also CSS

subscriptions, 63

T

tags, 156

targets, 295, 297

template stories, 297–298

    integrating data with the templates, 302

    retrieving data from the database, 300–301

    testing with hard-coded data, 298–300

Terms of Use, 5

test accounts, 212–214

test tool, 158–159

testing

    applications, 206–208

    interface, 251–252

    templates stories, 298–300

title data, 296

title template, 295–296

U

uid, 82, 243

URLs

    callback URLs, 205, 206

    Canvas page URL, 205, 206

    sharing, 163

US Politics application, 228–230

user API calls, 169–173

user id (uid), 15

utilities, implementing, 243–251

V

value, adding to Facebook with applications, 218–219

virality, 5–6

W

Wall, 11, 47–49
Web 2.0, 6
widths of Facebook objects, 128
World Wide Web Consortium (W3C),
    118, 122, 126

X

XHTML, 122
    attributes, 123–124
    debugging, 124–125
    div elements, 122–123
    id attribute, 124
    validating syntax, 124, 125
XML, 117–118
    attributes, 120
    capitalization, 119

document entity, 118
elements, 120–121
entities, 118
first line, 119
keywords, 120
logical structure, 119
namespaces, 121
physical structure, 118
root, 118
syntax, 119–120
values, 120–121

Z

zero-relative numbers, 304
Zuckerberg, Mark, 4, 5